Complete
Curry
Cookbook

250 Recipes from Around the World

Byron Ayanoglu and Jennifer MacKenzie

Robert
ROSE

For complete cataloguing information, see page 295.

Disclaimer
The recipes in this book have been carefully tested by our kitchen and our tasters. To
the best of our knowledge, they are safe and nutritious for ordinary use and users. For
those people with food or other allergies, or who have special food requirements or
health issues, please read the suggested contents of each recipe carefully and
determine whether or not they may create a problem for you. All recipes are used at
the risk of the consumer.

We cannot be responsible for any hazards, loss or damage that may occur as a
result of any recipe use.

For those with special needs, allergies, requirements or health problems, in the
event of any doubt, please contact your medical adviser prior to the use of any recipe.

Design and Production: Kevin Cockburn/PageWave Graphics Inc.
Editor: Sue Sumeraj
Proofreader: Sheila Wawanash
Indexer: Gillian Watts
Illustrations: Kveta
Photography: Colin Erricson
Food Styling: Kathryn Robertson
Prop Styling: Charlene Erricson

Cover image: Curried Pork with Sweet Peppers, Carrots and Coconut (page 126)

We acknowledge the financial support of the Government of Canada through the
Book Publishing Industry Development Program (BPIDP) for our publishing
activities.

Published by Robert Rose Inc.
120 Eglinton Avenue East, Suite 800, Toronto, Ontario, Canada M4P 1E2
Tel: (416) 322-6552 Fax: (416) 322-6936

Printed and bound in Canada

1 2 3 4 5 6 7 8 9 TCP 16 15 14 13 12 11 10 09 08

Contents

Introduction

The word "curry" has several favorable meanings, but its most frequent usage in the West is to encompass and be synonymous with Indian cuisine. However, Indians use the word only to curry our pleasure and familiarize us with saucy dishes on menus designed for foreigners. Indian cuisine is so complex, so regionally reformulated, so old and articulated, that it defies facile categories. Calling all saucy Indian culinary creations "curries" is like calling all the saucy dishes of French cuisine "stews." Neither name recognizes the traditions and expertise that have, over millennia, combined regional produce and temperament to create heirloom recipes.

But then again, all of that is just semantics, isn't it?

For the purposes of this book, the terms "curry" and "stew" are synonymous because it is our contention that the Indian curry is the parent of all the stews in the world. It was very much in place, aromatic and smooth, at a time when Europeans were just emerging from the caves and still dined on game meats charred on an open flame. It was India that enlightened our Western palate with its spices and cooking techniques, just as it informed our minds with its philosophy, theology, mythology and lifestyle, all of which we have adapted and reshaped to form the crux of our own civilization.

All saucy dishes of the world's major cuisines (with the arguable exception of Chinese cuisine) have roots that can be traced indisputably to Indian cookery. Saucy dishes start with oil-fried aromatics (onion, garlic, ginger), then other spices are added (turmeric, cumin, coriander seed, curry leaf), then some liquid to form a vibrant bath in which the main ingredient is simmered, briefly for vegetables and seafood, somewhat longer for chicken and longest for red meat. This is how saucy dishes are prepared all over the world, but no one does it better, or with more variations, than the Indians.

Some cuisines, such as Thai, Caribbean and Indian-style British, have borrowed unabashedly from the Indians and actually call their creations "curries." These dishes are the direct descendants of Indian cuisine and have a rightful place in this book.

More than any other criterion, an abundance of spices signifies the true essence of curry. This is sunbelt cooking, where spices grow in the wild and are widely available. Naturally, the sunbelt is also the territory of chiles, and an authentic curry is hot — for some, the hotter the better. On the other hand, if you use fewer chiles, other flavors and aromas can shine through. It's a matter of taste and priorities. There are even some curries in this book that use no chiles at all, relying on other flavors to inform and to satisfy the palate.

So sharpen those taste buds, pack some antacids (just in case), put a bib on to prevent soiling that fine shirt and get ready for prandial excitement and gustatory abandon. This is a lusty cuisine, and it deserves unqualified enthusiasm, almost devotion. If approached correctly, a curry meal becomes a revelation, rewarding us with timeless tastes and sensations.

Cooking Curry the Easy Way

Curry is traditionally cooked at the last minute — *à la minute*, as they say in French — because it is at its best fresh from the frying pan. This makes curry practical, and most of the actual cooking of our recipes takes less than a half-hour. There are exceptions, of course, just as there are exceptions to every rule. Red meats greatly benefit from a slow simmer, as do some of the other dishes you will encounter in this book. For your convenience, we have marked many of our recipes with the tags "Quick Sauté" (cooks in less than 30 minutes) or "Slow Simmer" (cooks for an hour or more).

However, as in all labor-intensive cultures that maintain traditional (almost ritualistic) cooking techniques, there is indeed work to be done. Every dish that comes out of an Indian (or other curry-related) kitchen requires a slew of chores to prepare for that brief half-hour of cooking. The purpose of this book, at the risk of offending purists, is to simplify that preparation and thus render curry-making more attractive to home cooks.

The most remarkable of our innovations, however, has nothing to do with saving time and labor; rather, it reduces calories, thereby contributing to better health. We recommend the use of small quantities of beneficial cooking fats to replace the commonly used mustard and coconut oils, and especially the ghee (clarified butter). Both mustard oil and coconut oil score badly in their saturated fat content. They can also prove difficult to find, and they are more expensive than corn or canola oils. Happily, most modern curry chefs can agree to the substitution.

Ghee, however, is much more sacred. Many cooks consider it an essential enrichment and believe that curry would be incomplete without it. But hey, we're talking about *butter*, a substance that is deemed unhealthy if used in excess. We have therefore limited its use to recipes that must have it, and even then we have added it in moderate quantities. Nevertheless, if you want to live dangerously, you can add a few drops of heated ghee on top of any dish in this book for that final and deeply satisfying enhancement.

The true taste of faraway cuisine is possible only with authentic ingredients. In the case of curry, this means particular spices and a variety of fresh chiles. It is possible to scour the markets of our big cities and find every single rare spice (though not often at its freshest) and unusual chile (which, having come from another continent, has not had the chance to ripen properly). But for those without access to the luxury of big-city leisurely shopping, and to make things easier all around, we recommend certain additive-free, supermarket-available curry pastes that are very useful, especially for meat and chicken dishes. Using the prepared ingredient obviates not only the special shopping trips, but also the grinding/pasting ordeal that intimidates a lot of home cooks, preventing them from preparing curries they would otherwise love to make and enjoy.

Quite a few of our recipes are made even simpler by the adoption of Basic Gravy, which was invented by Chef T. Siva Prasannan, owner-guru of Lonely Planet, the signature restaurant of Kovalam Beach in Kerala, the southernmost state of India. This homemade gravy takes minutes to prepare and achieves its texture easily in the food processor or blender (instead of the mortar and pestle), making it possible to put a curry on the table in well under half an hour, including prep time! It can be stored in the fridge for up to a week (and in the freezer in individual portions for up to 2 months), allowing you to make curry on the spur of the moment. Basic Gravy is an essential tool for those who like to make frequent gustatory voyages to the subcontinent without having to start the cooking process from scratch. The recipe appears at the end of this introduction.

Other less-than-orthodox but totally taste-acceptable shortcuts include preboiled beans and chickpeas (which are perfectly fine in cans) and some preboiled and frozen vegetables. The vegetables might be a contentious point, since in the Indian kitchen they are cooked in the sauce from raw. However, cooking from raw can be tricky, as it tends to diminish the sauce and sometimes results in undercooked vegetables. Using preboiled vegetables in a fully realized sauce allows for greater control, saves time and detracts only marginally from the true flavors and textures.

We offer many non-vegetable recipes that contain vegetables, even though in the original they would not. Curry cultures, especially the Indian, prefer vegetable recipes on their own, with the meat, chicken or fish on its own. But this requires cooking two separate dishes, as well as the staple rice or bread and a condiment such as raita or chutney. By combining the protein with the vegetable, you can get away with cooking one less dish and the result will still be delicious.

Finally, we've made things easier by adapting much of our cooking to a standard 12-inch (30 cm) skillet instead of using the wok-like kadahi, which is favored by chefs in the home country but needs careful cleaning and oiling. The best implement of all would be a modern, nonstick, easy-to-clean kadahi, and with the current popularity of curry we can hope that such an item will be on the market soon. In the meantime, use your skillet and make some curry. Your taste buds will be grateful.

Basic Gravy

This generic curry sauce enhancer speeds up curry recipes and works every time. It comes to us courtesy of Chef Prasannan of the Lonely Planet restaurant in Kovalam Beach, Kerala.

Tips

If you don't have a food processor, you can use a blender. Just add enough of the tomato purée to the onion mixture to help the blender purée more easily.

No food processor or blender? The onions, garlic and ginger can be minced by hand, and you can use a can of crushed (ground) tomatoes instead of whole tomatoes.

Let extra gravy cool completely, then transfer to an airtight container, cover and refrigerate for up to 1 week. Or divide into ½-cup (125 mL) and/or 1-cup (250 mL) portions in airtight containers and freeze for up to 2 months. Thaw overnight in the refrigerator or defrost in the microwave.

1	can (28 oz/796 mL) tomatoes with juice	1
2 cups	coarsely chopped onions	500 mL
⅓ cup	whole garlic cloves (about 12)	75 mL
⅓ cup	thinly sliced gingerroot	75 mL
2 tbsp	vegetable oil	25 mL
¼ cup	ground coriander	50 mL
1 tbsp	ground turmeric	15 mL
1 tbsp	garam masala	15 mL
2 tsp	salt	10 mL
1 tsp	cayenne pepper	5 mL

1. In a food processor, purée tomatoes with juice until smooth. Pour back into the can or into a bowl and set aside.

2. Add onions, garlic and ginger to food processor and pulse until very finely chopped but not juicy.

3. In a skillet, heat oil over medium heat. Add onion mixture and cook, stirring, until onions start to release their liquid, about 3 minutes. Stir in coriander, turmeric, garam masala, salt and cayenne. Cook, stirring, until well blended and mixture is starting to dry and get thick and paste-like, about 3 minutes.

4. Stir in puréed tomatoes and bring to a simmer, scraping up bits stuck to pan. Reduce heat and boil gently, stirring often, until slightly thickened and flavors are blended, about 5 minutes. Use as directed in recipes.

About These Recipes

Ingredients and Preparation

- **Bell peppers:** Remove the stem, core and seeds before chopping.
- **Hot chile peppers:** Some people prefer to remove the seeds from chile peppers before chopping; others leave them. The recipes will work either way. Leaving the ribs of the peppers in does increase the amount of heat slightly.
- **Gingerroot, garlic, onions, carrots:** Peel and trim ends before chopping, slicing or mincing.
- **Potatoes and sweet potatoes:** Unless otherwise specified in the recipe, it is your choice whether to peel or not. If leaving the skins on, be sure to scrub well under running water before chopping.
- **Fruit:** For any fruit with inedible skin, pits or seeds, we assume the fruit is peeled and pits are discarded before the fruit is chopped unless otherwise specified in the recipe.
- **Citrus juice and zest:** Recipes were tested with freshly squeezed limes, lemons and oranges. Bottled citrus juices will not necessarily produce the same results. To grate zest, use a fine-toothed Microplane type of grater or the fine side of a box cheese grater. It is much easier to grate the zest before squeezing out the juice.
- **Tomatoes and citrus fruits:** When these are chopped or sliced, the juices that accumulate on the cutting board are included with the flesh unless otherwise specified in the recipe.
- **Curry pastes, powders or masala blends:** Recipes were tested with commercially prepared products that are readily available at grocery stores. Experiment with different brands to see which you prefer. Homemade pastes and blends can be used if desired. If substituting a dry powder or masala blend for a paste, you may need to add a little more oil or moisture to prevent burning.
- **Chicken, beef and vegetable stock:** Recipes were tested with commercially prepared, high-quality stock in the form of ready-to-use broth and/or condensed broth diluted according to label directions. Sodium-reduced stock is preferred for many recipes and is noted accordingly. If you use homemade, unsalted stock, you will need to add more salt to enhance the other flavors.
- **Meat and poultry:** Recipes were tested with fresh, unseasoned meat and poultry. If you use seasoned meat that is infused with sodium phosphate, the cooking time, salt level and moisture level of recipes will be affected. Be sure to read fresh meat labels carefully when purchasing.
- **Chicken:** We prefer to use air-chilled chicken for the best flavor and texture. Conventional water-chilled chicken will work but can make sauces a little more watery, and the chicken may be chewy when simmered.
- **Fish and seafood:** Fresh fish is preferable as long as it is, indeed, fresh. Fresh fish has a pleasant, not fishy, aroma and no slippery film. If using frozen fish, thaw overnight in the refrigerator or according to package directions and use the day it is thawed. Rinse all fish and pat dry before using.
- **Shrimp:** Once caught, shrimp are generally frozen before shipping. Even the shrimp at the fresh fish and seafood counter have usually been thawed from frozen. For this

reason, it is preferable to buy frozen shrimp; otherwise, it's impossible for you to know how long it has been since it was thawed. When choosing a package of frozen shrimp, make sure there isn't much ice in the package and the shrimp aren't stuck together. These can be indicators of thawing and refreezing and result in an unpleasant taste and texture. Frozen shrimp with precut shells are handy and make peeling quick and easy. Thaw shrimp overnight in the package in a bowl in the refrigerator or, for immediate use, run cool water directly over shrimp in a colander in the sink. Rinse shrimp, drain well and pat dry before using.

- **Milk:** Recipes were tested with 2% milk. Other types of milk will work, although fat-free (skim) milk may cause sauces to be thin and look less appetizing.
- **Butter:** We use real butter. Recipes were tested with salted butter. If using unsalted butter, you may need to slightly increase the amount of salt to taste (about $\frac{1}{4}$ tsp/1 mL salt per cup/250 mL butter).
- **Vegetable oil:** Use whichever type of vegetable oil you prefer. A plain-flavored oil such as canola works well with the spicing in curries. If you prefer to use olive oil, use a very light-tasting oil to avoid overpowering the flavor of the other ingredients.
- **Whole spices and aromatics:** In many cultures, it is traditional to leave whole spices and aromatics (lime leaves, lemongrass, cinnamon sticks, etc.) in dishes when serving, but they aren't meant to be eaten. If you're serving guests who aren't accustomed to this, be sure to let them know not to eat the whole spices. If you prefer, discard whole spices before serving the dish.

- **Cinnamon:** The recipes were tested with 3-inch (7.5 cm) long cinnamon sticks. If you have shorter cinnamon sticks, add more; if you have longer cinnamon sticks, break into pieces as necessary.
- **Salt:** Many of the recipes add a measured amount of salt in the cooking process and then suggest adding more to taste at the end. This allows for variability in the salt level in added ingredients (stock, tomatoes, etc.). Adding salt at the end of cooking also heightens the flavors of the dish. If you leave salt out, the spices and other flavorings will be very dull.

To add salt to taste, first taste the cooked dish. If you are not sure whether it needs more salt, spoon a small amount of the curry into a bowl and add a pinch of salt. Stir it in and taste again. If it brightens the flavors, then add more salt to the pot — about $\frac{1}{4}$ tsp (1 mL) at a time is a good start. Stir and taste after each addition until you're happy with the flavor. Adding small amounts at a time and tasting each time is much better than adding a lot at once. If you over-salt, there is no remedy!

Measuring

- Produce is medium-sized unless otherwise specified.
- Where the exact quantity isn't imperative for vegetables and fruits, a number is given. Where it needs to be more precise, a volume is given (e.g., $\frac{1}{2}$ cup/125 mL chopped onions).

- Dry ingredients are measured in dry, nesting-style measuring cups. Ingredients such as flour are spooned in and leveled off, not tapped or packed.
- Liquid ingredients are measured in a liquid measuring cup with graduated volume markings, generally with a handle and a spout. The volume is read at eye level.

Make Ahead and Storage

- In general, the "Slow Simmer" curries can all be made ahead. In fact, many improve in taste after reheating. Transfer curry to a shallow container and let cool. Cover and refrigerate for up to 2 days. Return to pot and reheat over medium heat, stirring often, until hot and bubbling.
- Curries without potatoes or tender vegetables can be frozen for up to 2 months. Thaw overnight in the refrigerator before reheating.
- "Quick Sauté" curries are meant to be served immediately unless otherwise specified. Leftovers can be stored in an airtight container in the refrigerator for 2 to 3 days.
- Other storage information is included in specific recipes where applicable.

Soups & Salads

◆

Chilled Buttermilk Soup

Serves 4

A nutritious soup for hot weather, this rendering of lentils and buttermilk goes down smoothly with its meaningful spicing and velvety texture. It's a bit tricky to make and requires a low flame, a good stirring arm and some patience. On the plus side, it is made in advance and chilled, ready to please when the time is right.

Tip

After adding the buttermilk, make sure the mixture does not boil or the buttermilk may curdle. If you prefer, reheat the soup in the top of a double boiler.

½ cup	small yellow lentils (toor dal), rinsed	125 mL
½ tsp	ground turmeric	2 mL
3 cups	water	750 mL
1 cup	finely chopped onion	250 mL
¼ cup	finely chopped garlic	50 mL
½ tsp	hot pepper flakes	2 mL
1 tsp	freshly ground black pepper	5 mL
½ tsp	ground cumin	2 mL
2 cups	buttermilk	500 mL
10	curry leaves	10
	Salt	

1. In a pot, combine lentils, turmeric and water. Bring to a boil over high heat. Reduce heat and boil gently until lentils are very soft, about 25 minutes. Mash until smooth.

2. Stir in onion, garlic, hot pepper flakes, black pepper and cumin. Simmer over medium heat until onion is softened, about 5 minutes.

3. Remove from heat and stir in buttermilk, curry leaves and salt to taste. Return to low heat and heat, stirring constantly, just until steaming (do not boil).

4. Transfer to a bowl or container and let cool, stirring often. Cover and refrigerate until chilled, at least 4 hours, or for up to 1 day. Season to taste with more salt, if necessary. Serve cold.

Chilled Curried Banana Coconut Soup

Serves 6 to 8

This easy soup is packed with flavor. It becomes festive, almost decadent, if served in fine crystal glasses with appropriately decorative sprigs of mint.

Tips

If lime leaves aren't available, substitute ½ tsp (2 mL) grated lime zest and add with the lime juice.

For the best flavor and creamiest texture, be sure bananas are very ripe (speckled with brown spots).

¾ cup	coconut milk, divided	175 mL
2	wild lime leaves (see tip, at left)	2
1 tbsp	minced peeled gingerroot	15 mL
½ tsp	salt	2 mL
½ tsp	ground coriander	2 mL
¼ tsp	ground cumin	1 mL
1 tsp	mild Indian yellow curry paste or masala blend	5 mL
2 tbsp	freshly squeezed lime juice	25 mL
4	very ripe bananas	4
¾ cup	plain yogurt	175 mL
¾ cup	cold water	175 mL
1 tsp	granulated sugar, or to taste	5 mL
	Chopped fresh mint	

1. In a small skillet, heat 2 tbsp (25 mL) of the coconut milk over medium-low heat until bubbling. Add lime leaves and cook, stirring, until fragrant, about 2 minutes. Reduce heat to low. Add ginger, salt, coriander, cumin and curry paste; cook, stirring often, until ginger is softened and spices are fragrant, about 5 minutes. Remove from heat and stir in lime juice, scraping up any bits stuck to pan.

2. Discard lime leaves and transfer spice mixture to a blender. Add remaining coconut milk and bananas; purée until smooth.

3. Transfer to a bowl and whisk in yogurt and cold water. Cover and refrigerate until chilled, about 2 hours, or for up to 8 hours.

4. If soup is very thick, let stand at room temperature for 15 minutes to allow coconut milk to warm slightly. Whisk to blend and season to taste with sugar and salt. Ladle into chilled bowls and serve sprinkled with mint.

Curry-Roasted Squash and Apple Soup

Serves 6 to 8

The haute-cuisine popularity of blended squash or pumpkin soups might have started in the 1990s, but they have been around for a long time in cultures that have always loved the gourds for their buttery, creamy texture when baked or boiled. This particular squash soup will get extra kudos for its interesting spicing and the smoky taste of the oven.

Tip

The soup can be made ahead, cooled, covered and refrigerated for up to 2 days or frozen for up to 2 months (thaw overnight in the refrigerator). Reheat over medium heat until steaming and season to taste before serving.

- *Preheat oven to 450°F (230°C)*
- *Rimmed baking sheet, ungreased*

2 tsp	salt	10 mL
1 tsp	ground coriander	5 mL
1 tsp	ground cumin	5 mL
½ tsp	ground turmeric	2 mL
¼ tsp	ground cinnamon	1 mL
¼ tsp	freshly ground black pepper	1 mL
¼ cup	vegetable oil	50 mL
2 tbsp	cider or white wine vinegar	25 mL
4	cloves garlic	4
2	tart apples, peeled and chopped	2
1	butternut squash, peeled and cut into ½-inch (1 cm) pieces (about 8 cups/2 L)	1
1	large onion, chopped	1
6 cups	water (approx.)	1.5 L
½ tsp	garam masala, divided	2 mL

1. In a small bowl, combine salt, coriander, cumin, turmeric, cinnamon, pepper, oil and vinegar.

2. On baking sheet, combine garlic, apples, squash and onion. Drizzle with spice mixture and toss to coat evenly. Roast in preheated oven, stirring twice, for about 45 minutes or until softened and golden brown.

3. Transfer roasted vegetables to a large pot. Add water and bring to a boil over medium-high heat. Reduce heat and simmer, stirring occasionally, until vegetables are very soft and liquid is reduced by about one-third, about 30 minutes. Remove from heat.

4. Using an immersion blender in pot or transferring soup in batches to an upright blender, purée until very smooth. Return to pot, if necessary.

5. Reheat over medium heat until steaming, stirring often. Thin with a little water, if necessary, to desired consistency. Stir in half the garam masala and season to taste with salt and pepper. Ladle into warmed bowls and serve sprinkled with remaining garam masala.

Serving Suggestion

This soup is a nice starter to an Indian meal featuring Coconut Curried Chicken (page 72) or Beef Korma Curry with Almonds (page 93). It also works alongside a leftover Curry Lime Roasted Chicken (page 52) sandwich.

Variation

Replace squash with 2 large sweet potatoes, peeled and cut into ½-inch (1 cm) pieces.

Sweet Potato and Coconut Lime Soup

Serves 4 to 6

Creamy yet light, this soup marries the natural sugars of sweet potato and coconut with fragrant spices. It is an appetizing starter for the hefty fare of Caribbean and African curry meals, but also works well with main courses of other persuasions.

Tips

If lime leaves aren't available, substitute ½ tsp (2 mL) grated lime zest and add with the lime juice in step 3.

Reduced-sodium vegetable or chicken stock works best for this recipe. If it is not available, use 3 cups (750 mL) regular stock and 1 cup (250 mL) water.

The soup can be prepared through step 2, cooled, covered and refrigerated for up to 2 days.

Variation

Substitute 1 small pie pumpkin (about 2½ lbs/ 1.25 kg) for the sweet potatoes.

6 cups	cubed peeled sweet potatoes (about 2 large)	1.5 L
3	thin slices gingerroot	3
3	whole cloves	3
2	wild lime leaves (see tip, at left)	2
1	stick cinnamon	1
4 cups	vegetable or chicken stock	1 L
¾ cup	coconut milk	175 mL
½ cup	water or additional stock	125 mL
2 tbsp	freshly squeezed lime juice	25 mL
1 tsp	salt, or to taste	5 mL
¼ tsp	freshly ground black pepper, or to taste	1 mL
	Granulated sugar, optional	
	Coconut milk	
	Chopped fresh parsley	

1. In a large pot, combine sweet potatoes, ginger, cloves, lime leaves, cinnamon and stock. Bring to a boil over medium-high heat. Reduce heat to medium-low, cover and simmer until sweet potato is very soft and spices are infused, about 20 minutes. Discard ginger, cloves, lime leaves and cinnamon stick. Stir in coconut milk and water.

2. Using an immersion blender in pot or transferring soup in batches to an upright blender, purée until very smooth. Return to pot, if necessary.

3. Reheat over medium heat until steaming, stirring often. Whisk in lime juice. Season to taste with salt, pepper and sugar, if using. Ladle into warmed bowls and serve drizzled with coconut milk and sprinkled with parsley.

Golden Cauliflower Soup

Serves 4 to 6

Madame du Barry, the royal mistress of France's Louis XV, loved cauliflower so much that French recipes of the floral vegetable nearly always bear her name. She would have flipped for this easy-to-make soup, if only one of the thousand chefs at Versailles could have had this recipe.

Tips

If desired, remove about ½ cup (125 mL) of the cauliflower florets before puréeing soup and add some to each bowl when serving.

The soup can be made ahead, cooled, covered and refrigerated for up to 2 days or frozen for up to 2 months (thaw overnight in the refrigerator). Reheat over medium heat until steaming and season to taste before serving.

2 tbsp	vegetable oil	25 mL
1	large onion, chopped	1
4	cloves garlic, chopped	4
15	curry leaves	15
½ tsp	salt	2 mL
½ tsp	ground turmeric	2 mL
½ tsp	ground cumin	2 mL
Pinch	cayenne pepper, optional	Pinch
2 tsp	Indian yellow curry paste or masala blend	10 mL
1	all-purpose potato, peeled and diced	1
4 cups	vegetable or chicken stock (approx.)	1 L
4 cups	chopped cauliflower (about ½ large)	1 L
	Water, optional	
2 tbsp	freshly squeezed lemon juice	25 mL
	Fresh cilantro leaves	

1. In a large pot, heat oil over medium heat. Add onion and cook, stirring, until softened but not browned, about 5 minutes. Add garlic, curry leaves, salt, turmeric, cumin, cayenne, if using, and curry paste; cook, stirring, until softened and fragrant, about 2 minutes.

2. Add potato and stock; bring to a boil, scraping up bits stuck to pot. Reduce heat to medium-low, cover and boil gently until potatoes start to soften, about 5 minutes. Stir in cauliflower, cover and boil gently, stirring often, until cauliflower is soft, about 15 minutes. Remove from heat.

3. Discard curry leaves. Using an immersion blender in pot or transferring soup in batches to an upright blender, purée soup until very smooth. Return to pot, if necessary.

4. Reheat over medium heat until steaming, stirring often. Thin with more stock or a little water, if necessary, to desired consistency. Stir in lemon juice and season to taste with salt. Ladle into warmed bowls and float a few cilantro leaves on top of each.

Hot-and-Spicy Tomato Chile Soup

Serves 4

This lusty soup combines the spices and lentils of Asia with the tomatoes of the New World. It lifts the spirits as it teases the palate — how much more can a soup do?

Tips

Rinse lentils well in a sieve under cool running water and pick through to remove any stones and foreign particles. Drain well.

To make tamarind water, break 4 oz (125 g) of block tamarind into pieces and place in a heatproof bowl. Pour in 2 cups (500 mL) boiling water. Let stand until very soft, about 30 minutes, or for up to 8 hours. Press through a fine-mesh sieve, discarding seeds and skins.

½ cup	small yellow lentils (toor dal), rinsed	125 mL
1 tsp	ground turmeric	5 mL
4 cups	water, divided	1 L
2 cups	tamarind water (see tip, at left)	500 mL
4	cloves garlic, finely chopped	4
1	can (19 oz/540 mL) tomatoes with juice, finely chopped	1
10	curry leaves	10
1 tsp	garam masala	5 mL
¼ tsp	freshly ground black pepper	1 mL
1 tbsp	vegetable oil or ghee	15 mL
1 tsp	hot pepper flakes	5 mL
½ tsp	mustard seeds	2 mL
	Chopped fresh cilantro	

1. In a pot, combine lentils, turmeric and 2 cups (500 mL) of the water. Bring to a boil over high heat. Reduce heat and boil gently until lentils are very soft and most of the water is absorbed, about 25 minutes. Mash until smooth.

2. Stir in remaining water and tamarind water until blended. Stir in garlic, tomatoes with juice, curry leaves, garam masala and black pepper; bring to a boil. Cover, reduce heat and simmer, stirring occasionally, until well blended and soupy, 15 to 20 minutes.

3. Just before serving, in a small skillet, heat oil over medium heat until hot but not smoking. Add hot pepper flakes and mustard seeds; cook, stirring, until mustard seeds start to pop, about 1 minute. Stir into soup. Ladle into warmed bowls and serve sprinkled with cilantro.

Yellow Lentil Soup with Tamarind

Serves 4

Lentils are a miracle food. Easy to grow and fast to cook, they are a bundle of nourishment that replaces the need for meat in vegetarian diets. The Indian yellow lentils have the additional attribute of being deliciously nutty. This soup combines them with vegetables and the tartness of tamarind for a zesty, satisfying first course.

Tips

The soup can prepared through the end of step 2, cooled, covered and refrigerated for up to 2 days. Reheat over medium heat until steaming and complete step 3.

The addition of the fried spices on top of the soup is a traditional presentation but can be omitted if you prefer and the soup will still be delicious.

1 cup	small yellow lentils (toor dal), rinsed	250 mL
1 tsp	ground turmeric	5 mL
4 cups	water (approx.)	1 L
4	cloves garlic, chopped	4
2	hot green chile peppers, halved lengthwise	2
1 cup	cubed peeled eggplant	250 mL
½ cup	thinly sliced onion	125 mL
½ cup	lightly toasted sweetened shredded coconut	125 mL
2 cups	tamarind water (see tip, page 18)	500 mL
2 tsp	ground coriander	10 mL
1 tsp	freshly ground black pepper	5 mL
	Salt	
2 tbsp	vegetable oil (or half each oil and ghee)	25 mL
10	curry leaves	10
1 tbsp	mustard seeds	15 mL
½ tsp	fenugreek seeds	2 mL
	Chopped fresh cilantro	

1. In a saucepan, combine lentils, turmeric and water. Bring to a boil over high heat. Reduce heat and boil gently until lentils are very soft and most of the water is absorbed, about 25 minutes. Mash until smooth.

2. In a pot, combine garlic, chile peppers, eggplant, onion, coconut and tamarind water. Bring to a simmer over medium heat. Simmer until eggplant is slightly tender, about 5 minutes. Stir in lentils, coriander and black pepper. Simmer until vegetables are very soft and mixture is soupy, about 10 minutes (You may need to add a little water if it is too thick). Discard chile peppers. Season to taste with salt.

3. Just before serving, in a small skillet, heat oil over medium heat until hot but not smoking. Add curry leaves, mustard seeds and fenugreek seeds; cook, stirring, until mustard seeds just start to pop, about 1 minute. Remove from heat. Ladle soup into bowls, and drizzle with spices and oil. Serve sprinkled with cilantro.

Chickpea and Roasted Cumin Soup

Serves 4

This is a hearty soup for fans of meaty-nutty-tasting chickpeas, which respond so very well to the earthy flavor of cumin. It is ideal for lunch, as it needs only the addition of a sandwich to become a complete meal.

Tip

The soup can be prepared through the end of step 3, cooled, covered and refrigerated for up to 2 days. Reheat over medium heat until steaming and complete steps 4 and 5.

Variation

For a smooth soup, in step 4, using an immersion blender in pan or transferring soup in batches to an upright blender, purée until smooth. Return soup to pan, if necessary, and reheat over medium heat, adding a little more stock or water as necessary to thin to desired consistency.

1 tsp	cumin seeds	5 mL
2 tbsp	vegetable or olive oil	25 mL
1	large onion, chopped	1
2	cloves garlic, minced	2
1/4 tsp	salt	1 mL
1/8 tsp	ground turmeric	0.5 mL
1/4 cup	long-grain white rice	50 mL
1	can (19 oz/540 mL) chickpeas, drained and rinsed	1
4 cups	vegetable or chicken stock	1 L
2 tbsp	freshly squeezed lemon juice	25 mL
1 tbsp	chopped fresh cilantro	15 mL
2 tbsp	plain yogurt	25 mL

1. In a large saucepan, toast cumin seeds over medium heat, shaking pan almost constantly, until slightly darker brown and fragrant, 2 to 3 minutes.

2. Add oil to pan and swirl to coat. Add onion and cook, stirring, until starting to soften, about 2 minutes. Reduce heat to medium-low and cook, stirring often, until very soft and golden brown, 10 to 15 minutes. Add garlic, salt and turmeric; cook, stirring, for 1 minute. Stir in rice.

3. Add chickpeas and stock. Increase heat to medium-high and bring to a boil. Reduce heat to low, cover and simmer, stirring occasionally, until rice is soft and broth is flavorful, about 20 minutes. Remove from heat.

4. Using a potato masher or an immersion blender, mash about half of the chickpeas and rice, or mash to desired consistency. Stir in lemon juice and season to taste with salt.

5. In a small bowl, combine cilantro and yogurt. Ladle soup into warm bowls and serve with a dollop of yogurt mixture.

Mulligatawny Soup

Serves 4 to 6

This is your generic mix-and-match Indian meal-size soup, which comes in as many versions as there are Indian restaurants in Britain, all of which have it on their menu. You can add or substitute vegetables, or make it vegetarian by replacing the chicken with ½ cup (125 mL) yellow lentils.

Tips

Chicken breasts can be used, but they don't provide as much flavor and tend to dry out. If using breasts, cut in half crosswise before adding to pot and reduce cooking time in step 2 to 20 to 25 minutes.

The soup can be prepared through the end of step 3, cooled, covered and refrigerated for up to 2 days. Reheat over medium heat until steaming and complete step 4.

1 tbsp	vegetable oil	15 mL
1	large carrot, diced	1
1	large onion, chopped	1
2	cloves garlic, minced	2
1 tbsp	minced gingerroot	15 mL
1½ tsp	curry powder or masala blend	7 mL
1½ tsp	salt	7 mL
½ tsp	freshly ground black pepper	2 mL
¼ tsp	ground cumin	1 mL
¼ cup	long-grain white rice	50 mL
1 lb	skinless bone-in chicken pieces (thighs or drumsticks)	500 g
6 cups	water	1.5 L
1	tart apple, diced (peeled, if desired)	1
1 cup	very small cauliflower florets, optional	250 mL
2 tbsp	chopped fresh cilantro	25 mL
2 tbsp	freshly squeezed lemon juice	25 mL

1. In a large pot, heat oil over medium heat. Add carrot and onion; cook, stirring, until starting to soften, about 5 minutes. Add garlic, ginger, curry powder, salt, pepper and cumin; cook, stirring, until softened and fragrant, about 2 minutes. Stir in rice.

2. Stir in chicken and water. Increase heat to medium-high and bring to a boil. Reduce heat to low, cover and simmer, stirring occasionally, until chicken is falling off the bone, rice is soft and broth is flavorful, about 30 minutes. Remove from heat.

3. Using a slotted spoon, remove chicken from pot and transfer to a shallow bowl. Let stand until cool enough to handle, about 10 minutes. Remove meat from bones and discard bones. Cut or tear chicken into small pieces. Return chicken and any accumulated juices to pot.

4. Stir in apple and cauliflower, if using. Bring to a simmer over medium heat. Reduce heat and simmer gently until apple and cauliflower are just tender, about 5 minutes. Stir in cilantro and lemon juice. Season to taste with salt.

Marinated Cucumber Carrot Salad

Serves 4 to 6

Inspired by the Thai garnish/pickle, this refreshing salad works well alongside fiery Thai recipes or on its own as one of the salads in a festive buffet.

• ◆ •

Variation
Cucumber Carrot Salad Appetizers: Serve a platter of Thai shrimp chips or shrimp-flavored rice crackers with the salad and let guests top the crackers using tongs or a pickle fork.

½ cup	granulated sugar	125 mL
¼ tsp	hot pepper flakes	1 mL
¼ tsp	salt	1 mL
½ cup	seasoned rice vinegar	125 mL
1 tsp	grated lime zest	5 mL
⅓ cup	freshly squeezed lime juice	75 mL
2	carrots, shredded	2
1	English cucumber, halved lengthwise and thinly sliced	1

1. In a small saucepan, combine sugar, hot pepper flakes, salt, vinegar and lime juice. Bring to boil over medium heat, stirring until sugar is dissolved. Remove from heat and let cool for 5 minutes. Stir in lime zest.
2. In a bowl, combine carrots and cucumber. Pour hot vinegar mixture over vegetables and toss to coat. Let cool. Cover and refrigerate until vegetables are soft and infused with flavor, at least 2 hours, or for up to 1 day. Season to taste with salt.

Peanut and Cucumber Salad

Cucumber, tasty and juicy in any guise, assumes a number of enhanced dimensions in this quick salad. It's a crunchy, refreshing accompaniment to any grill or curry, and also makes for a light starter or palate teaser before nearly any main course on your menu.

Tip

This salad is best served immediately to make sure the vegetables are crunchy. If necessary, it can be chilled for up to 2 hours.

1	English cucumber	1
1	red bell pepper, halved and thinly sliced	1
1	hot green chile pepper, minced, or to taste	1
½ cup	roasted salted peanuts, chopped	125 mL
1 tbsp	chopped fresh cilantro or mint	15 mL
1 tsp	cumin seeds	5 mL
1 tbsp	granulated sugar	15 mL
¼ tsp	salt	1 mL
¼ cup	freshly squeezed lime juice	50 mL

1. Cut cucumber crosswise into 2-inch (5 cm) chunks. Cut each chunk lengthwise into thin slices. Stack slices and cut lengthwise into thin strips. Transfer to a bowl. Add red pepper, chile pepper, peanuts and cilantro. Set aside.

2. In a small skillet, toast cumin seeds over medium heat, shaking pan almost constantly, until slightly darker brown and fragrant, about 2 minutes. Remove from heat and stir in sugar, salt and lime juice, stirring until sugar is dissolved. Pour over cucumber mixture and toss to coat.

Thai Yellow Curry Mango Salad

Serves 4

This is our salute to one of Thai cuisine's most famous salads, using the green mangoes that are ubiquitous in that tropical country and can be easily found in Asian markets on this side of the globe.

Tip

Green mangoes are firm enough to peel with a sharp vegetable peeler or paring knife. Peel off skin and cut flesh away from the pit in slices. Cut each slice crosswise into thin strips.

2 tbsp	vegetable oil	25 mL
1 tsp	Thai yellow curry paste	5 mL
1	clove garlic, minced	1
2 tbsp	packed brown or palm sugar	25 mL
2 tbsp	freshly squeezed lime juice	25 mL
1 tbsp	fish sauce or soy sauce	15 mL
1/4 tsp	Asian chili sauce	1 mL
1	large green mango (or 2 small), peeled and julienned	1
1/2	red bell pepper, diced	1/2
1/4 cup	very thinly sliced red onion	50 mL
1 tbsp	chopped fresh cilantro	15 mL
1 tsp	chopped fresh mint	5 mL
	Salt, optional	
	Ground or chopped roasted peanuts	

1. In a small saucepan, heat oil over medium-low heat. Add curry paste and cook, stirring, until softened and fragrant, about 2 minutes. Add garlic, brown sugar, lime juice, fish sauce and chili sauce; cook, stirring occasionally, just until sugar is dissolved, about 1 minute. Transfer to a bowl and let cool completely.

2. In a large bowl, combine mango, red pepper, onion, cilantro and mint. Add dressing and toss to coat. Season to taste with salt, if using. Serve sprinkled with peanuts. Serve immediately or cover and refrigerate for up to 8 hours. Let stand at room temperature for 30 minutes before serving.

Caribbean Curried Black–Eyed Pea and Potato Salad

Serves 4 to 8

Here's a potato salad with a difference: legumes for protein and generous spice for enjoyment. We need never settle for the bland, fatty mayo version again. This dish is better at room temperature than cold, so it sits well on outdoor summer buffets.

Tip

Softening the spices in oil is essential to creating a pleasant curry flavor for salads. It may seem like extra work, but the results are worth it.

Variation

In place of canned black-eyed peas, you can soak and cook 1 cup (250 mL) dried.

4	boiling or all-purpose potatoes, cut into ³⁄₄-inch (2 cm) cubes	4
	Cold water	
1 tsp	salt, divided	5 mL
¹⁄₃ cup	vegetable oil, divided	75 mL
4	green onions, sliced	4
2	cloves garlic, minced	2
½	Scotch bonnet pepper, minced, or to taste	½
1 tbsp	curry powder, preferably Caribbean-style	15 mL
1	can (14 to 19 oz/398 to 540 mL) black-eyed peas, drained and rinsed	1
¹⁄₃ cup	water	75 mL
¼ cup	white wine vinegar	50 mL
1 tsp	dry or Dijon mustard	5 mL
1 tsp	chopped fresh thyme	5 mL
	Freshly ground black pepper	

1. In a pot, cover potatoes with cold water. Add ½ tsp (2 mL) of the salt and bring to a boil over high heat. Reduce heat and boil gently until potatoes are just tender, about 15 minutes. Drain and transfer to a bowl. Let cool slightly.

2. Meanwhile, in a skillet, heat 2 tbsp (25 mL) of the oil over medium heat. Add green onions, garlic, Scotch bonnet pepper, curry powder and remaining salt; cook, stirring, until onions are softened and spices are fragrant, about 3 minutes.

3. Stir in black-eyed peas until coated with spices. Pour in the ¹⁄₃ cup (75 mL) water and cook, scraping up bits stuck to pan and stirring occasionally, until liquid is almost all absorbed, about 5 minutes. Pour over potatoes in bowl and toss to coat. Let cool to room temperature or refrigerate until chilled, about 2 hours.

4. In a small bowl, whisk together remaining oil, vinegar, mustard, thyme and pepper to taste. Pour over potato mixture and toss to coat. Season to taste with salt. Serve immediately or cover and refrigerate for up to 1 day.

Apricot Curry Mixed Rice Salad

Serves 4 to 6

Perfect for a summer picnic, this rice-based salad satisfies while it delights. It is fruity and light, but robust with its multi-flavor dressing. And it travels well. Lakeside-friendly dishes don't get much better than this.

• ◆ •

Tips

Use a prepackaged blend of different varieties of rice or combine two or more of your favorites. Just one type of rice will work, but the different varieties add terrific textures and flavors. Depending on the variety of rice, you'll need 1 to 2 cups (250 to 500 mL) uncooked rice.

The best way to cool rice for this salad while preserving the firm texture is to spread hot cooked rice out on a rimmed baking sheet lined with parchment paper and let cool.

• ◆ •

Variation

Substitute 1 cup (250 mL) chopped fresh apricots or peaches for the dried apricots.

Dressing

⅓ cup	vegetable oil, divided	75 mL
1	hot green or red chile pepper, minced	1
1 tbsp	minced gingerroot	15 mL
1 tsp	ground coriander	5 mL
½ tsp	ground cumin	2 mL
⅛ tsp	ground cinnamon	0.5 mL
½ tsp	Indian yellow curry paste or masala blend	2 mL
⅓ cup	white wine vinegar	75 mL
½ tsp	salt	2 mL
1 tbsp	liquid honey	15 mL
1 tsp	Dijon or dry mustard	5 mL
4 cups	cooked mixed rice, cooled (see tips, at left)	1 L
1 cup	grapes, halved	250 mL
½ cup	finely chopped red onion	125 mL
½ cup	diced dried apricots	125 mL
	Salt	
2 tbsp	chopped fresh cilantro and/or mint	25 mL

1. *Prepare the dressing:* In a small skillet, heat 2 tbsp (25 mL) of the oil over medium-low heat. Reduce heat to low and add chile pepper, ginger, coriander, cumin, cinnamon and curry paste; cook, stirring, until softened and fragrant, about 3 minutes. Remove from heat and add vinegar, scraping up bits stuck to pan. Transfer to a large bowl. Whisk in salt, honey, mustard and remaining oil. (The dressing can be used immediately or covered and refrigerated for up to 1 day.)

2. Add rice, grapes, onion and apricots to dressing and toss to coat. Serve at room temperature or cover and refrigerate until chilled, about 1 hour, or for up to 1 day. Season to taste with salt. Stir in cilantro and/or mint.

Curried Egg Salad

Serves 4 to 6

This egg salad with a bite may not be ideal for the school lunches of uninitiated preteens, but for people with a spice-sophisticated palate it's absolutely the ticket for a quick lunch item.

Tips

Some bottled curry pastes caution against consuming without cooking. If you prefer to use paste in this salad, be sure to read the label carefully.

This salad can be served immediately or transferred to an airtight container and refrigerated for up to 1 day.

Variation

Replace the celery with cucumber and the cilantro with 2 tsp (10 mL) chopped fresh dill.

8	eggs	8
	Cold water	
1 tsp	curry powder or masala blend	5 mL
½ tsp	salt	2 mL
½ tsp	ground coriander	2 mL
⅛ tsp	ground cumin	0.5 mL
½ cup	plain yogurt	125 mL
¼ cup	mayonnaise	50 mL
1 tsp	Dijon mustard	5 mL
½ cup	finely diced celery	125 mL
1 tbsp	chopped fresh cilantro	15 mL

1. In a large saucepan, cover eggs with cold water by about 1 inch (2.5 cm). Bring to a boil over high heat. Remove from heat, cover and let stand for 15 minutes. Place pan in the sink and run cold water into pan until water is completely cold. Let eggs stand in cold water, refreshing as necessary, until chilled. Drain and peel off shells. Rinse eggs and drain well.

2. In a large bowl, using a potato masher or pastry blender, mash eggs until finely chopped.

3. In another bowl, combine curry powder, salt, coriander, cumin, yogurt, mayonnaise and mustard. Add to eggs and stir until blended. Stir in celery and cilantro.

Curry Chicken, Apple and Raisin Salad

Serves 4 to 6

A favorite at Nuttshell Next Door, the café co-owned by Jennifer and her husband, Jay Nutt, this refreshing, delicious salad redefines the idea of chicken salad. Serve it in a wrap, on top of greens or on its own as part of a buffet.

Tip
Some bottled curry pastes caution against consuming without cooking. If you prefer to use paste in this salad, be sure to read the label carefully.

Variation
Substitute 2 ripe peaches for the apple and dried sour cherries for the raisins.

1 tsp	curry powder or masala blend	5 mL
¼ tsp	ground cumin	1 mL
1 tbsp	freshly squeezed lemon or lime juice	15 mL
½ cup	mayonnaise	125 mL
⅓ cup	plain yogurt	75 mL
2 tsp	liquid honey	10 mL
1	tart apple, diced (peeled, if desired)	1
1	green onion, finely chopped	1
3 cups	shredded or chopped cooked chicken (about 12 oz/375 g)	750 mL
⅓ cup	raisins	75 mL
	Salt	

1. In a bowl, whisk together curry powder, cumin and lemon juice until blended. Whisk in mayonnaise, yogurt and honey. (The dressing can be used immediately or covered and refrigerated for up to 2 days.)

2. Add apple, green onion, chicken and raisins to dressing and toss to coat. Season to taste with salt. Serve immediately or cover and refrigerate for up to 8 hours.

Sizzling Curry Lime Shrimp Salad

Serves 4 to 8

Shrimp, a popular treat, lie waiting in their marinade to get a quick transformation into sizzle and succulence in mere minutes of cooking. Here, they are presented on a bed of lettuce as a "warm" salad. For additional dressing on the greens, sprinkle with some extra drops of lime juice and a scant drizzle of olive oil.

Variation

Omit the mixed greens and serve shrimp hot with toothpicks as appetizers.

1 tsp	grated lime zest	5 mL
1/4 tsp	ground cumin	1 mL
1/4 tsp	ground coriander	1 mL
Pinch	salt	Pinch
2 tbsp	Indian yellow curry paste or masala blend	25 mL
1 tbsp	vegetable oil	15 mL
1 lb	large raw shrimp, peeled, deveined and patted dry	500 g
1/4 cup	freshly squeezed lime juice	50 mL
8 cups	mixed salad greens	2 L
1 cup	sliced cucumber	250 mL
	Chopped fresh cilantro	

1. In a large bowl or resealable plastic bag, combine lime zest, cumin, coriander, salt, curry paste and oil. Add shrimp and toss to coat. Cover or seal bag and refrigerate for at least 4 hours or up to 2 days.

2. Heat a large skillet over medium-high heat until very hot but not smoking. Cook shrimp, in batches, stirring, until pink and opaque, about 3 minutes per batch. Transfer cooked shrimp to a clean bowl and reheat pan between batches.

3. Add all shrimp back to the skillet and pour in lime juice. Cook, stirring, just until sizzling, about 1 minute. Let cool slightly. Season to taste with salt.

4. To serve, divide salad greens among serving plates. Top with cucumber and shrimp, drizzling any juice from the pan over top. Sprinkle with cilantro.

Curry Shrimp and Papaya Salad

Serves 6 to 8

A recipe that Jennifer's mom, Patricia, used to make back in the '70s is the inspiration for this salad. For special occasions, she would make a similarly sauced shrimp and white asparagus salad. We've given it an updated twist here with papaya. We dedicate this recipe to her.

Tip

Buy the best-quality salad shrimp you can find. Some are very soft and mushy and overall unpleasant. Good-quality ones have a much better taste and texture. They're worth the price.

2 tbsp	vegetable oil	25 mL
1	hot green chile pepper, minced	1
1/4 tsp	ground cumin	1 mL
1 tsp	Indian yellow curry paste or masala blend	5 mL
1/4 cup	mayonnaise	50 mL
1/4 cup	plain yogurt	50 mL
1 tsp	grated lemon or lime zest	5 mL
2 tbsp	freshly squeezed lemon or lime juice	25 mL
12 oz	cooked salad shrimp, drained and patted dry	375 g
2 cups	diced peeled papaya	500 mL
1	green onion, sliced	1
	Chopped fresh mint or basil	

1. In a small skillet, heat oil over medium-low heat. Add chile pepper, cumin and curry paste; cook, stirring, until softened and fragrant, about 2 minutes. Transfer to a bowl and let cool slightly. Stir in mayonnaise, yogurt, lemon zest and lemon juice until blended. (The dressing can be served immediately or covered and refrigerated for up to 1 day.)

2. Just before serving, in a bowl, combine shrimp and papaya. Add dressing and toss gently to coat. Transfer to a shallow serving dish and serve sprinkled with green onion and mint.

Curry-Marinated Scallop Salad

Serves 4 to 8

Delicate bay scallops flavored with spices and topped by toothsome vegetables make for a luxurious addition to any array of party appetizers. The only caveat: avoid overcooking the scallops to retain their texture and their sweetness.

Tips

It is important to pat the scallops dry to make sure they sear quickly in the pan rather than boil in liquid, which can cause them to become rubbery.

Removing the small connecter muscle attached to the scallops is tedious, but it really improves the texture of the salad.

1 lb	frozen bay scallops, thawed	500 g
2 tbsp	olive or vegetable oil	25 mL
2	cloves garlic, minced	2
1 or 2	hot green chile peppers, minced	1 or 2
½ tsp	Indian yellow curry paste or masala blend	2 mL
1	yellow or green zucchini, halved lengthwise and thinly sliced	1
½	red, orange or yellow bell pepper, halved crosswise and thinly sliced	½
2 tbsp	white wine vinegar	25 mL
½ tsp	salt	2 mL
	Chopped fresh cilantro and/or basil	

1. Drain scallops in a colander and rinse with cool water. Drain well. Using a sharp paring knife, carefully remove the small white muscle from each scallop. Place on a paper towel–lined plate and pat dry.

2. In a large skillet, heat oil over medium-high heat. Add garlic, chile peppers and curry paste; cook, stirring, until softened and fragrant, about 30 seconds. Add scallops and cook, stirring, until coated in spices and just starting to firm up, 1 to 2 minutes. Remove from heat. Using a slotted spoon, immediately transfer scallops to a shallow dish, leaving as much oil in the pan as possible. Set aside.

3. Return pan to medium-high heat and heat for 30 seconds. Add zucchini and red pepper; cook, stirring, just until starting to wilt, about 1 minute. Pour over scallops in dish. Sprinkle with vinegar and salt and toss to coat. Let cool. Cover and refrigerate until chilled, about 1 hour, or for up to 4 hours.

4. Just before serving, season to taste with salt. Serve sprinkled with cilantro and/or basil.

Lemongrass Curried Calamari Salad

Serves 4 to 6

Tender, barely cooked calamari, livened by the tangy perfume of lemongrass and garnished with the sweet tartness of fresh grapefruit, is an irresistible notion for all fans of this oh-so-fashionable squiggly seafood. It's an excellent alternative to the ubiquitous fried version.

• ◆ •

Tips

If lime leaves are not available, substitute 1 tsp (5 mL) grated lime zest and use lime juice instead of lemon. Add zest with juice in step 3.

The key to keeping calamari tender is to cook it in a hot pan and very quickly. Be sure the pan is hot before adding the calamari, stir it briskly and watch carefully, removing from heat just as the calamari starts to firm up.

1	stalk lemongrass	1
2 tbsp	vegetable or olive oil	25 mL
4	wild lime leaves (see tip, at left)	4
1 tsp	minced gingerroot	5 mL
1/2 tsp	salt	2 mL
1/4 tsp	ground turmeric	1 mL
1 tsp	Indian or Thai yellow curry paste or masala blend	5 mL
12 oz	frozen calamari rings, thawed, drained and patted dry	375 g
1/4 cup	freshly squeezed lemon or lime juice	50 mL
	Boston or butter lettuce leaves	
1 cup	pink grapefruit segments (about 1 large)	250 mL
2 tbsp	chopped fresh cilantro	25 mL

1. Trim off root end of lemongrass and peel off outer stalks. Cut remaining stalk into 2-inch (5 cm) sections. Cut the thickest two sections in half lengthwise and pull out the two or three tender inner layers. Mince the tender layers very finely to make about 1 tsp (5 mL).

2. In a large skillet, heat oil over medium-low heat. Add chopped and minced lemongrass and lime leaves; cook, stirring, until fragrant, about 2 minutes. Add ginger, salt, turmeric and curry paste; cook, stirring, until softened and fragrant, about 2 minutes.

3. Increase heat to medium-high and heat for 30 seconds. Add calamari and cook, stirring, until coated in spices and just starting to firm up, about 30 seconds. Remove from heat and immediately transfer calamari to a shallow dish. Add lemon juice to pan and scrape up any bits stuck to pan. Pour over calamari and toss to coat. Let cool. Cover and refrigerate until chilled, about 1 hour, or for up to 4 hours.

4. Just before serving, discard lime leaves and large pieces of lemongrass. Season salad to taste with salt. Line chilled serving plates with lettuce and top with calamari and grapefruit segments, drizzling with any marinade from dish. Serve sprinkled with cilantro.

Chilled Curried Banana Coconut Soup (page 13)

Mulligatawny Soup (page 21)

Curry Shrimp and Papaya Salad (page 30)

Fruity Mango Papaya Chutney (page 37)

Condiments

Cold Coconut Chutney

Makes about
1 cup (250 mL)

A blender is all that is
needed for this easy but
supremely aromatic chutney
that highlights the natural
taste of coconut with
exotic flavors. It can
be served alongside just
about any curry.

Tips

To shred fresh coconut,
peel off brown outer layer
and use the coarse side of a
box cheese grater, or pulse in
a food processor until finely
chopped but not smooth.
Frozen coconut is available
at Asian specialty stores; thaw
and drain well before using.

In a pinch, packaged dried
unsweetened coconut can
be used. Soak about ¾ cup
(175 mL) in boiling water for
1 hour, drain well and
measure out 1 cup (250 mL).

Store any extra chutney in
an airtight container in the
refrigerator for up to 5 days.

1	hot green chile pepper, coarsely chopped	1
1 cup	fresh or frozen unsweetened shredded coconut (see tips, at left)	250 mL
½ tsp	finely chopped gingerroot	2 mL
6	curry leaves	6
¼ tsp	salt	1 mL
1 cup	warm water (approx.)	250 mL

1. In a blender, combine chile pepper, coconut, ginger, curry leaves, salt and warm water. Let stand for 30 minutes, then blend until slightly coarse and a little runny. If too thick, add a little water and blend. Serve immediately or transfer to a bowl or container, cover and refrigerate until chilled, about 1 hour.

Serving Suggestions

Use as a filling for Easy Masala Dosas (page 276) or as a topping for Uthappam (page 275).

Serve with Sweet-and-Tangy Curry of Quail and Peaches (page 84), Slow-Braised Beef Curry with Turnips (page 98) or any of the tomato-based vegetable curries.

Hot Coconut Chutney

This cooked version of coconut chutney allows for the use of spices that shine best when heated.

Tips

To shred fresh coconut, peel off brown outer layer and use the coarse side of a box cheese grater, or pulse in a food processor until finely chopped but not smooth. Frozen coconut is available at Asian specialty stores; thaw and drain well before using.

In a pinch, packaged dried unsweetened coconut can be used. Soak about ⅓ cup (75 mL) in boiling water for 1 hour, drain well and measure out ½ cup (125 mL).

If you like extra zing, include the green chile pepper. If you want only a little zing, remove the seeds and ribs from the chile.

½ cup	fresh or frozen unsweetened shredded coconut (see tips, at left)	125 mL
½ cup	warm water (approx.)	125 mL
1 tbsp	vegetable oil	15 mL
1 tsp	finely chopped gingerroot	5 mL
1 tsp	mustard seeds	5 mL
¼ tsp	hot pepper flakes	1 mL
1	hot green chile pepper, chopped, optional	1
8	curry leaves	8
¼ tsp	ground coriander	1 mL

1. In a blender, combine coconut and warm water. Let stand for 30 minutes, then blend until slightly coarse and a little runny. If too thick, add a little water and blend. Transfer to a bowl and set aside.

2. In a skillet, heat oil over medium heat until hot but not smoking. Add ginger, mustard seeds and hot pepper flakes; cook, stirring, until the seeds start to pop, about 1 minute. Add chile pepper, if using, curry leaves and coriander; cook, stirring, for 1 minute. Immediately add coconut mixture and cook, stirring, until smooth and bubbling, 3 to 4 minutes. Remove from heat and serve immediately.

Serving Suggestion

Serve with Chicken and Vegetable Curry (page 64), Tomato Masala Curry Beef Kabobs (page 91) or Baked or Fried Samosas (pages 280 and 282).

Major Grey–Style Mango Chutney

Makes about 3 cups (750 mL)

Mango chutney, as redefined by the British during the Raj, has always been one of the staples (and maybe the greatest attraction) of curry houses outside India. Its sweet-tartness performs magic on the palate when eaten with hot curries and spicy tandooris. Here's a recipe that will last you a month of curries.

Tip

This recipe hasn't been tested for hot water processing and room temperature storage. It is best to make it in small enough batches to store in the refrigerator and use within a month.

Variation

Major Grey–Style Pear Chutney: Substitute peeled, cored very ripe pears for the mangoes. Pears that hold their flavor after cooking, such as Bartlett, Bosc or Packham varieties, are best.

• *Three 1-cup (250 mL) glass canning jars*

⅓ cup	packed brown sugar	75 mL
2 tsp	mustard seeds	10 mL
1 tsp	pickling or kosher salt	5 mL
½ tsp	ground cinnamon	2 mL
½ tsp	ground coriander	2 mL
¼ tsp	ground cloves	1 mL
⅛ tsp	ground cardamom	0.5 mL
½ cup	cider vinegar	125 mL
⅓ cup	light (fancy) molasses	75 mL
3	cloves garlic, minced	3
1	seedless orange, peeled and chopped	1
½	small lime (peel and fruit), seeds removed, finely chopped	½
¼	lemon (peel and fruit), seeds removed, finely chopped	¼
2½ cups	chopped peeled sweet mangoes (about 2 large)	625 mL
½ cup	finely chopped onion	125 mL
2 tbsp	finely chopped gingerroot	25 mL
½ cup	raisins	125 mL

1. Warm canning jars by filling with hot water. Set aside.
2. In a large pot, combine brown sugar, mustard seeds, salt, cinnamon, coriander, cloves, cardamom, vinegar and molasses. Stir in garlic, orange, lime, lemon, mangoes, onion, ginger and raisins. Bring to a boil over medium heat, stirring often. Reduce heat and boil gently, stirring often, until onions, lemon and lime rinds are very soft and mixture is thick, about 40 minutes.
3. Empty jars and pour in hot chutney. Let cool, cover and refrigerate for at least 1 day. Store in the refrigerator for up to 1 month. Bring to room temperature before serving.

Fruity Mango Papaya Chutney

Fruitier than plain mango chutney, this version will add zest to vegetable curries and works well with meat. It is also delicious as a spread for cheese sandwiches, especially those made with aged Cheddar.

Tips

Look for the rich-flavored mangoes with the yellow skin for a wonderful flavor and texture for this chutney. There are several varieties, such as Atulfo or Alfonso.

Storing chutney in clean glass canning jars preserves the quality better than storing in plastic containers as the jars can be sterilized to prevent contamination and off flavors from affecting the chutney.

• *Three 1-cup (250 mL) glass canning jars*

½ cup	finely chopped sweet onion	125 mL
2 tbsp	minced gingerroot	25 mL
1 cup	packed brown sugar	250 mL
½ tsp	salt	2 mL
½ tsp	ground cinnamon	2 mL
¼ tsp	ground nutmeg, preferably freshly grated	1 mL
⅛ tsp	ground cloves	0.5 mL
¾ cup	cider vinegar	175 mL
½ cup	water	125 mL
1	hot green or red chile pepper, minced	1
3 cups	chopped peeled sweet mangoes (about 2 large)	750 mL
1 cup	chopped peeled papaya	250 mL
½ tsp	grated lime zest	2 mL
2 tbsp	freshly squeezed lime juice	25 mL

1. Warm canning jars by filling with hot water. Set aside.

2. In a large saucepan, combine onion, ginger, brown sugar, salt, cinnamon, nutmeg, cloves, vinegar and water. Bring to a boil over medium heat, stirring until sugar is dissolved. Reduce heat and boil gently until onion is soft and liquid is slightly reduced.

3. Stir in chile pepper, mangoes and papaya. Increase heat to medium and boil gently, stirring often, until fruit is translucent, 10 to 15 minutes. Stir in lime zest and juice.

4. Empty jars and pour in hot chutney. Let cool, cover and refrigerate for at least 1 day. Store in the refrigerator for up to 1 month. Bring to room temperature before serving.

Serving Suggestion

Serve with Curry Lime Roasted Chicken (page 52), Jamaican Chicken Curry and Sweet Potatoes (page 56) or Guyanese Goat Curry (page 150).

Pickled Peach Chutney

**Makes about
2 cups (500 mL)**

This is a cross between a
chutney and a fresh pickle.
The fruity sweetness of
the wine and the fragrant
Indian spices are combined
with peaches for a summery
taste sensation.

Tips

Peaches don't seem to have
as much fuzz these days, so a
gentle scrub with your hands
under running water is
usually enough to remove it.
If you prefer to peel the
peaches, blanch them in
boiling water for 30 seconds,
then plunge them into cold
water to make peeling easier.

Using sliced peaches gives
this chutney a slightly
different texture than most;
if you prefer, you can chop
the peaches for a more
traditional texture.

This recipe hasn't been tested
for hot water processing and
room temperature storage.
It is best to make it in small
enough batches to store in
the refrigerator and use
within a month.

- 2-cup (500 mL) glass canning jar

1	stick cinnamon, about 2 inches (5 cm) long	1
1 tsp	mustard seeds	5 mL
⅛ tsp	cumin seeds	0.5 mL
⅛ tsp	fenugreek seeds	0.5 mL
Pinch	hot pepper flakes	Pinch
½ cup	Gewürztraminer, Vidal or other off-dry white wine	125 mL
½ cup	cider vinegar	125 mL
2½ cups	sliced peaches, peeled if desired (about 4)	625 mL
2 tsp	minced gingerroot	10 mL
⅓ cup	packed brown sugar	75 mL
½ tsp	kosher or sea salt	2 mL
1 tbsp	chopped fresh cilantro, optional	15 mL

1. Warm canning jar by filling with hot water. Set aside.
2. Heat a saucepan over medium heat until hot. Add cinnamon stick, mustard seeds, cumin seeds, fenugreek seeds and hot pepper flakes; toast, shaking pan constantly, until the seeds are fragrant and start to pop, about 2 minutes.
3. Carefully pour in wine and vinegar. Stir in peaches, ginger, brown sugar and salt; bring to a boil over medium-high heat. Reduce heat and simmer just until peaches start to soften and turn translucent, about 3 minutes. Remove from heat.
4. Empty jar and use a slotted spoon to transfer peaches and cinnamon stick to jar, packing lightly. Set aside.
5. Return pan to medium-high heat and boil syrup until thickened and reduced by about half, about 5 minutes. Stir in cilantro, if using. Pour syrup into jar, pressing peaches gently with a thin spatula to release air bubbles. Make sure peaches are covered with syrup. Let cool, cover and refrigerate for at least 2 days. Store in the refrigerator for up to 1 month.

Fresh Cilantro Mint Chutney

Makes about
½ cup (125 mL)

This herbal chutney adds perfume and freshness to curries, and particularly to tandoori meats.

Tip
Toast cumin seeds in a dry small skillet over medium heat, shaking pan almost constantly, until seeds are slightly darker and have a toasted aroma. Immediately transfer to a bowl.

1 or 2	hot green chile peppers, chopped	1 or 2
1 cup	packed fresh cilantro leaves	250 mL
¼ cup	packed fresh mint leaves	50 mL
1 tsp	granulated sugar	5 mL
½ tsp	toasted cumin seeds (see tip, at left)	2 mL
¼ tsp	salt	1 mL
2 tbsp	freshly squeezed lemon juice	25 mL
2 tbsp	water (approx.)	25 mL

1. In a food processor or blender, combine chile peppers, cilantro, mint, sugar, cumin seeds, salt and lemon juice. Purée, adding just enough water to make a smooth paste and scraping the sides of the bowl or jug as necessary to incorporate the ingredients.
2. Serve immediately or transfer to an airtight container and refrigerate for up to 3 days. Stir to recombine ingredients and let warm to room temperature before serving.

Fresh Banana Mint Chutney

Makes about
¾ cup (175 mL)

Banana is probably the most difficult fruit to tame into a condiment, yet it works like a charm in this simple recipe.

Tip
If tamarind concentrate isn't available, substitute 2 tbsp (25 mL) thick tamarind water (see page 18).

2	very ripe bananas	2
1 tsp	chopped fresh mint	5 mL
½ tsp	minced gingerroot	2 mL
1 tbsp	tamarind concentrate (see tip, at left)	15 mL
1 tbsp	freshly squeezed lime juice	15 mL
¼ tsp	Asian chili sauce	1 mL
	Salt	

1. In a bowl, mash bananas until fairly smooth but with a few small pieces remaining. Stir in mint, ginger, tamarind, lime juice and chili sauce. Season to taste with salt. Serve immediately or cover and refrigerate for up to 8 hours. Bring to room temperature before serving.

Banana Tamarind Chutney

This tart and lively chutney with a complex taste combination will serve smoothly and meaningfully when sweetness is needed to alleviate the heat of a curry.

Tips

Check your package of tamarind to see if there is salt added. If not, increase the salt to ½ tsp (2 mL).

Chutney can be served the day it is made, but it benefits from standing for at least 1 day to allow the flavors to develop.

• *Two 1-cup (250 mL) glass canning jars*

2 oz	piece tamarind block, broken into small pieces (see tip, at left)	60 g
1 cup	boiling water	250 mL
1	small onion, finely chopped	1
1 tbsp	minced gingerroot	15 mL
¼ cup	raisins or chopped dates	50 mL
2 tbsp	packed brown sugar	25 mL
½ tsp	garam masala	2 mL
¼ tsp	salt	1 mL
¼ tsp	ground cumin	1 mL
Pinch	cayenne pepper	Pinch
2	very ripe bananas	2

1. In a heatproof bowl, combine tamarind and boiling water. Let stand until soft, about 30 minutes. Press pulp through a sieve into a saucepan, discarding seeds and skins.

2. Warm canning jars by filling with hot water. Set aside.

3. Add onion, ginger, raisins, brown sugar, garam masala, salt, cumin and cayenne to tamarind pulp. Bring to a boil over medium heat, stirring until sugar is dissolved. Reduce heat and boil gently, stirring occasionally, until onion is very soft and mixture has a jammy consistency, about 20 minutes. Remove from heat.

4. Add bananas and mash until fairly smooth. Return to medium-low heat and boil gently, stirring often, until banana is blended and chutney is slightly thickened, about 10 minutes.

5. Empty jars and pour in hot chutney. Let cool. Serve at room temperature or cover and refrigerate. Store in the refrigerator for up to 1 month. Bring to room temperature before serving.

> ## Serving Suggestion
>
> Serve as a dip for Vegetable Pakoras (page 278).

Rhubarb Chutney

❦

Rhubarb lends its sweet-tart wholesomeness to jams and pie fillings, and now to this tasty side dish for curries.

• ◆ •

Tips

In place of tamarind concentrate or paste, you can substitute 2 tbsp (25 mL) thick tamarind water (see page 18).

Chutney can be served the day it is made, but it benefits from standing for at least 1 day to allow the flavors to develop.

This recipe hasn't been tested for hot water processing and room temperature storage. It is best to make it in small enough batches to store in the refrigerator and use within a month.

• *Three 1-cup (250 mL) glass canning jars*

1	onion, chopped	1
2 cups	chopped rhubarb	500 mL
2 tbsp	minced gingerroot	25 mL
1½ cups	packed light brown sugar	375 mL
2 tsp	mustard seeds	10 mL
¼ tsp	ground cumin	1 mL
¼ tsp	salt	1 mL
Pinch	hot pepper flakes	Pinch
1¼ cups	cider vinegar	300 mL
1 tbsp	tamarind concentrate or paste (see tip, at left)	15 mL

1. Warm canning jars by filling with hot water. Set aside.

2. In a saucepan, combine onion, rhubarb, ginger, brown sugar, mustard seeds, cumin, salt, hot pepper flakes, vinegar and tamarind. Bring to a boil over medium heat, stirring until sugar is dissolved. Reduce heat and boil gently, stirring occasionally, until rhubarb is very soft and mixture is thick, about 40 minutes.

3. Empty jars and pour in hot chutney. Let cool. Serve at room temperature or cover and refrigerate. Store in the refrigerator for up to 1 month. Bring to room temperature before serving.

Tomato Chutney

1 tbsp	vegetable oil	15 mL
½ tsp	mustard seeds	2 mL
½ cup	chopped onion	125 mL
1 tbsp	finely chopped garlic	15 mL
1 tbsp	finely chopped gingerroot	15 mL
8	curry leaves	8
½ tsp	hot pepper flakes	2 mL
½ tsp	salt	2 mL
¼ tsp	ground turmeric	1 mL
2 cups	finely chopped fresh or canned tomatoes with juice	500 mL

1. In a saucepan, heat oil over medium heat until hot but not smoking. Add mustard seeds and cook, stirring, until the seeds start to pop, about 1 minute. Add onion, garlic, ginger and curry leaves; cook, stirring, until onion starts to soften, 1 to 2 minutes. Add hot pepper flakes, salt and turmeric; cook, stirring, for 30 seconds.

2. Add tomatoes and bring to a simmer, stirring until well mixed. Simmer, stirring often, until chutney is reduced and thickened, about 15 minutes. Remove from heat and let cool.

3. Transfer to a blender or food processor and purée until saucy and smooth. Transfer to a bowl or container, cover and refrigerate until chilled, about 1 hour. Serve cold.

Sweet Onion and Date Chutney

• *2-cup (500 mL) glass canning jar*

1½ cups	finely chopped sweet onion	375 mL
1 cup	chopped dates	250 mL
1 tbsp	minced gingerroot	15 mL
¼ cup	packed brown sugar	50 mL
1 tbsp	mustard seeds	15 mL
½ tsp	pickling or kosher salt	2 mL
Pinch	freshly ground black pepper	Pinch
½ cup	cider or white wine vinegar	125 mL
½ cup	water	125 mL

1. Warm canning jar by filling with hot water. Set aside.
2. In a saucepan, combine onion, dates, ginger, brown sugar, mustard seeds, salt, pepper, vinegar and water. Bring to a boil over medium heat, stirring until sugar is dissolved. Reduce heat and boil gently, stirring occasionally, until onion is very soft and mixture has a jammy consistency, 15 to 20 minutes.
3. Empty jar and pour in hot chutney. Let cool, cover and refrigerate for at least 1 day. Store in the refrigerator for up to 1 month. Bring to room temperature before serving.

Fresh Mint Raita

**Makes about
1 cup (250 mL)**

Delightful and minty,
this refreshing sauce will
complement any meat curry,
and especially lamb or goat.

1 cup	thick plain yogurt (see tip, below left)	250 mL
1 tbsp	freshly squeezed lime juice	15 mL
¼ tsp	salt	1 mL
⅛ tsp	ground cumin	0.5 mL
¼ cup	finely chopped fresh mint	50 mL

1. In a bowl, stir yogurt until smooth and blended. Stir in lime juice, salt and cumin. Fold in mint until well mixed. Transfer to a serving bowl, if desired. Serve at room temperature.

Tomato Garlic Raita

**Makes about
1½ cups (375 mL)**

Gently spiced and tomato-
tart, this yogurt sauce makes
a pleasant side sauce and also
works well as a dip for chips
or raw vegetables.

Tip
Use full-fat, Greek-style
or Balkan-style yogurt for
the best texture. To use a
lower-fat yogurt, place
about 1½ cups (375 mL)
into a coffee filter– or
cheesecloth-lined sieve placed
over a bowl. Refrigerate and
let drain until thickened but
not dry, about 4 hours.

1 cup	thick plain yogurt (see tip, at left)	250 mL
¼ tsp	salt	1 mL
1 cup	finely diced seeded tomato	250 mL
1 tbsp	vegetable oil	15 mL
¼ tsp	cumin seeds	1 mL
2 tbsp	minced garlic	25 mL
	Chopped fresh cilantro	

1. In a bowl, stir yogurt and salt until smooth and blended. Fold in tomato until well mixed. Set aside.

2. In a small skillet, heat oil over medium heat until hot but not smoking. Add cumin seeds and cook, stirring, until the seeds start to pop, about 1 minute. Add garlic and cook, stirring, just until garlic is wilted, about 30 seconds. Remove from heat and stir gently into the yogurt mixture. Transfer to a serving bowl, if desired, and sprinkle with cilantro. Serve at room temperature.

Fruit Raita

Makes about

1½ cups (375 mL)

Cool and refreshing, this easy fruit and yogurt sauce does wonders to put out the fires that erupt from eating curry. Serve it beside all curries, and particularly the hot ones.

1 cup	thick plain yogurt (see tip, page 44)	250 mL
1 tbsp	freshly squeezed lemon juice	15 mL
¼ tsp	salt	1 mL
1 cup	finely diced fruit (apple, pear, mango, papaya, in any combination)	250 mL
Pinch	garam masala	Pinch
	Vegetable oil	

1. In a bowl, stir yogurt until smooth and blended. Stir in lemon juice and salt. Fold in fruit until well mixed. Transfer to a serving bowl, if desired. Sprinkle with garam masala and a few drops of oil. Serve at room temperature.

Cucumber Raita

Makes about

1¾ cups (425 mL)

The grandparent of Greek tzatziki, this sauce is ideal alongside tandoori meats, to which it adds yet another gustatory dimension.

Tip

This raita is best eaten soon after it is made. If stored longer than a few hours, the cucumber tends to release its juices, making the texture watery and unpleasant.

1 cup	thick plain yogurt (see tip, page 44)	250 mL
1 tbsp	freshly squeezed lemon juice	15 mL
¼ tsp	salt	1 mL
1	hot green chile pepper, finely chopped	1
¾ cup	finely diced seeded cucumber	175 mL
¼ cup	finely diced red onion	50 mL
Pinch	garam masala	Pinch
	Vegetable oil	

1. In a bowl, stir yogurt until smooth and blended. Stir in lemon juice and salt. Fold in chile pepper, cucumber and red onion until well mixed. Transfer to a serving bowl, if desired. Sprinkle with garam masala and a few drops of oil. Serve at room temperature.

Caramelized Mango Relish

**Makes about
2 cups (500 mL)**

Here's a brilliant method
(if we do say so ourselves) of
caramelizing mango without
softening its texture, for a
relish that might become the
highlight of the meal it's
meant to enhance.

¼ cup	granulated sugar	50 mL
¼ cup	white vinegar	50 mL
1	large sweet mango, peeled and diced	1
1	small red bell pepper, diced	1
¼ cup	finely chopped red onion	50 mL
¼ tsp	hot pepper flakes	1 mL
¼ tsp	ground cumin	1 mL
¼ tsp	freshly ground black pepper	1 mL
	Salt	
1 tbsp	chopped fresh cilantro	15 mL

1. In a small saucepan over low heat, gently heat sugar and
   vinegar, stirring until sugar is dissolved. Increase heat to
   medium and bring to a gentle boil. Boil without stirring,
   swirling pan gently as the color appears, until syrup turns
   a golden caramel color, about 8 minutes. Remove from heat
   and let cool just until bubbles subside.

2. Meanwhile, in a heatproof bowl, combine mango, red
   pepper, onion, hot pepper flakes, cumin and black pepper.
   Pour in syrup (it will harden upon contact with the mango
   mixture and then soften again).

3. Cover and refrigerate until caramel is dissolved and flavors
   are blended, about 1 hour, or for up to 1 day. Season to taste
   with salt and stir in cilantro.

Fresh Mango Pineapple Relish

Makes about 2½ cups (625 mL)

This spicy, tropical fruit salad adds flavor and lightness to meat and chicken curries.

Tip

This relish is best made just before serving but can be covered and refrigerated for up to 2 hours.

Variations

Fresh Mango Melon Relish: Replace half or all of the pineapple with diced peeled melon, such as cantaloupe, Crenshaw, honeydew or Santa Claus melon.

Fresh Sweet Mango Pineapple Relish: Replace the green mango with 1 large firm ripe sweet mango and omit the honey.

1	large green mango (or 2 small), peeled and diced	1
1½ cups	diced fresh pineapple	375 mL
1 tbsp	chopped fresh cilantro	15 mL
1 tsp	minced fresh hot chile pepper, or to taste	5 mL
¼ tsp	salt	1 mL
1 tsp	grated lime zest	5 mL
2 tbsp	freshly squeezed lime juice	25 mL
1 tbsp	liquid honey	15 mL

1. In a bowl, combine mango, pineapple, cilantro, chile pepper, salt, lime zest, lime juice and honey. Toss gently to combine. Season with additional chile pepper and salt, if desired.

Serving Suggestion

Serve with Braised Pork with Caribbean Coconut Lime Curry (page 115), Grilled Tilapia in Jamaican Curry (page 161) or Caribbean Curry Rice and Peas (page 262).

Green Mango Pickle

**Makes about
2 cups (500 mL)**

Green mangoes are readily
available in Asian markets.
They are aromatic and
slightly tart, and have a
sturdy texture for easy dicing
and pickling. Their fruity
taste makes an excellent
counterpoint to curries.

● *2-cup (500 mL) glass canning jar*

2 cups	diced peeled green mangoes (about 2)	500 mL
1 tbsp	pickling or kosher salt	15 mL
2 tsp	fenugreek seeds	10 mL
½ tsp	fennel seeds	2 mL
⅔ cup	vegetable oil	150 mL
5	curry leaves	5
2 tsp	mustard seeds	10 mL
¼ tsp	hot pepper flakes, or to taste	1 mL
⅛ tsp	ground turmeric	0.5 mL

1. In a heatproof bowl, combine mangoes and salt. Let stand
   at room temperature for 1 hour. Drain off liquid but do not
   rinse. Return to bowl.

2. Warm canning jar by filling with hot water. Set aside.

3. In a small dry skillet, toast fenugreek seeds and fennel seeds
   over medium heat, shaking pan almost constantly, until
   slightly darker and fragrant. Transfer to a spice grinder
   or mortar and grind to a powder. Set aside.

4. In the same skillet, heat oil over medium heat until hot
   but not smoking. Add curry leaves, mustard seeds and hot
   pepper flakes. Cook, stirring, until mustard seeds darken
   slightly but are not yet popping, about 30 seconds. Remove
   from heat and stir in ground fenugreek mixture and
   turmeric. Pour over mangoes and toss to coat evenly.

5. Empty jar and pour in mango mixture. Insert a thin spatula
   into jar to remove any air bubbles and pack pieces down to
   ensure mangoes are covered with oil. Let cool, cover and
   refrigerate for at least 3 days. Store in the refrigerator for
   up to 1 month. Bring to room temperature before serving.

Spicy Pickled Green Beans

Makes about 4 cups (1 L)

Layers of flavors and barely cooked green beans combine to produce a simple but surprisingly satisfying pickle. It does wonders alongside creamy curries, providing crunch and freshness.

Tips

Keep in mind that Scotch bonnet peppers will add quite a bit of heat to these pickles — go for it if you like them fiery!

This recipe hasn't been tested for boiling water processing. Be sure to keep filled jars refrigerated.

- Two 2-cup (500 mL) glass canning jars

1 lb	green beans	500 g
½ cup	granulated sugar	125 mL
1 tbsp	pickling or kosher salt	15 mL
1 tsp	celery seeds	5 mL
1 tsp	mustard seeds	5 mL
½ tsp	cumin seeds	2 mL
1¾ cups	white wine vinegar	425 mL
⅔ cup	water	150 mL
1 or 2	hot chile peppers, seeded and quartered (long red chile, jalapeño or Scotch bonnet)	1 or 2

1. Warm canning jars by filling with hot water. Set aside.

2. Rinse green beans well under cold running water. Drain well. Cut off stems and discard any imperfect beans. Set aside.

3. In a large saucepan, combine sugar, salt, celery seeds, mustard seeds, cumin seeds, vinegar and water. Bring to a boil over medium heat, stirring until sugar is dissolved. Add beans, pressing to immerse in liquid, and return to a boil. Remove from heat.

4. Empty jars and place half the chile pepper pieces in each jar. Add beans, packing lightly but leaving room for liquid. Fill jars with enough pickling liquid to cover beans. Let cool, cover and refrigerate for at least 3 days. Store in refrigerator for up to 1 month.

Spicy Peanut Sauce

Makes about 1 cup (250 mL)

A generic sauce of Thai and Indonesian cuisines, peanut sauce's most famous use is with satay, but it can dress up any marinated and grilled meat, or can even be thinned out with warm water for a salad dressing.

Tip

If you want to make the sauce ahead, do not add the garlic in step 1. Cover and refrigerate sauce for up to 1 week, adding garlic and reheating gently over low heat before serving.

1	small clove garlic, minced	1
1 tsp	minced gingerroot	5 mL
1/2 tsp	granulated sugar	2 mL
1/4 tsp	hot pepper flakes	1 mL
1/3 cup	coconut milk	75 mL
1 tbsp	freshly squeezed lime or lemon juice or rice vinegar	15 mL
2 tsp	soy sauce	10 mL
1/2 cup	smooth peanut butter	125 mL

1. In a small saucepan over low heat, combine garlic, ginger, sugar, hot pepper flakes, coconut milk, lime juice and soy sauce. Cook, stirring until sugar is dissolved, just until steaming, about 2 minutes. Remove from heat.

2. Whisk in peanut butter just until melted. Serve immediately or cover and refrigerate for up to 1 day. Bring to room temperature or warm slightly before serving.

Poultry

— ◆ —

Curry Lime Roasted Chicken

Serves 4

Burnished, crispy roast chicken with a curried sauce and a honey-sweet finish. This one is special enough for the meat course of Sunday dinner. Celebrate it with a couple of vegetable curries and a festive rice on the side.

Tips

Be sure your roasting pan is suitable for use on the stovetop. Those with nonstick coatings often aren't. If your pan can't be used on the burner, transfer the stock and drippings to a saucepan.

To use curry powder or masala blend in place of curry paste, add 1 tsp (5 mL) of vegetable oil, or just enough to make a thick, smooth paste. If the paste is too thin, it will run off the chicken rather than coating it nicely.

- *Roasting pan with rack*
- *Meat thermometer*

1	roasting chicken (about 3 lbs/1.5 kg)	1
	Salt and freshly ground black pepper	
½	lime	½
½ tsp	ground cumin	2 mL
4 tsp	Indian yellow curry paste	20 mL
¼ cup	liquid honey	50 mL
¼ cup	chicken stock, optional	50 mL
	Lime wedges	

1. Rinse chicken inside and out and pat dry. Place on rack in roasting pan and sprinkle inside and out with salt and pepper.

2. Finely grate zest and squeeze juice from lime. Set both aside separately. Place lime rind inside chicken cavity. Tie legs and tuck wings under back.

3. In a bowl, combine cumin, curry paste and 1 tbsp (15 mL) of the lime juice. Spread evenly over chicken. Let stand at room temperature for 15 minutes. Meanwhile, preheat oven to 325°F (160°C).

4. In a separate bowl, combine honey, lime zest and remaining lime juice. Set aside.

5. Roast chicken for 75 minutes. Gently baste with about one-third of the honey mixture and roast, basting two more times with remaining honey mixture, until thermometer inserted in thickest part of thigh reaches 180°F (82°C), about 30 minutes. Transfer to a cutting board, tent with foil and let rest for 15 minutes before carving.

6. If desired, add stock to drippings in roasting pan. Place pan over medium heat (see tip, at left) and bring drippings to a boil, scraping up bits stuck to pan. Boil until slightly reduced, about 2 minutes.

7. Carve chicken and serve with pan juices, if using, and lime wedges to squeeze over top.

Beginner's Curry Chicken and Rice

Serves 4

Developed by Jennifer for the Dairy Farmers of Canada's Milk Calendar, this recipe uses milk, rice and chicken in a mildly curried sauce. It's a great introduction to curry, and usually quite a favorite with kids.

• ◆ •

Tip

To satisfy more adventurous palates, serve an Asian hot chili sauce or hot chutney as a topping.

• ◆ •

Variation

Substitute another frozen mixed vegetable blend, such as California mix or one of the Asian blends, for the peas and carrots.

1 tbsp	butter	15 mL
1 lb	boneless skinless chicken thighs	500 g
3	cloves garlic, minced	3
1	onion, chopped	1
1 tsp	salt	5 mL
1 tbsp	mild Indian yellow curry paste or powder	15 mL
1 cup	parboiled long-grain white rice	250 mL
2 tbsp	all-purpose flour	25 mL
2 cups	milk	500 mL
1 cup	chicken stock	250 mL
2 cups	frozen mixed peas and carrots, thawed	500 mL
½ cup	plain yogurt	125 mL
	Lime or lemon wedges	

1. In a large nonstick skillet, melt butter over medium-high heat. Add chicken and cook, turning once, until well browned, 2 to 3 minutes per side. Transfer to a bowl.

2. Reduce heat to medium. Add garlic, onion, salt and curry paste to pan and cook, stirring, until softened, about 3 minutes. Stir in rice until coated in spices.

3. Whisk flour into milk and gradually stir into pan. Stir in stock and bring to a boil, scraping up bits stuck to pan. Nestle chicken pieces into rice in a single layer and add any accumulated juices to pan.

4. Reduce heat to medium-low, cover and simmer until rice is almost tender, about 20 minutes. Gently stir in peas and carrots. Cover and cook until juices run clear when chicken is pierced and rice is tender, about 5 minutes. Remove from heat and let stand, covered, for 5 minutes. Serve topped with yogurt and garnished with lime wedges to squeeze over top.

Tropical Chicken, Pineapple and Banana Curry

Serves 4

Jennifer's friends Rob and Carey Moluchi generously shared their favorite chicken curry recipe with us. It is a hit at parties with its combination of sweet and savory. They often make two or even three versions with progressively more heat to please all of the partygoers. "Texmati" or basmati rice is the perfect accompaniment.

Tips

This version is on the mild side. If you prefer more heat, just add more cayenne or pass some Caribbean hot sauce at the table for those guests who like to spice it up.

If you don't have Caribbean-style curry powder, substitute Indian curry powder. It will likely be a little spicier, so you may want to decrease the cayenne pepper to a pinch, unless you want it fiery.

4 tsp	curry powder, preferably Caribbean-style	20 mL
¾ tsp	salt	3 mL
¼ tsp	cayenne pepper	1 mL
½ cup	chicken stock	125 mL
2 tbsp	freshly squeezed lemon juice	25 mL
2 tbsp	olive or vegetable oil	25 mL
1	clove garlic, smashed	1
8	skinless bone-in chicken thighs or drumsticks, trimmed	8
1	large sweet onion, such as Vidalia, chopped	1
1	red bell pepper, halved and sliced	1
1	green bell pepper, halved and sliced	1
1 cup	drained canned or fresh pineapple chunks	250 mL
½ cup	raisins, preferably sultanas	125 mL
1 tbsp	cornstarch	15 mL
⅓ cup	rum	75 mL
2	firm ripe bananas	2
½ cup	salted roasted cashews	125 mL

1. In a bowl, combine curry powder, salt, cayenne, stock and lemon juice. Set aside.

2. In a large, deep skillet, heat oil over medium heat. Add garlic and cook, stirring, until fragrant. Transfer to a bowl.

3. Add chicken to pan, in batches if necessary, and cook, turning, until browned on all sides, about 10 minutes. Transfer to another bowl.

4. Spoon off all but 1 tbsp (15 mL) of the oil. Add onion and reserved garlic to pan and cook, stirring, until onion is softened, about 5 minutes. Add stock mixture to pan and bring to a simmer, scraping up bits stuck to pan.

5. Return chicken and accumulated juices to pan, turning chicken to coat in sauce. Reduce heat to low, cover and simmer, stirring and turning chicken once, for 20 minutes. Stir in red and green peppers, pineapple and raisins. Increase heat to medium-low, cover and simmer until juices run clear when chicken is pierced, about 10 minutes.

6. Meanwhile, in a small bowl, whisk cornstarch into rum. Slice bananas. Using tongs, transfer chicken to a warmed serving dish and keep warm.

7. Stir rum mixture and bananas into skillet. Increase heat to medium and bring to a boil, stirring gently. Boil, stirring often, until sauce is thickened and glossy, about 3 minutes. Season to taste with salt. Pour over chicken in dish and serve sprinkled with cashews.

Serving Suggestion

Create a Caribbean-themed meal with appetizer-size Jamaican Curried Beef Patties (page 108), serve the chicken curry with rice or Chile Pepper Cornbread (page 272) and with Curried Okra (Bindi) Masala (page 229), and finish off with fresh melon scented with mint. To drink? Rum punch, of course.

Tip

For maximum convenience, look for skinless bone-in chicken (preferably air-chilled). If skinless is not available, to remove skin from drumsticks, use the tip of a paring knife to slit the skin lengthwise down the drumstick, being careful not to pierce the meat. Using a paper towel to help grip the skin, peel from the thick end to the narrow and cut the skin off at the knuckle.

Jamaican Chicken Curry and Sweet Potatoes

Serves 4

The Caribbean got its curry dishes courtesy of the British, who imported the notion from their colonies on the subcontinent. In Jamaica, the most British of all the Caribbean nations, they developed their own versions of highly flavored curries, which, more often than not, are fiery hot with Scotch bonnet chiles. This dish combines chicken with sweet potatoes for a meaningful taste that lingers on the taste buds long after it's eaten. It also reheats very well.

Tips

Be very cautious when chopping Scotch bonnet peppers. Wear disposable gloves and wash all utensils and cutting boards well.

To add more body to the sauce, leave about 6 pieces of sweet potato in the pot and mash into sauce while boiling in step 4.

2 tbsp	curry powder, preferably Jamaican- or other Caribbean-style	25 mL
½ tsp	ground allspice	2 mL
¼ tsp	salt	1 mL
	Juice of 1 lime	
8	skinless bone-in chicken thighs, trimmed (or 4 breasts, cut in half)	8
1 tbsp	vegetable oil	15 mL
4	cloves garlic, minced	4
3	green onions, sliced	3
½	Scotch bonnet pepper, minced, or to taste	½
1 tbsp	minced gingerroot	15 mL
2 cups	chicken stock or water	500 mL
1	large sweet potato, peeled and cut into 1½-inch (4 cm) chunks	1

1. In a non-reactive bowl, combine curry powder, allspice, salt and lime juice. Add chicken and toss to coat evenly. Cover and refrigerate for at least 1 hour or for up to 1 day. Let stand at room temperature for 15 minutes.

2. In a large pot, heat oil over medium heat. Add garlic, onions, Scotch bonnet pepper and ginger; cook, stirring, until onions are softened but not browned, about 2 minutes. Add chicken mixture and cook, stirring, just until chicken turns white, about 3 minutes. Add stock and bring to a simmer, scraping up bits stuck to pan. Stir in sweet potato.

3. Reduce heat to low, cover and simmer, stirring and turning chicken pieces occasionally, until juices run clear when chicken is pierced and potatoes are tender, 30 to 40 minutes. Using a slotted spoon, transfer chicken and potatoes to a warmed serving dish and keep warm.

4. Increase heat to medium-high and boil sauce, uncovered, until slightly thickened, about 5 minutes. Season to taste with salt. Pour over chicken and potatoes.

Guyanese Curry Chicken and Potatoes

Serves 4

The deep, mellow spices and melt-in-your-mouth chicken in a deep golden sauce make this dish a wonderful taste of Guyana.

Tip

Garam masala from Guyana is a blend of roasted spices. If you have unroasted garam masala, toast in a dry small skillet over medium heat, stirring constantly, until the color darkens and spices smell toasted, about 2 minutes.

Serving Suggestion

Serve with fried plantain or Curried Plantain with Raisins and Pecans (page 215).

8	bone-in chicken thighs, trimmed (or 4 breasts, cut in half), skin removed if desired	8
½ tsp	salt	2 mL
¼ tsp	freshly ground black pepper	1 mL
4	cloves garlic	4
1	onion, cut into 8 pieces	1
2 tbsp	curry powder, preferably Guyanese- or other Caribbean-style	25 mL
2 tsp	garam masala, preferably Guyanese-style	10 mL
¼ cup	water	50 mL
1 tbsp	vegetable oil	15 mL
4	small boiling or all-purpose potatoes, cut into quarters	4
1	large ripe tomato, chopped	1
1½ cups	chicken stock	375 mL

1. In a bowl, sprinkle chicken with salt and pepper. Toss to coat evenly. Let stand at room temperature for 15 minutes.
2. In a blender or food processor, purée garlic, onion, curry powder, garam masala and water until fairly smooth.
3. In a large pot, heat oil over medium heat. Add puréed mixture and cook, stirring, until fragrant and starting to thicken, about 3 minutes. Add chicken and cook, stirring, until most of the liquid has evaporated and chicken turns white, about 3 minutes.
4. Stir in potatoes and tomato. Add stock and bring to a simmer, scraping up bits stuck to pan. Reduce heat to low, cover and simmer, stirring and turning chicken pieces once, until chicken is no longer pink inside and potatoes are tender, 30 to 40 minutes. Using a slotted spoon, transfer chicken to a warmed serving dish and keep warm.
5. Increase heat to medium-high and boil sauce and potatoes gently, uncovered, reducing heat slightly if necessary, until sauce is slightly thickened, about 5 minutes. Season to taste with salt. Pour sauce over chicken.

African Curried Chicken with Pumpkin

Serves 4

This stew picks up on flavors of sub-Saharan Africa. The characteristic peanuts, often called groundnuts, lend richness to the gravy and blend subtly with curry, providing deep flavor to chicken and pumpkin. It's deliciously comforting on any continent.

Tips

If using peanuts, they give the best texture to the sauce if pulsed in a food processor to a coarse meal (without processing too much into butter). You may need to do more than ¼ cup (50 mL), depending on the size of your food processor. Extra ground nuts can be frozen for future use.

Pumpkin can be difficult to peel, depending on its firmness and the thickness of the rind (and the sharpness of your peeler). If necessary, cut pumpkin into wedges, scoop out seeds and place wedges on a baking sheet. Bake in a 400°F (200°C) oven just until skin and flesh start to soften, about 10 minutes.

1 tbsp	vegetable oil	15 mL
4	whole cloves	4
1	stick cinnamon, broken in half	1
2 tsp	mustard seeds	10 mL
2	onions, chopped	2
2 or 3	hot green or red chile peppers, minced	2 or 3
1 tbsp	minced gingerroot	15 mL
2 tbsp	curry powder	25 mL
½ tsp	salt	2 mL
8	skinless bone-in chicken thighs, trimmed (or 4 breasts, cut in half)	8
1½ cups	chicken stock or water	375 mL
¼ cup	finely ground peanuts or peanut butter (see tip, at left)	50 mL
3 cups	cubed (1-inch/2.5 cm) peeled pie pumpkin or butternut squash	750 mL
	Juice of ½ lemon	

1. In a large pot, heat oil over medium heat until hot but not smoking. Add cloves, cinnamon and mustard seeds; cook, stirring, until toasted and fragrant, about 1 minute. Add onions and cook, stirring, until onions are softened, about 5 minutes. Add chile peppers, ginger, curry powder and salt; cook, stirring, for 2 minutes.

2. Add chicken and cook, stirring often, just until chicken turns white, about 3 minutes. Add stock and peanuts; bring to a simmer, scraping up bits stuck to pan. Reduce heat to low, cover and simmer for 15 minutes.

3. Stir in pumpkin, cover and simmer, stirring and turning chicken pieces occasionally, until juices run clear when chicken is pierced and pumpkin is tender, 25 to 30 minutes. Using a slotted spoon, transfer chicken and pumpkin to a warmed serving dish and keep warm.

4. Increase heat to medium-high and boil sauce, uncovered, until slightly thickened, about 5 minutes. Discard cloves and cinnamon stick, if desired. Stir in lemon juice and season to taste with salt. Pour sauce over chicken and pumpkin.

Filipino Chicken Adobo

Serves 4

Here's a curry-like stew with mild spice and no chiles, a kind of fusion between Asia and Europe, much like the Philippines themselves, where it originated. It has an uplifting taste with its use of vinegar and soy, and is designed for universal appeal.

Tips

For the best flavor and color, use a high-quality naturally brewed soy sauce. Check the label carefully, as some products sold as soy sauce have very little soy and loads of salt and coloring.

When browning the chicken, be sure not to turn it too soon or it will stick to the pan and shred. When it is well browned, it should lift off easily.

Serving Suggestion

Serve with mashed potatoes or Cilantro Lime Sweet Potatoes (page 246) or over Spinach Rice Pilau (page 255) or Golden Curried Pineapple Rice (page 259).

2 tbsp	vegetable oil	25 mL
8	bone-in chicken thighs, trimmed (or 4 breasts, cut in half), skin removed if desired	8
2	onions, chopped	2
6	cloves garlic, minced	6
4	bay leaves	4
1 tsp	paprika	5 mL
1/2 tsp	ground turmeric	2 mL
1/4 tsp	freshly ground black pepper	1 mL
1 cup	water	250 mL
1/2 cup	rice vinegar or white vinegar	125 mL
1/3 cup	soy sauce	75 mL
	Salt	

1. In a large, deep skillet, heat oil over medium-high heat until hot but not smoking. Add chicken, in batches if necessary, skin side down, and brown, turning once, for about 4 minutes per side. Transfer to a plate.

2. Spoon off all but 2 tbsp (25 mL) of the fat from pan. Reduce heat to medium-low. Add onions and cook, stirring, until very soft and golden brown, about 8 minutes. Add garlic, bay leaves, paprika, turmeric and pepper; cook, stirring, until fragrant, about 1 minute.

3. Add water, vinegar and soy sauce. Increase heat to medium-high and bring to a simmer, scraping up bits stuck to pan. Return chicken and any accumulated juices to pan. Reduce heat to low, cover and simmer, stirring and turning chicken once, until juices run clear when chicken is pierced, about 30 minutes. Using a slotted spoon, transfer chicken pieces to a bowl and keep warm.

4. Increase heat to medium-high and boil sauce, uncovered, stirring occasionally, until reduced by about half, about 10 minutes. Discard bay leaves. Season to taste with salt. Return chicken to pan, turning to coat in sauce, and heat through, about 2 minutes.

Chicken Korma Curry

Serves 8

Enriched with velvety cashew butter, cream and yogurt, this chicken curry is smooth and pleasantly unctuous. Try it with an aromatic rice and a crisp-textured vegetable curry on a cool autumn evening. It'll feel like summer all over again.

Tips

If cashew butter is not available, substitute ½ cup (125 mL) ground or finely chopped cashews or almonds or ⅓ cup (75 mL) almond butter or natural peanut butter.

When browning the chicken, be sure not to turn it too soon or it will stick to the pan and shred. When it is well browned, it should lift off easily.

Serving Suggestion

Serve with Curried Green Beans Masala (page 216) or another tender-crisp green vegetable and Lemon Coriander Rice (page 257) or Spinach Rice Pilau (page 255).

2 tbsp	vegetable oil (approx.)	25 mL
¼ cup	raisins	50 mL
8	skinless bone-in chicken thighs, trimmed (or 4 breasts, cut in half)	8
1	onion, finely chopped	1
3	cloves garlic, minced	3
2 tbsp	minced gingerroot	25 mL
1 tsp	each ground coriander and garam masala	5 mL
¾ tsp	salt	3 mL
½ tsp	ground cumin	2 mL
Pinch	cayenne pepper	Pinch
1 cup	chicken stock or water	250 mL
½ cup	whipping (35%) cream	125 mL
⅓ cup	cashew butter	75 mL
¼ cup	plain yogurt, at room temperature (see tip, page 68)	50 mL
	Chopped fresh mint or cilantro	

1. In a large skillet, heat oil over medium-high heat until hot but not smoking. Add raisins and cook, stirring, until starting to puff, about 15 seconds. Using a slotted spoon, transfer to a bowl, leaving as much oil in pan as possible.

2. Add chicken to pan, in batches if necessary, and brown, turning once, about 4 minutes per side. Transfer to another bowl.

3. Reduce heat to medium-low and add a little more oil to pan, if necessary, to coat the pan. Add onion and cook, stirring, until softened and starting to brown, about 3 minutes. Add garlic, ginger, coriander, garam masala, salt, cumin and cayenne; cook, stirring, until spices are blended and fragrant, about 1 minute.

4. Increase heat to medium-high. Add stock, cream and cashew butter; bring to a boil, scraping up any bits stuck to pan and stirring until blended. Return chicken and any accumulated juices to pan, turning chicken pieces to coat in sauce. Reduce heat to low, cover and simmer, stirring and turning chicken twice, until juices run clear when chicken is pierced, about 30 minutes.

5. Remove from heat and stir in yogurt. Season to taste with salt. Serve sprinkled with reserved raisins and mint.

Chicken and Tart Apple Curry

Serves 4

Fruity and multi-flavored, this is a quick and inexpensive chicken curry for a memorable weekday meal. It also works well accompanied by one or two vegetable curries.

Tip

For more kick, use a medium or hot curry paste.

Serving Suggestion

Serve with Naan (page 268) or over Lemon Coriander Rice (page 257) or plain basmati.

1 tbsp	vegetable oil	15 mL
8	skinless bone-in chicken thighs, trimmed	8
1 tbsp	mustard seeds	15 mL
1 tsp	cumin seeds	5 mL
1	onion, sliced lengthwise	1
2 tbsp	minced gingerroot	25 mL
¼ tsp	salt	1 mL
¼ tsp	ground cinnamon	1 mL
Pinch	ground cardamom	Pinch
4 tsp	Indian yellow curry paste or masala blend	20 mL
1½ cups	chicken stock, divided	375 mL
1	tart apple, thinly sliced (peeled if desired)	1
½ cup	whipping (35%) cream	125 mL
2 tbsp	freshly squeezed lime juice	25 mL
	Chopped fresh mint or cilantro	

1. In a large, deep nonstick skillet, heat oil over medium-high heat until hot but not smoking. Add chicken, in batches if necessary, and cook, turning once, until well browned, about 4 minutes per side. Transfer to a plate.

2. Reduce heat to medium-low. Add mustard seeds and cumin seeds; cook, stirring, until just starting to pop, about 30 seconds. Add onion, ginger, salt, cinnamon, cardamom and curry paste; cook, stirring, adding 2 tbsp (25 mL) of the stock as necessary to prevent burning, until onion is softened, about 5 minutes.

3. Add remaining stock and bring to a simmer, scraping up bits stuck to pan. Return chicken and any accumulated juices to pan. Reduce heat to low, cover and simmer, stirring and turning chicken once, for 20 minutes.

4. Increase heat to medium-low and stir in apple and cream. Simmer, uncovered, stirring occasionally, until juices run clear when chicken is pierced and apples are tender, about 10 minutes. Stir in lime juice and season to taste with salt. Serve sprinkled with mint.

Bombay (Mumbai)

Bombay and I go back some 24 years, and in that time it has changed not only its complexion, but also its name, to Mumbai. Under any name, it remains one of the most fascinating places on earth, and it is now, as it ever was, among the most successful transplants of the Western mind on a faraway and ancient country.

Home to 40 million citizens and India's hub for all business, including movies, Mumbai is as modern as tomorrow's cybernetic innovation, yet as traditional as a Bengali shami kebab (a sort of burger that requires a good six hours and a couple of kitchen helpers to prepare). Born out of the Anglo imagination, the city stands on landfill where there had been only a deep bay and a fishing village and was constructed to grand imperial standards, designed as the bastion and home away from home of the mighty Raj, the most profitable of the many tentacles of the British Empire, which was our civilization's most articulated experiment to dominate the world.

I'm here to research the secrets of Indian cuisine. In my two previous visits, I managed to penetrate food-crazed Mumbai society through my exploits with food (though my ego would have had me believe it was because of my charm and profound worldliness), but this time I hit the jackpot. I am housed in a huge room, smack in front of the Gate of India in the 140-year-old Royal Bombay Yacht Club. I dine in the breezy ambience of the Bombay Gymkhana, and in the male-bonding confines of the Cricket Club of India, and in the musty elegance of an 18th-century palace built on the peak of Malabar Hill that belongs still to a ship-building family from long ago (they built the ships that helped Nelson win Trafalgar), and in the home of Marianne Q., who has recently become mother-in-law to a famous English actress.

I am eating far too much (well, I've made it my life's work to eat), but I'm also beginning to understand what the Indian palate demands from its plate of daily nourishment. In a word, it is "flavor," backed up by a second word, "spice." Be it a humble plate of chickpeas with puri (a deep-fried bread), or the Goan specialties of the Gymkhana, or the melting meats of Lucknow served at the Cricket Club, or the coconut-based Mangalorean delicacies of Mrs. Q., or the delights of the city's most famous seafood eatery, Trishna, it is flavor and the kick of spice that drive the engine of this cuisine and deliver the sighs of contentment from the constituents.

An Indian meal is much like Indian music, Indian sunsets or even Indian romance. It starts slowly, with mellow resonance and gentle stress. One or two flavors and some textural treats segue fairly soon into juicy, lusty, intensely colorful stews and grills and stir-fries that fire up the palate as they fuel the imagination and feed one's deepest and most secret desires, becoming sheer pleasure and unforgettable entertainment.

My best glimpse into what an Indian meal is all about comes on the ancient terrace of the erstwhile shipping tycoons. The terrace, with its marble floor, its sculpted walls and parapets and its comprehensive view of Marine Drive and downtown, is an extension of the museum piece of a residence from which it springs.

Home to two unmarried heiresses until their recent and consecutive deaths in their 90s, this palace is Bombay as it used to be for the super-rich: white-gloved service from servants, an abundance of European art and sculpture, lavish dining rooms, ballrooms, a twin office for the sisters and even a 1940s-style bar in vinyl and chrome (a centerpiece for drinking alcohol in a city that still frowns on drinking when it wants to), the whole package under 30-foot (9 m), ornately molded ceilings.

Apparently, the sisters spent all their capital and spared no effort to keep the house and its style intact through all that has happened in the world, and particularly in India, in the last 50 years. Now that they are gone, it is logical that one day soon the building and its huge lawns, which lie in Bombay's pricey Malabar neighborhood (second only to Juhu Beach, where all the movie rich live) will be sold for many millions to a developer who will put up several high-rise condos in its stead.

For the moment, however, I am sitting in a wicker chair that has been contoured to the human behind by the many that have lounged in it, nibbling on a homemade samosa that is crispy outside and subtly spicy and smooth inside. The sunset ends dramatically and suddenly, giving way to the pitch black of the tropical night, full of animal sounds and floral perfumes. I am talking to my friend, the great-great-granddaughter of the original owner, who, I discover, made most of his fortune by shipping opium to China. The family's transition from 18th-century dope barons to 20th-century gentility was painless; at the time, selling opium was seen not as a crime but simply as a successful business. It allowed subsequent generations to be unabashedly and permanently idle, taken care of hand and foot, with license to be melancholy.

When the meal is ready, the servants — who still live and serve as if the sisters will imminently return, as they used to from their annual summer trips to London, and catch them doing the wrong thing — ring the signifying bell. We walk down the alabaster stairs, holding on to the thick, jet black slickness of a priceless teak balustrade.

The dinner table, pristine in starched white linens, is arrayed with seafood, which I had requested. There is Bombay duck — not those dried-out fishy snacks we get over here, but the real thing, a mushy, bony fish that must be hand-picked of its bones and pressed for a few hours to firm up its flesh. In a sweet-and-sour, coconut-and-tomato-based Goa fish curry, garlic, curry leaf and a slew of compatible spices envelop filets of pomfret, the fish of choice from the sea that surrounds the city. For variety, there is also a vinegary pork vindaloo (a rarity in pork-forbidding India).

After dinner, we go for a tour of the antique furniture and artwork in the reception rooms, the library and the office (with its two-person desk), all of which remain exactly as the sisters arranged them. We return to the dining room for a dessert of rather rubbery rajmalai, a milk-based quenelle that is usually fluffy and smooth. "It is canned," says my friend. Then she smiles. She and I both know this would never have been acceptable if the old gals had still been alive. — B.A.

Chicken and Vegetable Curry

Serves 4

An easy one-dish meal, this dish comes out succulent every time, and it practically cooks itself on the simmer. It also reheats to advantage. Comfort food doesn't get much easier or tastier than this.

Variation

Substitute blanched or thawed frozen green beans for the peas.

2 tbsp	vegetable oil, divided	25 mL
1	stick cinnamon, broken in half	1
1 tsp	cumin seeds	5 mL
4	small boiling or all-purpose potatoes, cut into ½-inch (1 cm) cubes	4
½ tsp	salt	2 mL
8	skinless bone-in chicken thighs, trimmed	8
1½ cups	Basic Gravy (see recipe, page 7)	375 mL
½ cup	chicken stock or water	125 mL
2 cups	small cauliflower florets	500 mL
1 cup	frozen green peas, thawed	250 mL
	Chopped fresh cilantro	

1. In a large, deep skillet, heat half the oil over medium-high heat until hot but not smoking. Add cinnamon and cumin seeds; cook, stirring, until seeds start to pop, about 1 minute. Add potatoes and salt; cook, stirring, until starting to soften and brown, about 3 minutes. Transfer potatoes to a bowl.

2. Reduce heat to medium and add remaining oil to pan. Add chicken, in batches if necessary, and brown, turning once, for about 4 minutes per side. Return all chicken to pan. Add gravy and cook, stirring, for 1 minute. Add stock and bring to a simmer, scraping up bits stuck to pan. Stir in reserved potatoes.

3. Reduce heat to low, cover and simmer, stirring and turning chicken once, until potatoes are slightly tender, about 15 minutes. Stir in cauliflower and peas. Cover and simmer until juices run clear when chicken is pierced and vegetables are tender, about 15 minutes. Discard cinnamon stick, if desired. Season to taste with salt. Serve sprinkled with cilantro.

Indian-Style Butter Chicken

Serves 4 to 6

Serves 4 to 6

Tandoori-roasted, refried in butter and finished in a spice-spiked tomato sauce: is there no end to these Indian efforts to squeeze as much pleasure as possible from chicken? Hopefully not, as the results are fit for royalty.

Tip

A deep saucepan prevents the tomato sauce from splattering the stove too much as it simmers. If you have a very wide, deep saucepan, you can use it instead of the skillet in step 4.

8	pieces cooked Tandoori Chicken (see recipe, page 66)	8
2	hot green chile peppers, chopped	2
1 tbsp	minced gingerroot	15 mL
1	can (28 oz/796 mL) tomatoes with juice	1
1½ tsp	ground cumin	7 mL
1 tsp	ground coriander	5 mL
½ tsp	paprika	2 mL
⅛ tsp	ground cardamom	0.5 mL
Pinch	ground cloves	Pinch
¼ cup	butter, divided	50 mL
1 cup	whipping (35%) cream	250 mL
	Garam masala	
	Chopped fresh cilantro	

1. Remove bones from chicken and discard. Tear chicken into bite-size pieces. Set aside.

2. In a deep saucepan, combine chile peppers, ginger, tomatoes with juice, cumin, coriander, paprika, cardamom and cloves. Bring to a boil over medium-high heat, breaking up tomatoes with a spoon. Reduce heat and simmer, stirring occasionally, until thickened and flavorful, about 15 minutes.

3. Using an immersion blender in pan or transferring to an upright blender or food processor, purée tomato mixture until smooth; set aside.

4. In a large skillet, melt half the butter over medium-high heat. Add chicken pieces, in three batches, and cook, turning once, until browned and crispy, about 3 minutes per batch, adding more of the butter as necessary between batches. Transfer to a bowl.

5. Carefully pour tomato sauce into pan (it will splatter) and cook, scraping up bits stuck to pan, for 2 minutes. Stir in reserved chicken pieces and cream; bring to a simmer. Reduce heat and simmer, stirring often, until slightly thickened, about 10 minutes. Remove from heat.

6. Cut remaining butter into small pieces and stir into sauce until melted. Season to taste with salt. Serve sprinkled with garam masala and cilantro.

Tandoori Chicken

Serves 4

To create tandoori chicken, skinless chicken permeated with many flavors in a spicy yogurt marinade is roasted in a barrel-shaped clay oven for a smoky, aromatic taste and a succulence beyond belief. Happily, we can achieve practically the same results with a regular barbecue or even a home oven.

● ━◆━ ●

Tips

A lower-fat yogurt can be used, but make sure it does not contain gelatin. When cooked, gelatin in yogurt can cause the yogurt to split and create a curdled texture.

If you prefer the traditional bright red color of tandoori chicken that you often see in restaurants, add red and yellow food coloring to the yogurt marinade.

To barbecue, you'll need a gas grill with at least 2 burners. If using a charcoal barbecue, use your favorite method of indirect cooking. If you don't have a working thermometer on your barbecue, place an oven thermometer beside the chicken.

● *Rimmed baking sheet, lined with greased foil (for oven-baked method)*

8	skinless bone-in chicken thighs, trimmed (or 4 bone-in breasts)	8
1 tbsp	freshly squeezed lemon juice	15 mL
½ tsp	salt	2 mL
1½ tsp	garam masala	7 mL
1 tsp	ground cumin	5 mL
1 tsp	ground coriander	5 mL
⅛ tsp	ground cardamom	0.5 mL
1	clove garlic, minced	1
1 tsp	minced hot green chile pepper	5 mL
1 tsp	minced gingerroot	5 mL
1½ tsp	paprika	7 mL
½ cup	plain yogurt, preferably full-fat (see tip, at left)	125 mL
	Lemon wedges	

1. If using chicken breasts, cut each in half crosswise. Cut 3 shallow slashes in the meaty side of each chicken thigh or breast piece. In a shallow dish, sprinkle lemon juice and salt over chicken and toss to coat evenly. Let stand at room temperature for 15 minutes.

2. Meanwhile, in a dry small skillet over medium heat, toast garam masala, cumin, coriander and cardamom, stirring constantly, just until spices have a toasted aroma and are starting to darken, 1 to 2 minutes. Immediately transfer to a small bowl. Stir in garlic, chile pepper, ginger, paprika and yogurt. Pour over chicken in dish and stir to coat evenly. Cover and refrigerate for at least 4 hours or for up to 1 day. Let stand at room temperature for 30 minutes before cooking.

3. *To grill:* Preheat barbecue to high (see tip, at left). Turn off one burner. Remove chicken from marinade, leaving a coating of marinade on the chicken. Discard any excess marinade. Place chicken, meaty side up, on grill over unlit side and close lid. Grill, maintaining heat at 450°F (230°C) or as close as possible, until chicken is no longer pink inside for breasts or juices run clear when chicken is pierced for thighs, 25 to 30 minutes. Place chicken over hot side of grill and cook, turning once, just until grill marks appear, about 5 minutes.

4. *To bake in oven:* Preheat oven to 450°F (230°C). Remove chicken from marinade, leaving a coating of marinade on the chicken. Discard any excess marinade. Place chicken on prepared baking sheet, leaving as much space as possible between pieces, and bake until chicken is no longer pink inside for breasts or juices run clear when chicken is pierced for thighs, 25 to 30 minutes. Broil, if desired, turning once, until chicken is lightly browned, about 4 minutes.

5. *For both versions:* Let chicken stand for 5 minutes before serving. Serve with lemon wedges to squeeze over top.

Tips

If making the oven version, add a little smoky flavor by adding ¼ tsp (1 mL) smoked paprika with the regular paprika.

If you want to make Indian-Style Butter Chicken (page 65), double the recipe to make sure you have leftovers.

British-Style Butter Chicken

Serves 6

Smooth and comforting, this combination of dairy, spice and chicken was one of the most restorative prandial pleasures of the British during the Raj. It continues to please in countless curry houses of Britain today. This simplified version was created by Jennifer for the Dairy Farmers of Canada's Milk Calendar.

Tip

For the best results, avoid using fat-free yogurt and any yogurt that contains gelatin. When cooked, gelatin in yogurt can cause the yogurt to split and create a curdled texture.

• Preheat oven to 375°F (190°C)
• 13- by 9-inch (3 L) glass baking dish

2 tbsp	butter, divided	25 mL
1 tbsp	minced gingerroot	15 mL
2 tsp	minced hot green chile pepper	10 mL
1 tsp	ground cumin	5 mL
1 tsp	paprika	5 mL
2 tbsp	tandoori or tikka curry paste, divided	25 mL
1	can (28 oz/796 mL) crushed (ground) tomatoes	1
1 cup	whipping (35%) cream	250 mL
1½ lbs	boneless skinless chicken thighs or breasts, cut into 1½-inch (4 cm) pieces	750 g
½ cup	plain yogurt (see tip, at left)	125 mL
¼ cup	chopped fresh cilantro	50 mL
2 tbsp	freshly squeezed lime or lemon juice	25 mL

1. Place half the butter in the glass baking dish. Place in preheated oven until melted, about 3 minutes. Swirl to coat dish and set aside.

2. In a large, deep pot, melt remaining butter over medium-high heat. Add ginger, chile pepper, cumin, paprika and half the tandoori paste; cook, stirring, until softened and fragrant, about 2 minutes. Add tomatoes and bring to a boil, stirring. Stir in cream and return to a boil. Reduce heat and simmer, stirring often, until sauce is thickened and flavorful, about 10 minutes.

3. Meanwhile, in a bowl, combine chicken, yogurt and remaining tandoori paste until chicken is evenly coated. Spread in a single layer in prepared dish. Bake for 10 minutes.

4. Pour tomato sauce evenly over chicken in dish. Bake until sauce is bubbling and chicken is no longer pink inside, about 10 minutes. Serve sprinkled with cilantro and lime juice.

Madras Chicken Curry

Serves 4

Another British adaptation from classic Indian cuisine, "Madras-style" usually denotes fiery hot and was designed for hardened Raj colonels at the Officers' Club. It lost much of its tough image when it became a staple of curry houses back home, and in any case, it can be mollified by using fewer chiles.

Tips

This version has a fair amount of heat, but it's not overwhelming. To turn up the heat even more, increase the chile peppers to 4 or 5.

To ensure that green beans cook evenly, it is best to blanch them before adding them to the tomato-based sauce. In a pot of boiling water, blanch green beans until bright green, about 2 minutes. Drain well.

3	dried red chile peppers, broken	3
2 tbsp	white wine vinegar	25 mL
1 tbsp	vegetable oil	15 mL
1 tbsp	mustard seeds	15 mL
1	onion, finely chopped	1
2 tbsp	Madras curry paste or masala blend	25 mL
1 lb	boneless skinless chicken thighs or breasts, cut into 1-inch (2.5 cm) pieces	500 g
1	can (28 oz/796 mL) diced tomatoes with juice	1
½ cup	coconut milk	125 mL
2 tbsp	tomato paste	25 mL
1½ cups	chopped green beans, blanched (see tip, at left)	375 mL
	Salt	
	Chopped fresh cilantro	

1. In a microwave-safe bowl or a small saucepan, combine chile peppers and vinegar. Bring just to a boil in microwave on High, about 1 minute, or in saucepan over high heat. Remove from heat, cover and let stand until chiles are soft, about 15 minutes, or for up to 1 day.

2. In a large skillet, heat oil over medium heat until hot but not smoking. Add mustard seeds and cook, stirring, until slightly toasted but not yet popping, about 15 seconds. Add onion and cook, stirring, until softened and starting to brown, about 5 minutes. Add chile mixture and curry paste; cook, stirring, until fragrant, about 1 minute.

3. Add chicken and stir until coated in spices. Stir in tomatoes with juice, coconut milk and tomato paste; bring to a simmer, scraping up bits stuck to pan. Reduce heat and simmer gently, stirring often, for 5 minutes. Stir in green beans and simmer until chicken is no longer pink inside and sauce is slightly thickened, about 5 minutes. Season to taste with salt. Serve sprinkled with cilantro.

Chicken Vindaloo Curry

Serves 4

When the Portuguese came to Goa, on India's west coast, they introduced vinegar to Indian cuisine. Tangy vindaloo curries (named after the "vin" in vinegar) quickly joined the lexicon of favorites, especially with ex-pat Europeans who like their spicy stews to have an acidic punch. This quick version for chicken is an easy introduction to the Goan specialty.

Tip

Vindaloo often indicates a fiery dish. If you want the heat, use a hot vindaloo paste. A mild paste will provide a tamer result but will still provide plenty of flavor.

¼ tsp	ground cinnamon	1 mL
Pinch	ground cardamom	Pinch
Pinch	ground cloves	Pinch
1 tbsp	vindaloo or Indian yellow curry paste or masala blend	15 mL
1 lb	boneless skinless chicken thighs or breasts, cut into 1-inch (2.5 cm) pieces	500 g
1 tbsp	vegetable oil	15 mL
1	onion, finely chopped	1
2 tbsp	all-purpose flour	25 mL
¼ cup	white vinegar	50 mL
1¼ cups	chicken stock	300 mL
¼ cup	tomato paste	50 mL
	Salt	
2 tbsp	chopped fresh cilantro	25 mL

1. In a bowl, combine cinnamon, cardamom, cloves and curry paste. Add chicken and toss to coat evenly. Let stand at room temperature for 15 minutes, or cover and refrigerate for up to 1 day.

2. In a large skillet, heat oil over medium heat. Add onion and cook, stirring, until softened and starting to brown, about 5 minutes. Add chicken mixture and cook, stirring, until chicken turns white, about 3 minutes. Sprinkle with flour and cook, stirring, for 1 minute. Stir in vinegar, scraping up any bits stuck to pan.

3. Increase heat to medium-high. Add stock and tomato paste; bring to a simmer, stirring. Reduce heat and simmer gently, stirring often, until chicken is no longer pink inside and sauce is slightly thickened, about 5 minutes. Season to taste with salt and stir in cilantro.

Thai Green Curry Chicken

Serves 4

The most popular chicken curry of Thailand often requires the services of the fire department in the home country, but we've made this version a touch milder to suit delicate North American palates.

Tip

This version is moderately spicy, but you can adjust the heat to your taste by using more or less green curry paste.

Variation

Replace the green curry paste with Thai yellow curry paste and the peas with snow peas, trimmed and halved diagonally.

1 tbsp	vegetable oil	15 mL
1	onion, thinly sliced lengthwise	1
1 tbsp	minced gingerroot	15 mL
4 tsp	Thai green curry paste	20 mL
1	red bell pepper, chopped	1
1 lb	boneless skinless chicken thighs or breasts, cut into 3/4-inch (2 cm) pieces	500 g
1 tsp	packed brown or palm sugar	5 mL
1	can (14 oz/400 mL) coconut milk	1
1/4 cup	water	50 mL
2 tbsp	fish sauce (nam pla)	25 mL
1 cup	frozen green peas, thawed	250 mL
2 tbsp	freshly squeezed lime juice	25 mL
	Salt, optional	
	Chopped roasted salted peanuts	
	Chopped fresh Thai or sweet basil and/or mint	

1. In a large skillet, heat oil over medium-high heat. Add onion and cook, stirring, until starting to soften, about 2 minutes. Stir in ginger and curry paste; cook, stirring, until spices are blended and fragrant, about 30 seconds.

2. Stir in red pepper and chicken until coated in spices. Add brown sugar, coconut milk, water and fish sauce; bring to a simmer, scraping up bits stuck to pan. Stir in peas. Reduce heat and simmer gently, stirring often, until chicken is no longer pink inside, about 8 minutes. Stir in lime juice and season to taste with salt, if using. Serve sprinkled with peanuts, basil and/or mint.

Coconut Curried Chicken

Serves 4

Deeply onion-scented and richly lustrous with coconut milk, this saucy chicken curry is an ideal partner to plain rice, for a happily slurpy repast. It comes to us from sunny Sri Lanka.

Tips

Two chile peppers add a moderate amount of heat. Use only 1 for a mild dish or add 1 or 2 more for a more fiery dish.

The onion can be chopped in a food processor; just be sure not to purée it to the point where it becomes juicy.

1 lb	boneless skinless chicken breasts or thighs, cut into 1½-inch (4 cm) pieces	500 g
½ tsp	salt	2 mL
¼ tsp	ground turmeric	1 mL
1 tbsp	vegetable oil	15 mL
2	bay leaves	2
1	stick cinnamon, about 2 inches (5 cm) long	1
2 tsp	cumin seeds	10 mL
4	cloves garlic, minced	4
2	hot green chile peppers, minced, or to taste	2
1	large onion, finely chopped (see tip, at left)	1
2 tbsp	minced gingerroot	25 mL
1	can (14 oz/400 mL) coconut milk	1
2	large ripe tomatoes, chopped	2
¼ tsp	garam masala	1 mL

1. In a bowl, combine chicken, salt and turmeric. Toss to coat evenly. Let stand at room temperature for 15 minutes.

2. In a large skillet, heat oil over medium heat until hot but not smoking. Add bay leaves, cinnamon and cumin seeds; cook, stirring, until seeds start to pop, about 1 minute. Add garlic, chile peppers, onion and ginger. Reduce heat to medium-low and cook, stirring often, adding up to 2 tbsp (25 mL) water as necessary to prevent burning, until onions are deep golden brown, about 10 minutes.

3. Add chicken mixture and stir until coated with spices. Add coconut milk and bring to a simmer, scraping up bits stuck to pan. Reduce heat and simmer gently, stirring occasionally, until chicken is no longer pink inside and sauce is slightly thickened, about 10 minutes.

4. Stir in tomatoes and cook, stirring, just until heated through, about 2 minutes. Discard cinnamon stick, if desired. Season to taste with salt and serve sprinkled with garam masala.

Sweet Mango Curry Chicken

Serves 4

Quick and easy, this curry benefits greatly from the sweetness of mango and the smoothness of coconut milk. It works best over al dente rice noodles, though plain rice will also do.

Tip

Choose your heat level: use just 1 chile pepper and a mild curry paste for a mild but flavorful version, or use 2 or 3 chile peppers and/or a medium or hot curry paste to turn up the heat.

1 tbsp	vegetable oil	15 mL
1	onion, sliced lengthwise	1
1	hot green chile pepper, minced, or to taste	1
2 tbsp	minced gingerroot	25 mL
1 tbsp	Indian yellow curry paste or masala blend	15 mL
1 lb	boneless skinless chicken breasts or thighs, cut into 1½-inch (4 cm) pieces	500 g
½ cup	coconut milk	125 mL
½ cup	chicken stock or water	125 mL
1	large firm ripe sweet mango, peeled and sliced	1
½ tsp	salt, or to taste	2 mL
2	green onions, thinly sliced	2
¼ cup	thin strips red bell pepper	50 mL

1. In a large skillet, heat oil over medium heat. Add onion and cook, stirring, until softened and starting to brown, about 3 minutes. Stir in chile pepper, ginger and curry paste; cook, stirring, until softened and fragrant, about 1 minute.

2. Add chicken and stir until coated with spices. Stir in coconut milk and stock; bring to a simmer, scraping up bits stuck to pan. Reduce heat and simmer gently, stirring often, until chicken is no longer pink inside and sauce is slightly thickened, about 10 minutes.

3. Increase heat to medium and stir in mango. Cook, stirring gently, just until starting to soften, about 3 minutes. Stir in salt. Serve sprinkled with green onions and red pepper.

Green Mango Curry Chicken with Basil

Serves 4

This delightful, easy-to-make curry with Thai accents such as green mango and basil is suitable as a second offering alongside a more traditional Indian-style dish. It adds variety and gustatory counterpoint to a curry-themed dinner.

Tip

Look for green mango at Asian specialty stores or well-stocked grocery stores. They are often displayed with the vegetables rather than the fruit. In a pinch, an underripe, hard sweet mango can be used in place of a true green mango.

1 tbsp	vegetable oil	15 mL
1	large onion, sliced lengthwise	1
3	cloves garlic, minced	3
1	red bell pepper, chopped	1
1 tbsp	minced gingerroot	15 mL
1 tbsp	Thai red curry paste	15 mL
1 lb	boneless skinless chicken breast or thighs, cut into thin strips	500 g
1	large green mango (or 2 small), peeled and cut into thin strips	1
¾ cup	water or chicken stock	175 mL
2 tbsp	fish sauce (nam pla)	25 mL
2 tbsp	freshly squeezed lime juice	25 mL
2 tbsp	chopped fresh Thai or sweet basil	25 mL
	Salt	

1. In a large skillet, heat oil over medium-high heat. Add onion and cook, stirring, until softened and starting to brown, about 3 minutes. Add garlic, red pepper, ginger and curry paste; cook, stirring, until garlic is softened and spices are blended, about 1 minute.

2. Stir in chicken until coated with spices. Stir in mango. Add water, fish sauce and lime juice; bring to a simmer, scraping up bits stuck to pan. Reduce heat and simmer gently, stirring often, until chicken is no longer pink inside and mango is tender, about 5 minutes. Stir in basil and season to taste with salt.

Fiery Pineapple Chicken Curry

Serves 4

Almonds, raisins and pineapple elevate this simple chicken curry to specialty status, and it'll do you proud as part of a celebratory buffet. But it's so simple and easy to make that you'll be tempted to serve it on ordinary occasions and make them special.

Tip

If fresh pineapple isn't available, substitute one 19-oz (540 mL) can pineapple chunks, drained, and add in step 3 for the last 5 minutes of cooking.

1 tbsp	vegetable oil	15 mL
1/4 cup	chopped almonds	50 mL
1/4 cup	raisins	50 mL
2 to 3	hot red or green chile peppers, minced	2 to 3
1 1/2 cups	chopped fresh pineapple	375 mL
1/2 tsp	ground cumin	2 mL
1 cup	Basic Gravy (see recipe, page 7)	250 mL
1 lb	boneless skinless chicken thighs or breasts, cut into 1-inch (2.5 cm) pieces	500 g
1 cup	coconut milk	250 mL
1 tbsp	soy sauce (approx.)	15 mL
1 tbsp	chopped fresh cilantro	15 mL
2 tsp	chopped fresh mint, optional	10 mL

1. In a large skillet, heat oil over medium-high heat until hot but not smoking. Add almonds and raisins; cook, stirring, until almonds are toasted and raisins start to puff, about 30 seconds. Using a slotted spoon, transfer to a bowl, leaving as much oil in the pan as possible. Set aside.

2. Reduce heat to medium-low and add chile peppers, pineapple and cumin; cook, stirring, until fragrant and pineapple starts to release its juices, about 2 minutes. Add gravy and cook, stirring, for 1 minute.

3. Add chicken and stir until coated in gravy. Stir in coconut milk and soy sauce; bring to a simmer. Reduce heat and simmer gently, stirring often, until chicken is no longer pink inside, pineapple is tender and sauce is slightly thickened, about 10 minutes. Season to taste with soy sauce and stir in cilantro and mint, if using. Serve sprinkled with reserved almonds and raisins.

Caribbean Chicken Curry with Papaya and Lime

Serves 4

Here's a flash of the Caribbean for those of us who can afford the islands only on rare occasions. Papaya and lime combine into a sublime flavor that sings on the palate and adds layers and dimensions to the all-too-familiar taste of chicken.

Tips

If a very ripe tomato is not available, substitute 1 cup (250 mL) drained canned diced tomatoes.

One half of a Scotch bonnet lends noticeable heat to this curry. If you like it fiery, use a whole pepper.

Variation

If papaya is not available, substitute 1 cup (250 mL) cubed fresh pineapple and add with the chicken in step 2. Or substitute 1 small, firm, ripe sweet mango, peeled and cubed, adding in step 3 with the lime zest and juice.

1 tbsp	vegetable oil	15 mL
1	onion, sliced lengthwise	1
2 tbsp	minced gingerroot	25 mL
4 tsp	curry powder, preferably Caribbean-style	20 mL
¾ tsp	salt	3 mL
1	very ripe large tomato, chopped	1
½	Scotch bonnet pepper, minced, or to taste	½
1 lb	boneless skinless chicken breasts or thighs, cut into 1-inch (2.5 cm) pieces	500 g
1 cup	coconut milk	250 mL
¼ cup	water	50 mL
1 cup	cubed seeded peeled papaya	250 mL
1 tsp	grated lime zest	5 mL
2 tbsp	freshly squeezed lime juice	25 mL
2	green onions, thinly sliced	2

1. In a large skillet, heat oil over medium heat. Add onion and cook, stirring, until starting to soften, about 3 minutes. Add ginger, curry powder and salt; cook, stirring, until onion is soft and spices are fragrant, about 2 minutes. Stir in tomato and Scotch bonnet pepper; cook, stirring, until tomato starts to soften, about 2 minutes.

2. Add chicken and stir until coated with spices. Stir in coconut milk and water; bring to a simmer, scraping up bits stuck to pan. Reduce heat and simmer gently, stirring often, until chicken is no longer pink inside and sauce is slightly thickened, about 8 minutes.

3. Increase heat to medium and stir in papaya, lime zest and lime juice. Cook, stirring gently, just until papaya is heated through, about 2 minutes. Season to taste with salt. Serve sprinkled with green onions.

Chicken Curry with Exotic Mushrooms and Saffron

Serves 4 to 8

Saffron, fancy mushrooms and whipping cream render this chicken dish both expensive and calorific, but it tastes so terrific that it would be sinful to pass it up. One solution would be to serve a modest quantity along with another, more benign curry, and thus limit consumption to small (but unforgettable) portions.

- - ◆ - -

Tips

This will work with regular button mushrooms, but the depth of flavor from the exotic varieties really does add to the final result. Avoid any that are too dark (such as portobello), as they will discolor the sauce.

The whipping cream is essential, accenting the flavor of the saffron and creating a velvety texture. Don't be tempted to substitute a lower-fat cream in this one.

⅛ tsp	saffron threads	0.5 mL
1 cup	chicken stock, heated	250 mL
½ tsp	fennel seeds	2 mL
2 tbsp	butter or vegetable oil	25 mL
12 oz	exotic mushrooms (such as shiitake, cremini, oyster, king, etc.), trimmed and sliced	375 g
1 cup	Basic Gravy (see recipe, page 7)	250 mL
1 lb	boneless skinless chicken breasts or thighs, cut into 1½-inch (4 cm) pieces	500 g
½ cup	whipping (35%) cream	125 mL
	Salt	
	Chopped fresh cilantro	

1. In a measuring cup or bowl, combine saffron and stock; let stand for 15 minutes.

2. In a dry large skillet over medium-high heat, toast fennel seeds, stirring constantly, until fragrant, about 30 seconds. Add butter and swirl to coat pan. Add mushrooms and cook, stirring, until liquid is released and mushrooms are browned, about 8 minutes. Add gravy and cook, stirring, for 1 minute.

3. Add chicken and stir until coated. Add stock mixture and cream; bring to a simmer, scraping up bits stuck to pan. Reduce heat and simmer gently, stirring occasionally, until chicken is no longer pink inside and sauce is slightly thickened, about 10 minutes. Season to taste with salt and serve sprinkled with cilantro.

Chicken Tikka Curry with Roasted Red Peppers

Serves 4

Tenderly and aromatically baked chicken nuggets are poached in a perky, creamy sauce, along with the sweetness of roasted peppers. This colorful dish will make festive even a small family dinner.

Tips

Jarred or freshly roasted red bell peppers can be used. If using fresh, 2 peppers will give you about ½ cup (125 mL) sliced. If using the jarred variety, which are usually smaller, you'll need about 4. Drain well and pat dry before measuring.

The sweetness of canned tomatoes and roasted red peppers can vary (especially if you're using peppers from a jar). Adding a little sugar can cut the acidity and let the other flavors shine through without making the final result too sweet.

Marinated chicken can be covered and refrigerated for up to 1 day.

• *Rimmed baking sheet, lined with greased foil*

1 tsp	cornstarch	5 mL
¼ cup	plain yogurt (not fat-free, see tip, page 68)	50 mL
3 tbsp	tikka or tandoori curry paste, divided	45 mL
1 lb	boneless skinless chicken thighs or breasts, cut into 1-inch (2.5 cm) pieces	500 g
1 tbsp	butter or vegetable oil	15 mL
4	green onions, sliced	4
2	cloves garlic, minced	2
1	hot green chile pepper, minced	1
1 tsp	ground coriander	5 mL
½ tsp	ground cumin	2 mL
1 cup	canned crushed (ground) tomatoes	250 mL
¾ cup	water	175 mL
½ cup	drained sliced roasted red peppers	125 mL
⅓ cup	whipping (35%) cream	75 mL
	Granulated sugar	
	Salt	
	Chopped fresh cilantro or basil	

1. In a bowl, combine cornstarch, yogurt and 2 tbsp (15 mL) of the curry paste until blended and smooth. Add chicken and toss to coat. Let stand at room temperature for 15 minutes.

2. Preheat oven to 425°F (220°C).

3. On prepared baking sheet, spread chicken, with marinade. Bake until coating is starting to brown, about 10 minutes.

4. Meanwhile, in a large skillet, melt butter over medium heat. Add green onions, garlic, chile pepper, coriander, cumin and remaining curry paste; cook, stirring, until onions are softened and spices are fragrant, about 3 minutes. Stir in tomatoes and water; bring to a boil, scraping up bits stuck to pan. Boil for 2 minutes, stirring occasionally.

5. Using a slotted spatula, transfer chicken to sauce, discarding juices. Stir in red peppers and cream. Reduce heat and simmer gently, stirring often, until chicken is no longer pink inside and sauce is slightly thickened, about 5 minutes. Season to taste with sugar and salt. Serve sprinkled with cilantro.

Chicken and Eggplant Curry with Lemongrass

Serves 4

From Burma comes this lively chicken curry that features soft and fragrant eggplant and the perfume of lemongrass. It is easy to cook and surprises with its complex flavors and textures. A special dish for everyday dinners.

Tips

If lime leaves aren't available, substitute 1 tsp (5 mL) finely grated lime zest and stir in 5 minutes before the end of cooking in step 3.

The dried shrimp add a depth and saltiness to the sauce and are an essential element to Burmese curries. They can be omitted; just use more salt to bring out the other flavors.

If you don't have very ripe fresh tomatoes, substitute one 28-oz (796 mL) can diced tomatoes, drained. Omit the salt in step 1 and just season to taste in step 3.

1 tbsp	vegetable oil	15 mL
1	stick cinnamon, broken in half	1
1	onion, sliced lengthwise	1
1	stalk lemongrass, chopped and bruised (see tip, page 83)	1
4	wild lime leaves (see tip, at left)	4
1 tbsp	dried shrimp (see tip, at left)	15 mL
1/4 tsp	salt	1 mL
2	very ripe large tomatoes, chopped (see tip, at left)	2
1 cup	Basic Gravy (see recipe, page 7)	250 mL
1/4 cup	water	50 mL
8	boneless skinless chicken thighs or breasts, cut into 2-inch (5 cm) pieces	8
2 cups	diced eggplant	500 mL
	Chopped fresh Thai or sweet basil	

1. In a large skillet, heat oil over medium heat until hot but not smoking. Add cinnamon and cook, stirring, until fragrant, about 1 minute. Add onion, lemongrass, lime leaves, dried shrimp and salt; cook, stirring, until onion is softened and starting to brown, about 5 minutes.

2. Stir in tomatoes and cook, stirring, until starting to soften, about 2 minutes. Add gravy and cook, stirring, for 1 minute. Add water and bring to a simmer, stirring.

3. Stir in chicken and eggplant. Reduce heat to low, cover and simmer, stirring often, until eggplant is tender and chicken is no longer pink inside, about 20 minutes. Discard cinnamon, lime leaves and lemongrass, if desired. Season to taste with salt. Serve sprinkled with basil.

Red Curry Chicken with Snap Peas and Cashews

Serves 4

A certifiably Thai specialty, this curry offers the snap of fresh peas, the zap of red curry paste, the luxury of cashews and the succulence of quick-cooked chicken. It's like a sweet evening breeze after a sweltering day in Bangkok. Try it with jasmine rice or wide rice noodles.

Tips

If lime leaves aren't available, substitute ½ tsp (2 mL) finely grated lime zest and add with the lime juice in step 2.

The cashews give the best texture to the sauce if pulsed in a food processor to a coarse meal (without processing too much into butter). You may need to do more than ¼ cup (50 mL), depending on the size of your food processor. Extra ground nuts can be frozen for future use.

1 tbsp	vegetable oil	15 mL
1	red or yellow bell pepper, halved crosswise and thinly sliced	1
1 cup	sugar snap peas or frozen green peas	250 mL
2	wild lime leaves (see tip, at left)	2
¼ cup	salted roasted cashews, ground or finely chopped (see tip, at left)	50 mL
1 tbsp	packed brown or palm sugar	15 mL
1	can (14 oz/400 mL) coconut milk	1
¼ cup	water	50 mL
1 tbsp	Thai red curry paste	15 mL
1 lb	boneless skinless chicken breast or thighs, cut into thin strips	500 g
2 tbsp	freshly squeezed lime juice	25 mL
	Salt	
	Salted roasted cashews	
	Chopped fresh mint and/or Thai basil	
	Lime wedges	

1. In a large skillet, heat oil over medium heat. Add red pepper, peas and lime leaves; cook, stirring, until pepper is starting to soften, about 1 minute. Add ground cashews, brown sugar, coconut milk, water and curry paste; bring to a boil, stirring until blended. Reduce heat and boil gently, stirring often, until slightly thickened, about 2 minutes.

2. Stir in chicken and return to a simmer, stirring. Reduce heat and simmer gently, stirring often, until chicken is no longer pink inside and peas are tender-crisp, about 5 minutes. Discard lime leaves, if desired. Stir in lime juice and season to taste with salt. Serve sprinkled with cashews, mint and/or basil and garnished with lime wedges to squeeze over top.

Jamaican Chicken Curry and Sweet Potatoes (page 56)

Chicken and Vegetable Curry (page 64)

Red Curry Chicken with Snap Peas and Cashews (page 80)

Chile Lime Curry Beef Kabobs (page 90)

Thai Tamarind Chicken Curry with Zucchini

Serves 4

Zucchini is an underutilized vegetable that can be truly delightful in recipes created around it. In this Thai-inspired curry, it shines both for its comforting texture and for its fresh taste. It is a natural mate for chicken and works wonders with Thai sticky rice.

Tip

To make tamarind water, break a 2-oz (60 g) piece of block tamarind into small pieces and place in a heatproof bowl. Pour in 1 cup (250 mL) boiling water and let stand until very soft, about 30 minutes, or for up to 8 hours. Press through a fine-mesh sieve, discarding seeds and skins. Extra tamarind water can be stored in the refrigerator for up to 2 weeks.

1 tbsp	vegetable oil	15 mL
1	onion, finely chopped	1
2 tsp	packed brown or palm sugar	10 mL
1/4 tsp	ground cinnamon	1 mL
1/8 tsp	ground cardamom	0.5 mL
1 tbsp	Thai yellow curry paste	15 mL
2 cups	diced zucchini (about 2)	500 mL
1 lb	boneless skinless chicken thighs or breasts, cut into 1-inch (2.5 cm) pieces	500 g
1 cup	coconut milk	250 mL
1/2 cup	tamarind water (see tip, at left)	125 mL
1 tbsp	fish sauce (nam pla)	15 mL
	Salt, optional	
	Chopped roasted salted peanuts	
	Chopped fresh mint	

1. In a large skillet, heat oil over medium heat. Add onion and cook, stirring, until starting to soften, about 2 minutes. Add brown sugar, cinnamon, cardamom and curry paste; cook, stirring, until onion is softened and starting to brown, about 3 minutes. Add zucchini and cook, stirring, for 2 minutes.

2. Add chicken and stir until coated with spices. Add coconut milk, tamarind water and fish sauce; bring to a simmer, stirring often. Reduce heat and simmer gently, stirring often, until chicken is no longer pink inside, zucchini is tender and sauce is slightly thickened, about 10 minutes. Season to taste with salt, if using. Serve sprinkled with peanuts and mint.

Spicy Cream Curry Chicken with Cucumbers

Serves 6 to 8

Jennifer's friend Mary-Jane Pilgrim created this succulent chicken recipe for a contest. She didn't win the contest, but we think it's a winner! The cucumbers are an unusual addition but lend a crispness that contrasts the sauce nicely. Serve over fluffy hot jasmine or basmati rice.

Tip

For a super-quick version, purchase one rotisserie chicken. Remove all skin and bones and cut the meat into large chunks. Omit adding the chicken in step 2 and add cooked chicken with the cream in step 3.

2 tbsp	olive oil	25 mL
1	onion, chopped	1
2	cloves garlic, minced	2
1 tbsp	minced gingerroot	15 mL
2 tsp	ground turmeric	10 mL
1 tsp	chili powder	5 mL
½ tsp	salt	2 mL
¼ tsp	ground cinnamon	1 mL
¼ tsp	freshly ground black pepper	1 mL
⅛ tsp	cayenne pepper	0.5 mL
1½ lbs	boneless skinless chicken breasts and/or thighs, cut into 1-inch (2.5 cm) pieces	750 g
1	English cucumber, peeled, halved lengthwise, seeded and cut into 1-inch (2.5 cm) chunks	1
1	can (28 oz/796 mL) diced tomatoes with juice	1
2 tbsp	tomato paste	25 mL
2 tbsp	freshly squeezed lime juice	25 mL
1 tbsp	liquid honey	15 mL
⅓ cup	cream (any type)	75 mL
	Fresh cilantro leaves, torn	
	Plain yogurt or sour cream and lime wedges	

1. In a large, deep skillet, heat oil over medium heat. Add onion and cook, stirring, until softened, about 5 minutes. Add garlic, ginger, turmeric, chili powder, salt, cinnamon, black pepper and cayenne; cook, stirring, until spices are blended and fragrant, about 1 minute.

2. Add chicken and stir until coated with spices. Stir in cucumber, tomatoes with juice, tomato paste, lime juice and honey; bring to a simmer. Reduce heat to low, cover and simmer, stirring occasionally, until cucumber is slightly tender, about 10 minutes.

3. Increase heat to medium-low. Stir in cream and simmer gently, uncovered, until chicken is no longer pink inside and cucumber is tender-crisp, about 5 minutes. Season to taste with salt and pepper. Serve sprinkled with cilantro. Serve yogurt and lime wedges to pass at the table.

Spicy Coconut Curry Duck with Lemongrass

Serves 4

Duck is one of the most luxurious meats in a chef's arsenal. Here, it is flavored with several spices, including the deep citrus aromas of lemongrass. This is as rich as any other duck recipe and should be served in small portions, alongside vegetable and/or lentil dishes and, of course, rice.

Tips

To prepare lemongrass, trim off tough outer layers. Cut remaining stalk into 2-inch (5 cm) sections. Smash each piece with the broad side of a knife to bruise; this will help release the flavor when the lemongrass is cooked.

If very ripe fresh tomatoes aren't available, substitute 1½ cups (375 mL) drained canned diced tomatoes.

In step 4, be sure the sauce is at a simmer, with bubbles breaking the surface almost constantly, not too slowly and not vigorously, to ensure that the duck doesn't get rubbery. Adjust the heat as necessary.

4	duck leg quarters	4
½ tsp	salt, divided	2 mL
2 tbsp	vegetable oil	25 mL
2	stalks lemongrass, chopped and bruised	2
1	onion, chopped	1
3	cloves garlic, minced	3
2	hot green chile peppers, sliced	2
1 tbsp	minced gingerroot	15 mL
10	curry leaves	10
1 tbsp	ground coriander	15 mL
1 tsp	ground turmeric	5 mL
¼ tsp	cayenne pepper	1 mL
2	very ripe tomatoes, diced	2
1 cup	coconut milk	250 mL
½ cup	chicken stock or water	125 mL

1. Sprinkle duck with half the salt. Heat a large skillet over medium-high heat. Add duck and cook, turning once, until well browned. Remove from heat. Transfer duck to a bowl.

2. Spoon off all but 2 tbsp (25 mL) of the fat from the pan. Return pan to medium-low heat. Add lemongrass and onion; cook, stirring, until onion is softened, about 3 minutes. Add garlic, chile peppers, ginger, curry leaves, coriander, turmeric, cayenne and remaining salt; cook, stirring, until spices are softened and fragrant, about 1 minute.

3. Add tomatoes and cook, stirring, until softened. Increase heat to medium-high. Add coconut milk and stock; bring to a simmer, scraping up bits stuck to pan. Return duck and any juices to pan, turning to coat in sauce.

4. Reduce heat to low, cover and simmer, turning duck and stirring occasionally, for 1 hour. Uncover and simmer, turning duck and stirring often and spooning off fat as it accumulates, until duck is fork-tender, about 30 minutes. Transfer duck to a warmed serving platter; keep warm.

5. Increase heat to medium-high and boil sauce until slightly thickened, about 5 minutes. Discard lemongrass, if desired. Season to taste with salt.

Sweet-and-Tangy Curry of Quail and Peaches

2 tbsp	vegetable oil	25 mL
2 tsp	mustard seeds	10 mL
3	cloves garlic, chopped	3
1 or 2	hot green chile peppers, minced	1 or 2
1	2-inch (5 cm) piece gingerroot, cut into quarters	1
1 tbsp	curry powder	15 mL
¼ tsp	salt	1 mL
8	quails, quartered	8
1	large tomato, chopped	1
1½ cups	chicken stock	375 mL
3	peaches	3
	Chopped fresh cilantro	

1. In a large skillet, heat oil over medium-high heat until hot but not smoking. Add mustard seeds and cook, stirring, until slightly darker but not yet popping, about 15 seconds. Add garlic, chile peppers, ginger, curry powder and salt; cook, stirring, until softened and fragrant, about 2 minutes.

2. Add quail and stir until coated with spices and just starting to brown, about 3 minutes. Add tomato and cook, stirring, until starting to soften, about 2 minutes.

3. Stir in stock and bring to a simmer, scraping up bits stuck to pan. Reduce heat and simmer gently, stirring often, until sauce is slightly thickened and juices run clear when quail is pierced, about 15 minutes.

4. Meanwhile, slice peaches. Stir into sauce and simmer just until peaches are softened but still hold their shape, about 5 minutes. Discard ginger. Season to taste with salt and serve sprinkled with cilantro.

Beef

•◆•

Curry–Marinated Grilled Flank Steak

Serves 4 to 6

About halfway through every summer's barbecue season, we get tired of plain steak, delicious as it might be. The excitement we crave returns with this heroically proportioned marinade, which entices us to enjoy steak again. Perfect for dinner on the patio with a few friends and lots of beer.

Tips

This marinade freezes well and is perfect for toting to the cottage or making ahead for entertaining. Place the steak and marinade into a large resealable freezer bag. Remove air and seal bag. Freeze for up to 1 month. Thaw overnight in the refrigerator. Let stand at room temperature for 30 minutes and proceed with step 2.

This recipe doubles easily and is perfect for a crowd. If marinating in bags, divide the marinade in half and use 2 separate bags.

1/2 tsp	packed brown or palm sugar	2 mL
2 tbsp	hoisin sauce	25 mL
1 1/2 tsp	Thai yellow curry paste	7 mL
1 tsp	minced gingerroot	5 mL
2 tbsp	rice vinegar	25 mL
1 tbsp	soy sauce	15 mL
1/2 tsp	Asian chili sauce	2 mL
1	beef flank steak (about 1 1/2 lbs/750 g)	1

1. In a large shallow dish or a resealable plastic bag, combine brown sugar, hoisin sauce and curry paste, mashing to blend. Stir in ginger, vinegar, soy sauce and chili sauce. Add steak, turning to coat. Cover and refrigerate for at least 8 hours or for up to 24 hours, turning occasionally. Let stand at room temperature for 30 minutes before grilling.

2. Preheat barbecue to medium-high and grease grill rack.

3. Remove steak from marinade, discarding marinade. Place steak on greased grill. Cover and grill, turning once, for 7 to 10 minutes for medium-rare. Transfer to a cutting board and tent with foil. Let rest for 10 minutes. Slice thinly, across the grain.

Serving Suggestion

Create a summery Asian feast with Marinated Cucumber Carrot Salad (page 22), Caramelized Mango Relish (page 46), Red Curry Fish with Lemongrass (page 158) and Basil and Mint–Scented Coconut Jasmine Rice (page 260).

Caribbean Sweet Mango Beef Curry

Serves 4

Memories of cherished vacations to the islands don't come any beefier or mango-sweeter than this quick and easy Caribbean curry. The only things missing are a beachside table and a warm breeze from the turquoise sea.

Tip

Half a Scotch bonnet pepper adds a pleasant, moderate heat. If you like a hot dish, use a whole pepper.

4 tsp	curry powder, preferably Caribbean-style, divided	20 mL
2 tbsp	freshly squeezed lime juice, divided	25 mL
1 lb	boneless beef grilling steak (such as strip loin or top sirloin), cut into thin strips	500 g
1 tbsp	vegetable oil	15 mL
1	onion, sliced lengthwise	1
3	cloves garlic, minced	3
½	Scotch bonnet pepper, minced	½
1 tbsp	minced gingerroot	15 mL
1 tsp	salt	5 mL
1 cup	coconut milk	250 mL
1	ripe but firm sweet mango, peeled and sliced	1
2	green onions, sliced	2
	Chopped fresh cilantro	

1. In a bowl, combine half each of the curry powder and lime juice. Add beef and toss to coat evenly. Let stand at room temperature for 15 minutes.

2. In a large skillet, heat oil over medium-high heat. Add onion and cook, stirring, until softened and starting to brown, about 3 minutes. Add remaining curry powder, garlic, Scotch bonnet pepper, ginger and salt; cook, stirring, until spices are fragrant, about 1 minute.

3. Add beef mixture and cook, stirring, for 1 minute. Add coconut milk and bring to a simmer, scraping up bits stuck to pan. Stir in mango. Reduce heat and simmer gently, stirring often, until beef is just slightly pink inside and mango is tender, about 3 minutes, or until desired doneness. Stir in remaining lime juice. Season to taste with salt and serve sprinkled with green onions and cilantro.

Serving Suggestion

Served with plain cooked rice or Dry Curry of Potatoes and Onions (page 242) and a tender-crisp green vegetable.

Red Curry Beef with Thai Basil

Serves 4

Thinly sliced steak quickly poached in a rollickingly spiced, thin but meaningful sauce means beefy nirvana for those who like their meat-eating on the lean side. Thai sticky rice is the ideal canvas on which this curry can shine.

Tip

Without the chile peppers, this has a moderate amount of heat. Add 1 chile for a bit more kick. If you like it fiery, add 2.

2 tbsp	vegetable oil, divided	25 mL
1 tbsp	Thai red curry paste, divided	15 mL
1 lb	boneless beef grilling steak (such as strip loin or top sirloin), cut into thin strips	500 g
1	onion, sliced lengthwise	1
3	cloves garlic, minced	3
1 or 2	Thai red chile peppers, minced, optional	1 or 2
1 tbsp	minced gingerroot	15 mL
1½ cups	chopped fresh or drained canned tomatoes	375 mL
1 tsp	packed brown or palm sugar	5 mL
¼ cup	beef stock or water	50 mL
2 tbsp	freshly squeezed lime juice	25 mL
1 tbsp	fish sauce (nam pla)	15 mL
	Salt, optional	
2 tbsp	chopped fresh Thai or sweet basil	25 mL

1. In a bowl, combine 1 tbsp (15 mL) of the oil and 1 tsp (5 mL) of the curry paste. Add beef and toss to coat evenly. Let stand at room temperature for 15 minutes.

2. In a large skillet, heat remaining oil over medium-high heat. Add onion and cook, stirring, until starting to soften, about 3 minutes. Add remaining curry paste, garlic, chile peppers, if using, and ginger; cook, stirring, until blended and fragrant, about 1 minute. Add tomatoes and cook, stirring, until starting to soften, about 2 minutes.

3. Add beef mixture and cook, stirring, for 1 minute. Add brown sugar, stock, lime juice and fish sauce; bring to a simmer, scraping up bits stuck to pan. Reduce heat and simmer gently, stirring often, until beef is just slightly pink inside, about 3 minutes, or until desired doneness. Season to taste with salt, if using, and stir in basil.

Malaysian Red Curry Beef

Serves 4

Flavorful and zesty, this recipe with its tasty sauce, cashews and raisins adds a new dimension to beef. Borrowing from both Thai and Chinese cuisines, it offers tastes and textures that transport the palate to Southeast Asia. As an added bonus, it's easy to assemble and cooks up in next to no time.

Tip

A tender, well-aged grilling steak gives the best flavor and melt-in-your-mouth texture.

2 tbsp	vegetable oil, divided	25 mL
¼ cup	unsalted raw cashews	50 mL
¼ cup	raisins	50 mL
1 lb	boneless beef grilling steak (such as strip loin or top sirloin), cut into thin strips	500 g
2 or 3	hot red or green chile peppers, minced	2 or 3
1	red bell pepper, chopped	1
1 cup	Basic Gravy (see recipe, page 7)	250 mL
1 cup	coconut milk	250 mL
1 tbsp	soy sauce	15 mL
1 tbsp	chopped fresh cilantro	15 mL
2 tsp	chopped fresh mint, optional	10 mL
	Salt	

1. In a large skillet, heat half the oil over medium-high heat until hot but not smoking. Add cashews and raisins; cook, stirring, until cashews are toasted and raisins start to puff. Using a slotted spoon, transfer to a bowl, leaving as much oil in the pan as possible. Set aside.

2. Add beef to pan, in two or three batches, and brown on both sides, adding more of the oil as necessary between batches. Transfer to a bowl.

3. Reduce heat to medium and add any remaining oil to pan. Add chile peppers and bell pepper; cook, stirring, until starting to soften, about 2 minutes. Stir in gravy and cook, stirring, for 1 minute. Add beef with any accumulated juices and stir until coated. Add coconut milk and soy sauce; bring to a simmer, scraping up any bits stuck to pan.

4. Reduce heat and simmer, stirring often, until sauce is slightly thickened, flavors are blended and beef is cooked to desired doneness, about 8 minutes for medium. Stir in cilantro and mint, if using, and season to taste with salt. Serve sprinkled with reserved cashews and raisins.

Chile Lime Curry Beef Kabobs

Serves 4 to 6

Turn your summer patio into an instant kabob house with these zingy skewers that will please young and old alike. Your teenagers will love them even more if you serve some sort of crispy potato on the side. You can also turn them into pita wraps, with a smear of raita and shreds of lettuce.

● ◆ ●

Tip

Kabobs made with just meat, rather than a mix of meat and vegetables, don't look as pretty but do cook more evenly, giving the beef a better texture and flavor. If you want vegetable kabobs as well, double the marinade and marinate vegetables in a separate dish, then thread them onto separate skewers.

● ◆ ●

Variation

Substitute lean boneless lamb leg for the beef.

● *Four to six 8-inch (20 cm) metal or bamboo skewers*
● *Baking sheet, lined with greased foil (for broiler method)*

1 tbsp	vegetable oil	15 mL
2	dried red chile peppers, crumbled (or ¾ tsp/3 mL hot pepper flakes)	2
½ tsp	ground cumin	2 mL
½ tsp	ground coriander	2 mL
2 tbsp	Indian yellow curry paste or masala blend	25 mL
1 tsp	grated lime zest	5 mL
¼ cup	freshly squeezed lime juice	50 mL
1½ lbs	boneless beef sirloin or marinating steak, cut into 1-inch (2.5 cm) cubes	750 g
¼ tsp	salt	1 mL
	Lime wedges	

1. In a small skillet, heat oil over medium-low heat. Add chile peppers, cumin, coriander and curry paste; cook, stirring, until softened and fragrant, about 2 minutes. Remove from heat and let bubbles subside. Add lime zest and juice, scraping up bits stuck to pan. Pour into a shallow dish and let cool completely.

2. Add beef to marinade and toss to coat evenly. Cover and refrigerate for at least 8 hours or for up to 1 day.

3. If using bamboo skewers, soak skewers in a shallow dish for at least 30 minutes or for up to 4 hours.

4. Preheat barbecue to medium and grease grill rack, or preheat broiler with rack 6 inches (15 cm) from burner.

5. Remove beef from marinade, discarding remaining marinade, and sprinkle beef with salt. Thread beef onto skewers, leaving about ⅛ inch (3 mm) between pieces.

6. Place skewers on greased grill or on prepared baking sheet if broiling. Grill or broil, turning skewers to brown all sides, until beef is cooked to desired doneness, about 8 minutes for medium. Let stand for 5 minutes before serving. Serve with lime wedges to squeeze over top.

Tomato Masala Curry Beef Kabobs

Serves 4 to 6

Curry-flavored kabobs, tenderized by the acidity of tomato, grill into a succulence that must be tasted to be believed. Go the full monty on these by serving them with a fancy rice and an upscale salad as well as the recommended raita.

Tip

Disposable latex or rubber gloves are handy not only for chopping hot chile peppers, but also to prevent the curry from staining your hands while you're skewering the meat.

Variation

Substitute lean boneless lamb leg for the beef.

• *Four to six 8-inch (20 cm) metal or bamboo skewers*
• *Baking sheet, lined with greased foil (for broiler method)*

1 tbsp	vegetable oil	15 mL
1 or 2	hot green chile peppers, minced	1 or 2
10	curry leaves	10
½ tsp	garam masala	2 mL
½ cup	Basic Gravy (see recipe, page 7)	125 mL
½ cup	canned crushed (ground) tomatoes	125 mL
½ cup	water	125 mL
2 tsp	soy sauce	10 mL
1½ lbs	boneless beef sirloin or marinating steak, cut into 1-inch (2.5 cm) cubes	750 g
	Chopped fresh cilantro	
	Fresh Mint Raita (see recipe, page 44) or plain yogurt, optional	

1. In a small saucepan, heat oil over medium heat until hot but not smoking. Add chile peppers, curry leaves and garam masala; cook, stirring, until fragrant, about 1 minute. Add gravy and cook, stirring, for 1 minute. Add tomatoes, water and soy sauce; bring to a boil, stirring. Reduce heat and simmer, stirring often, until slightly thickened, about 10 minutes. Pour into a shallow dish and let cool completely.

2. Add beef to marinade and toss to coat evenly. Cover and refrigerate for at least 8 hours or for up to 1 day.

3. If using bamboo skewers, soak skewers in a shallow dish for at least 30 minutes or for up to 4 hours.

4. Preheat barbecue to medium and grease grill rack, or preheat broiler with rack 6 inches (15 cm) from burner.

5. Remove beef from marinade, leaving a thin coating of marinade on meat and discarding remaining marinade. Thread beef onto skewers, leaving about ⅛ inch (3 mm) between pieces.

6. Place skewers on greased grill or on prepared baking sheet if broiling. Grill or broil, turning skewers to brown all sides, until beef is cooked to desired doneness, about 8 minutes for medium. Let stand for 5 minutes before serving. Sprinkle with cilantro and serve with raita for dipping, if desired.

Beef Curry with Many Onions

Serves 8

Beef and onions have an affinity that verges on the romantic. They blend with each other totally and appear together as the prime ingredients of stews internationally. This Asian version has the added advantage of a bouquet of other, equally complementary flavors.

Tip

This seems like a lot of onions to chop, but chopping them by hand gives the finished dish a much better texture than using a food processor.

Serving Suggestion

Serve with Cilantro Lime Sweet Potatoes (page 246) or your favorite mashed or roasted potatoes and a crisp green vegetable.

2 lbs	boneless beef for stew, cut into 1-inch (2.5 cm) pieces	1 kg
¼ cup	white wine vinegar	50 mL
2 tbsp	Madras curry paste or masala blend, divided	25 mL
2 tbsp	vegetable oil	25 mL
2	dried red chile peppers, crumbled	2
2	bay leaves	2
1	stick cinnamon, broken in half	1
1 tbsp	mustard seeds	15 mL
1 tsp	cumin seeds	5 mL
3	large onions, chopped (about 5 cups/1.25 L)	3
6	cloves garlic, chopped	6
1 cup	beef stock	250 mL
	Salt	
	Chopped fresh cilantro	

1. In a large bowl, combine beef, vinegar and half the curry paste. Toss to coat evenly. Let stand at room temperature while proceeding with steps 2 and 3.

2. In a large pot, heat oil over medium heat until hot but not smoking. Add chile peppers, bay leaves, cinnamon, mustard seeds and cumin seeds; cook, stirring, until seeds are slightly toasted but not yet popping, about 15 seconds. Add onions and cook, stirring, until starting to soften, about 2 minutes.

3. Stir in garlic. Reduce heat to medium-low and cook, stirring often, until onions are very soft and starting to turn golden, about 30 minutes. Add remaining curry paste and cook, stirring, until blended and fragrant, about 1 minute.

4. Add beef mixture and stir until coated in onions. Stir in stock. Increase heat to medium-high and bring to a simmer, scraping up bits stuck to pot. Reduce heat to medium-low, cover and simmer, stirring occasionally, until beef is fork-tender, 1 to 1½ hours. Discard bay leaves and cinnamon stick. Season to taste with salt and serve sprinkled with cilantro.

Beef Korma Curry with Almonds

Serves 8

Rich and flavorful, this long-simmered combination of beef, almonds and cream makes a worthy centerpiece for a celebratory dinner party. The smooth sauce makes it luxurious, but if you're avoiding excessive calories, half-and-half (10%) cream works nearly as well as whipping cream.

Variation

Instead of simmering on the stovetop, after returning beef to pot in step 4, transfer to a 325°F (160°C) oven (be sure the pot is ovenproof or transfer to a casserole dish) and bake, covered, for about 2 hours.

6	cloves garlic	6
½ cup	blanched almonds	125 mL
¼ cup	coarsely chopped gingerroot	50 mL
1 cup	water, divided	250 mL
2 tbsp	vegetable oil, divided	25 mL
2 lbs	boneless beef for stew, cut into 1-inch (2.5 cm) pieces	1 kg
4	whole cloves	4
1	stick cinnamon, broken in half	1
1 tbsp	whole coriander seeds	15 mL
2 tsp	cumin seeds	10 mL
2	onions, chopped	2
1½ tsp	salt	7 mL
½ tsp	ground cardamom	2 mL
¾ cup	whipping (35%) cream	175 mL
½ tsp	garam masala	2 mL

1. In a blender or food processor, purée garlic, almonds, ginger and half the water until smooth. Set aside.

2. In a large pot, heat half the oil over medium-high heat until hot but not smoking. Add beef, in three batches, and brown on all sides, adding more of the oil between batches as necessary. Transfer to a bowl.

3. Reduce heat to medium-low and add any remaining oil to pot. Add cloves, cinnamon, coriander seeds and cumin seeds; cook, stirring, until seeds start to pop, about 1 minute. Add onions, salt and cardamom; cook, stirring, until onions are softened and starting to brown, about 5 minutes. Add puréed mixture and cook, stirring, until fragrant and starting to thicken, about 3 minutes.

4. Stir in remaining water and cream. Increase heat to medium-high and bring to a boil, scraping up any bits stuck to pot. Return beef and any accumulated juices to pot. Reduce heat to medium-low, cover and simmer, stirring occasionally, until beef is fork-tender, 1½ to 2 hours. Discard cloves and cinnamon stick, if desired. Season to taste with salt and serve sprinkled with garam masala.

Tamarind Curried Beef and Potatoes

Serves 8

A simplified version of masaman, southern Thailand's richly sauced sweet-and-sour curry, this meat-and-potatoes dish will bring summertime to the coldest days of deep winter, for which its hefty nourishment is so suitable.

Tip

To make tamarind water, break a 2-oz (60 g) piece of block tamarind into small pieces and place in a heatproof bowl. Pour in 1 cup (250 mL) boiling water and let stand until very soft, about 30 minutes, or for up to 8 hours. Press through a fine-mesh sieve, discarding seeds and skins. Extra tamarind water can be stored in the refrigerator for up to 2 weeks.

Variation

The fish sauce can be replaced with 1 tsp (5 mL) salt in step 3 and more to taste as necessary in step 4.

2 tbsp	vegetable oil, divided	25 mL
2 lbs	boneless beef for stew, cut into 1½ inch (4 cm) pieces	1 kg
1	large onion, chopped	1
1	stick cinnamon, broken in half	1
¼ tsp	ground cardamom	1 mL
2 tbsp	Thai yellow curry paste	25 mL
1 tbsp	packed brown or palm sugar	15 mL
1	can (14 oz/400 mL) coconut milk	1
1 cup	tamarind water (see tip, at left)	250 mL
2 tbsp	fish sauce (nam pla)	25 mL
4	small boiling or all-purpose potatoes, cut into ¾-inch (2 cm) cubes	4
¼	cucumber, cut into thin strips	¼
	Chopped roasted salted peanuts	

1. In a large, deep pot, heat half the oil over medium-high heat until hot but not smoking. Add beef, in three batches, and brown on all sides, adding more of the oil between batches as necessary. Transfer to a bowl.

2. Reduce heat to medium-low and add any remaining oil to pot. Add onion, cinnamon and cardamom; cook, stirring, adding up to 2 tbsp (25 mL) water if necessary to prevent burning, until onion is softened and starting to brown, about 3 minutes. Add curry paste and cook, stirring, until fragrant, about 1 minute.

3. Add brown sugar, coconut milk, tamarind water and fish sauce; bring to a boil, scraping up any bits stuck to pot. Return beef and any accumulated juices to pot. Reduce heat to medium-low, cover and simmer, stirring occasionally, for 45 minutes.

4. Stir in potatoes, cover and simmer, stirring occasionally, until potatoes and beef are fork-tender, about 40 minutes. Discard cinnamon stick, if desired. Season to taste with fish sauce. Serve sprinkled with cucumber and peanuts.

Caribbean Curried Beef and Chickpeas

Serves 8

This is a beef version of the famous Jamaican goat curry, just as meaty and zesty as its cousin and further fortified with the goodness and substance of chickpeas. It simmers for a long time, more or less unattended while you perform other kitchen duties, filling the air with its aromatic promise.

Tips

Half of a Scotch bonnet pepper will give a pleasant but detectable heat. A whole one will provide a definite kick.

Garam masala from Guyana is a blend of roasted spices. If you have unroasted garam masala, toast in a dry small skillet over medium heat, stirring constantly, until the color darkens and spices smell toasted, about 2 minutes.

Reduced-sodium stock is best for this recipe. If using regular stock, use 1 cup (250 mL) stock and ½ cup (125 mL) water.

2 lbs	boneless beef for stew, cut into 1-inch (2.5 cm) pieces	1 kg
1	onion, finely chopped	1
½ to 1	Scotch bonnet pepper, minced	½ to 1
3 tbsp	curry powder, preferably Caribbean-style, divided	45 mL
2 tbsp	freshly squeezed lime juice	25 mL
2 tbsp	vegetable oil	25 mL
3	cloves garlic, minced	3
1 tbsp	minced gingerroot	15 mL
1 tbsp	garam masala, preferably Guyanese-style	15 mL
1	large ripe tomato, chopped	1
1½ cups	beef stock	375 mL
2	cans (14 to 19 oz/398 to 540 mL) chickpeas, drained and rinsed	2
2 tsp	chopped fresh thyme	10 mL
	Salt	
4	green onions, sliced	4

1. In a large bowl, combine beef, onion, Scotch bonnet pepper, 2 tbsp (25 mL) of the curry powder and the lime juice. Toss to coat evenly. Cover and marinate at room temperature for 30 minutes or refrigerate overnight.

2. In a large pot, heat oil over medium-high heat. Add remaining curry powder, garlic, ginger and garam masala; cook, stirring, until softened and fragrant, about 30 seconds. Add beef mixture with marinade and stir until coated with spices and beef starts to turn white, about 2 minutes.

3. Stir in tomato and stock; bring to a simmer. Reduce heat to medium-low, cover and simmer, stirring occasionally, for 45 minutes. Stir in chickpeas and simmer, covered, until beef is fork-tender, 45 to 60 minutes.

4. Stir in thyme. Increase heat to medium and simmer, uncovered, until sauce is slightly thickened, about 10 minutes. Season to taste with salt and serve sprinkled with green onions.

Beef Curry with Green Beans and Yogurt

Serves 8

Tender beef, freshly crisp green beans and benignly creamy yogurt sauce combine their appetizing tastes and textures for a deeply satisfying and visually attractive main course. A chutney and some rice will complete the picture.

Tips

Full-fat yogurt provides the best texture. A lower-fat yogurt will work, but avoid fat-free yogurt and any with added gelatin. When cooked, gelatin in yogurt can cause the yogurt to split and create a curdled texture.

Blanching the green beans before adding them to the curry ensures that they will get tender. Acidic ingredients, such as tomatoes, can cause green beans to be tough if they're not first blanched.

Marinated beef can be refrigerated for up to 1 day.

2 lbs	boneless beef for stew, cut into 1-inch (2.5 cm) pieces	1 kg
1½ cups	plain yogurt, preferably full-fat, divided	375 mL
⅓ cup	tandoori or tikka curry paste, divided	75 mL
2 tbsp	vegetable oil, divided	25 mL
2	onions, chopped	2
1 or 2	hot green chile peppers, minced, optional	1 or 2
2 tbsp	minced gingerroot	25 mL
2 tsp	ground turmeric	10 mL
1 tsp	salt	5 mL
2	cans (each 28 oz/796 mL) diced tomatoes with juice	2
4 cups	chopped green beans, blanched, or thawed if frozen (about 1 lb/500 g)	1 L
	Chopped fresh cilantro or mint	
	Chopped roasted cashews or almonds	

1. In a bowl, combine beef, ⅓ cup (75 mL) of the yogurt and 2 tbsp (25 mL) of the curry paste, tossing to coat evenly. Cover and let stand at room temperature for 30 minutes.

2. In a large, deep pot, heat half the oil over medium-high heat until hot but not smoking. Add beef mixture, in two or three batches, and brown on all sides, adding more of the oil between batches as necessary. Transfer to a bowl.

3. Reduce heat to medium and add any remaining oil to pot. Add remaining curry paste, onions, chile peppers, if using, ginger, turmeric and salt; cook, stirring, adding up to 2 tbsp (25 mL) water if necessary to prevent burning, until onions are softened, about 3 minutes.

4. Add tomatoes with juice and bring to a boil, scraping up any bits stuck to pot. Return beef and any accumulated juices to pot. Reduce heat to medium-low, cover and simmer, stirring and mashing tomatoes occasionally, until beef is fork-tender, 1 to 1½ hours.

5. Stir in green beans and simmer until beans are tender-crisp, about 5 minutes. Remove from heat. Stir remaining yogurt until creamy and smooth, then stir into pot. Season to taste with salt. Serve sprinkled with cilantro and nuts.

Baked Beef and Root Vegetable Curry

Serves 8

Here's a substantial beef, parsnip and carrot stew that bakes long and blissfully in a perky sauce. Enriched with yogurt, it's comfort food of the highest order. Plain rice or naan will lend all the support this curry needs.

Tips

Reduced-sodium beef stock works best for this recipe. If it is not available, use 1½ cups (375 mL) regular beef stock and 1 cup (250 mL) water.

Full-fat yogurt provides the best texture. A lower-fat yogurt will work, but avoid fat-free yogurt and any with added gelatin. When cooked, gelatin in yogurt can cause the yogurt to split and create a curdled texture.

If you don't have an ovenproof pot, transfer beef mixture to a 16-cup (4 L) casserole dish after step 2.

• Preheat oven to 325°F (160°C)

1 tbsp	vegetable oil	15 mL
4	bay leaves	4
2	sticks cinnamon, broken in half	2
1 tbsp	cumin seeds	15 mL
1	large onion, chopped	1
1 or 2	hot green chile peppers, minced	1 or 2
¼ cup	chopped gingerroot	50 mL
1 tsp	ground turmeric	5 mL
½ tsp	freshly ground black pepper	2 mL
½ tsp	ground cardamom	2 mL
2 lbs	boneless beef for stew, cut into 1-inch (2.5 cm) pieces	1 kg
4	small parsnips, peeled and cut into chunks	4
4	carrots, cut into chunks	4
2 cups	beef stock	500 mL
4	all-purpose potatoes, cut into chunks	4
	Salt	
¾ cup	plain yogurt	175 mL
½ tsp	garam masala	2 mL
	Chopped fresh basil or cilantro	

1. In a large, deep ovenproof pot, heat oil over medium heat until hot but not smoking. Add bay leaves, cinnamon and cumin seeds; cook, stirring, until seeds start to pop, about 1 minute. Add onion and cook, stirring, until softened and starting to brown, about 5 minutes. Add chile peppers, ginger, turmeric, pepper and cardamom; cook, stirring, until softened and fragrant, about 1 minute.

2. Stir in beef until well coated with spices, about 2 minutes. Add parsnips, carrots and stock; bring to a simmer, scraping up bits stuck to pot.

3. Cover and bake in preheated oven, stirring once, for 1 hour. Stir in potatoes, cover and bake, stirring once, until beef and vegetables are fork-tender, about 1 hour. Remove lid and bake until slightly thickened, about 20 minutes. Discard bay leaves and cinnamon sticks. Season to taste with salt. Serve topped with yogurt and sprinkled with garam masala and basil.

Slow–Braised Beef Curry with Turnips

Serves 8

Inspired by a staple of Canadian Maritimes cuisine, this recipe marries beef with nutritious turnip and accents them with fragrant spices, adding sparkle to a classic stew.

* ◆ •

Tips

If you have freshly harvested turnips with tender skins, there is no need to peel them. Just trim off the ends and give them a good scrub under running water.

Reduced-sodium beef stock works best for this recipe. If it is not available, use 2 cups (500 mL) regular beef stock and 1 cup (250 mL) water.

1 tbsp	vegetable oil	15 mL
10	curry leaves	10
1	stick cinnamon, broken in half	1
1 tsp	cumin seeds	5 mL
2	large onions, sliced lengthwise	2
8	white turnips, peeled and cut into wedges (about 2 lbs/500 g)	8
2 or 3	hot green chile peppers, minced	2 or 3
2 tbsp	minced gingerroot	25 mL
2 tbsp	Indian yellow curry paste or masala blend	25 mL
2 lbs	boneless beef for stew, cut into 1-inch (2.5 cm) pieces	1 kg
3 cups	beef stock	750 mL
	Salt	
½ tsp	garam masala	2 mL
	Chopped fresh cilantro	

1. In a large, deep pot, heat oil over medium heat until hot but not smoking. Add curry leaves, cinnamon and cumin seeds; cook, stirring, until seeds start to pop, about 1 minute. Add onions and cook, stirring, for 2 minutes. Reduce heat to medium-low and cook, stirring often, until onions are very soft and golden brown, 10 to 15 minutes. Add turnips, chile peppers, ginger and curry paste; cook, stirring, until well blended, about 2 minutes.

2. Stir in beef until well coated with spices, about 2 minutes. Stir in stock. Increase heat to medium-high and bring to a simmer, scraping up any bits stuck to pan. Reduce heat to medium-low, cover and simmer, stirring often, until beef and turnips are fork-tender, 1 to 1½ hours.

3. Uncover, increase heat to medium and simmer until sauce is slightly thickened, about 5 minutes. Discard cinnamon stick, if desired. Season to taste with salt. Serve sprinkled with garam masala and cilantro.

Braised Beef Curry with Chiles, Lime and Lemongrass

Serves 8

Burmese influences such as aromatic spices, hot chiles and dried shrimp contribute perfume and fire to this long-braised, meltingly tender beef. You'll need plenty of plain rice with this one.

• ◆ •

Tips

If lime leaves aren't available, substitute 1 tsp (5 mL) finely grated lime zest and stir in at the beginning of step 3.

It is traditional to leave the lime leaves and lemongrass in the finished dish, but they're not meant to be eaten. You can discard them before serving, if you prefer — or warn your guests!

For the beef, buy a boneless cross rib, blade or chuck roast and cut into strips, or buy precut strips, rather than purchasing precut stewing beef, which often comes in random shapes.

1 tbsp	vegetable oil	15 mL
1	stick cinnamon, broken in half	1
2	onions, chopped	2
2	stalks lemongrass, chopped and bruised (see tip, page 83)	2
4	wild lime leaves (see tips, at left)	4
2 or 3	hot green chile peppers, minced	2 or 3
2 tbsp	minced gingerroot	25 mL
2 tbsp	dried shrimp (see tip, page 79)	25 mL
2 tbsp	Indian yellow curry paste or masala blend	25 mL
2 lbs	boneless beef for stew (see tip, at left), cut into 1/4-inch (0.5 cm) thick strips	1 kg
1	can (28 oz/796 mL) tomatoes with juice, chopped	1
	Salt	
	Chopped fresh Thai or sweet basil	

1. In a large, deep pot, heat oil over medium heat until hot but not smoking. Add cinnamon and cook, stirring, until fragrant, about 1 minute. Add onions, lemongrass and lime leaves; cook, stirring, until onions are softened, about 5 minutes. Add chile peppers, ginger, shrimp and curry paste; cook, stirring, until well blended, about 1 minute.

2. Stir in beef until well coated with spices, about 2 minutes. Add tomatoes with juice and bring to a simmer, scraping up any bits stuck to pan. Reduce heat to medium-low, cover and simmer, stirring often, until beef is fork-tender, 1 to 1 1/2 hours.

3. Uncover and simmer until sauce is slightly thickened, about 10 minutes. Discard cinnamon stick, lemongrass and lime leaves, if desired. Season to taste with salt. Serve sprinkled with basil.

Ground Beef Curry with Potatoes and Peas

Serves 4

A basic curry with everyday, inexpensive ingredients, this curry-house staple is a viable option for a casual lunch that is tasty and uplifting as well as fast. Rice or naan and a small salad complete the simple menu.

Tip

We prefer lean ground beef for the optimal balance of fat and flavor. Extra-lean beef doesn't have enough beef flavor and can be dry and tough. Higher-fat ground beef can make the dish greasy.

1 lb	lean ground beef	500 g
1	onion, chopped	1
1 tsp	ground cumin	5 mL
4	small boiling or all-purpose potatoes, cut into ½-inch (1 cm) cubes	4
1 cup	Basic Gravy (see recipe, page 7)	250 mL
1½ cups	beef stock or water	375 mL
1 cup	frozen green peas	250 mL
1 tbsp	chopped fresh cilantro	15 mL
	Salt	

1. In a large skillet over high heat, brown ground beef, onion and cumin, breaking up beef with a spoon, until beef is no longer pink and onion is softened, about 8 minutes. Drain off all but 1 tbsp (15 mL) fat.

2. Reduce heat to medium. Add potatoes and cook, stirring, until starting to soften, about 3 minutes. Add gravy and cook, stirring, for 1 minute. Stir in stock and bring to a boil. Reduce heat to medium-low, cover and simmer, stirring occasionally, until potatoes are almost tender, about 15 minutes.

3. Stir in peas, cover and simmer until peas are heated through and flavors are blended, about 5 minutes. Stir in cilantro and season to taste with salt.

Serving Suggestion

Serve topped with Cucumber Raita (page 45) or Fresh Mint Raita (page 44) and a fruit chutney such as Pickled Peach Chutney (page 38) or Rhubarb Chutney (page 41).

Thai Green Curry Ground Beef and Zucchini

Serves 4

Easygoing lunches need appropriately unpretentious food, but there's no need to sacrifice novelty or flavor. This affordable recipe combines meat and vegetables in a lovely coconut-rich sauce. It's an ideal partner to rice or noodles.

Tip

Good-quality coconut milk makes a big difference in the flavor and texture of this recipe. Be sure to use one with as little added water as possible.

Variation

Substitute 1 Japanese eggplant, thinly sliced, for the zucchini and add 1 tsp (5 mL) mint with the basil.

1 lb	lean ground beef	500 g
2	cloves garlic, minced	2
1	onion, finely chopped	1
2 tbsp	minced gingerroot	25 mL
1	zucchini, halved lengthwise and thinly sliced	1
4 tsp	Thai green curry paste	20 mL
1	can (14 oz/400 mL) coconut milk	1
1 tbsp	fish sauce (nam pla)	15 mL
	Salt, optional	
2 tbsp	chopped fresh Thai basil	25 mL
	Lime wedges	

1. In a large skillet over medium-high heat, brown ground beef, garlic, onion and ginger, breaking up beef with a spoon, until beef is no longer pink and onion is softened, 8 to 10 minutes. Add zucchini and curry paste; cook, stirring, until zucchini starts to soften, about 2 minutes. Drain off any fat.

2. Add coconut milk and fish sauce; bring to a boil, scraping up any bits stuck to pan. Reduce heat and simmer, stirring often, until about half the liquid is absorbed and flavors are blended, about 10 minutes. Season to taste with salt, if using. Serve sprinkled with basil and garnished with lime wedges to squeeze over top.

African Curried Beef and Sweet Potato Casserole

Serves 8 to 10

This blend of traditional South African bobotie and the North American favorite shepherd's pie will bring a lively twist to the dinner table. It's perfect for entertaining or a potluck, as it can be made ahead.

Tips

If you want moderate heat in the meat mixture, use 2 chile peppers.

To make ahead, cool meat mixture and topping completely. Assemble in baking dish without butter and almonds. Cover and refrigerate for up to 2 days. Drizzle with butter and bake, increasing time to about 1 hour, covering topping loosely with foil if it starts to get too brown. Add almonds for the last 15 minutes.

• *12-cup (3 L) shallow baking dish, greased*

2 lbs	lean ground beef	1 kg
1	onion, finely chopped	1
½ tsp	ground cinnamon	2 mL
2 or 3	hot green or red chile peppers, minced	2 or 3
1 cup	Basic Gravy (see recipe, page 7)	250 mL
½ cup	raisins and/or chopped dried apricots	125 mL
1 cup	beef stock or water	250 mL
	Salt	

Sweet Potato Topping

3 lbs	sweet potatoes (about 3 large), peeled and cut into chunks	1.5 kg
1½ tsp	salt, divided	7 mL
¼ tsp	freshly ground black pepper	1 mL
¼ tsp	ground cinnamon	1 mL
2 tbsp	freshly squeezed lemon juice	25 mL
2	eggs, beaten	2
1 tbsp	chopped fresh cilantro	15 mL
2 tbsp	butter, melted	25 mL
¼ cup	sliced almonds	50 mL

1. In a large skillet over high heat, brown ground beef, onion and cinnamon, breaking up beef with a spoon, until beef is no longer pink and onion is softened, about 10 minutes. Add chile peppers and cook, stirring, for 1 minute.

2. Add gravy and cook, stirring, for 1 minute. Stir in raisins and/or apricots. Add stock and bring to a boil. Reduce heat and simmer, stirring occasionally, until most of the liquid is absorbed, about 15 minutes. Season to taste with salt.

3. *Meanwhile, prepare the topping:* In a large pot, cover sweet potatoes with cold water and add ½ tsp (2 mL) of the salt. Bring to a boil over high heat. Reduce heat and boil gently until potatoes are fork-tender, about 15 minutes. Drain and return to pot. Add remaining salt, pepper, cinnamon and lemon juice; mash until smooth. Stir in eggs and cilantro.

4. Preheat oven to 350°F (180°C).

5. Spread beef mixture in prepared baking dish. Spread topping in an even layer over meat. Drizzle with melted butter and sprinkle with almonds. Bake until meat filling is heated through and topping is slightly puffed and browned, about 30 minutes. Let stand for 10 minutes before serving.

Serving Suggestion

Serve with Peanut and Cucumber Salad (page 23) or with a crisp green salad with a citrus dressing.

Tip

Be sure to keep the sweet potatoes cooking at a gentle boil rather than a hard boil to prevent the outsides from breaking up and getting mushy before the insides are cooked.

Variation

Replace the ground beef with ground lamb and add 1 cup (250 mL) frozen green peas, thawed, just before assembling.

Meatballs in Tomato Onion Curry

Serves 4

Tender meatballs, smooth and creamy from their rice filler, sit invitingly in a perky tomato curry sauce. This affordable lunch or dinner will elicit kudos every time.

● ◆ ●

Tips

A gentle hand while mixing and shaping the meatballs is important to prevent the meat from getting overworked and tough.

The meatballs can be prepared ahead, covered and refrigerated for up to 1 day or frozen for up to 3 months (thaw overnight in the refrigerator).

Meatballs

1	egg	1
¾ cup	cold cooked rice	175 mL
1 tbsp	chopped fresh cilantro	15 mL
¼ tsp	salt	1 mL
1 tbsp	tandoori or tikka curry paste or masala blend	15 mL
1 lb	lean ground beef	500 g

Tomato Onion Curry

1 tbsp	vegetable oil	15 mL
1	stick cinnamon, broken in half	1
1 tsp	cumin seeds	5 mL
2	onions, chopped	2
1 or 2	hot green chile peppers, minced, optional	1 or 2
½ cup	Basic Gravy (see recipe, page 7)	125 mL
1	can (28 oz/796 mL) diced tomatoes with juice	1
	Salt	
	Chopped fresh cilantro	

1. *Prepare the meatballs:* In a large bowl, using a fork, combine egg, rice, cilantro, salt and curry paste. Blend in ground beef. Form into thirty-six 1-inch (2.5 cm) balls.

2. In a large nonstick skillet over medium heat, brown meatballs on all sides, about 5 minutes. Transfer to a bowl.

3. *Prepare the curry:* Wipe out skillet. Return to medium heat and heat oil until hot but not smoking. Add cinnamon and cumin seeds; cook, stirring, until seeds are starting to pop, about 1 minute. Add onions and cook, stirring, until softened and deep golden brown, about 8 minutes. Add chile peppers, if using, and gravy; cook, stirring, for 1 minute. Stir in tomatoes with juice and bring to a boil.

4. Add meatballs and any accumulated juices and stir gently to coat in sauce. Reduce heat and simmer, stirring gently and turning meatballs occasionally, until meatballs are no longer pink inside and sauce is thickened, about 10 minutes. Season to taste with salt and serve sprinkled with cilantro.

Meatballs in Zesty Coconut Curry

Serves 4

Meatballs, as Italian cuisine has taught us, can be not just an inexpensive dinner, but a tasty delight. It's all in the additions and the sauce. These Asian meatballs pass all the criteria, elevating them to gourmet.

Tip

The meatballs can be prepared ahead, covered and refrigerated for up to 1 day or frozen for up to 3 months (thaw overnight in the refrigerator).

Variation

Substitute Thai yellow curry paste for the Indian, lime zest and juice for the lemon, and Thai basil for the cilantro.

Meatballs

1	egg	1
½ cup	fresh bread crumbs	125 mL
1 tbsp	chopped fresh cilantro	15 mL
¼ tsp	salt	1 mL
1 tbsp	freshly squeezed lemon juice	15 mL
1 tsp	Indian yellow curry paste or masala blend	5 mL
1 lb	lean ground beef	500 g

Coconut Curry Sauce

1 tbsp	vegetable oil	15 mL
1 or 2	hot green or red chile peppers, minced, optional	1 or 2
1	small onion, sliced lengthwise	1
½ tsp	salt	2 mL
1 tbsp	Indian yellow curry paste or masala blend	15 mL
¼ cup	sweetened flaked coconut	50 mL
1	can (14 oz/400 mL) coconut milk	1
1 tsp	finely grated lemon zest	5 mL
1 tbsp	freshly squeezed lemon juice	15 mL
	Chopped fresh cilantro	
	Lemon wedges	

1. *Prepare the meatballs:* In a large bowl, using a fork, combine egg, bread crumbs, cilantro, salt, lemon juice and curry paste. Blend in ground beef. Form into twenty 1½-inch (4 cm) balls.

2. In a large nonstick skillet over medium heat, brown meatballs on all sides, about 8 minutes. Transfer to a bowl.

3. *Prepare the sauce:* Wipe out skillet. Return to medium heat and heat oil. Add chile peppers, if using, onion, salt and curry paste; cook, stirring, until onion is softened and starting to brown, about 3 minutes. Add coconut and coconut milk; bring to a boil, stirring until blended.

4. Add meatballs and any accumulated juices and stir gently to coat in sauce. Reduce heat and simmer, stirring gently and turning meatballs occasionally, until meatballs are no longer pink inside and sauce is slightly thickened, 5 to 10 minutes. Stir in lemon zest and juice and season to taste with salt. Serve sprinkled with cilantro and with lemon wedges.

Baked Curried Beef Koftas and Vegetables

Serves 4

Meatballs by another name and in a different shape, koftas are spiced to tease the palate and increase the appetite. Here, they luxuriate in an assertive tomato curry alongside soothingly tender carrots and eggplant.

Tips

The addition of oats to the meat mixture is not traditional by any means, but it does help the baked koftas retain moisture.

A gentle hand while mixing and shaping the beef is important to prevent the meat from getting overworked and tough.

- Preheat oven to 400°F (200°C)
- 13- by 9-inch (3 L) glass baking dish, greased

Koftas

1	egg	1
½ cup	quick-cooking rolled oats	125 mL
2 tbsp	chopped fresh parsley	25 mL
½ tsp	salt	2 mL
½ tsp	garam masala	2 mL
1 tbsp	Indian yellow curry paste or masala blend	15 mL
1 lb	lean ground beef	500 g

Vegetable Curry

1 tbsp	vegetable oil	15 mL
2	carrots, chopped	2
1	onion, sliced lengthwise	1
10	curry leaves	10
1 or 2	hot green chile peppers, minced	1 or 2
½ tsp	ground cumin	2 mL
4 tsp	Indian yellow curry paste or masala blend	20 mL
2 cups	cubed eggplant (½-inch/1 cm cubes)	500 mL
½ tsp	salt	2 mL
1 cup	drained canned diced tomatoes	250 mL
1 cup	beef stock	250 mL
½ tsp	garam masala	2 mL
	Chopped fresh parsley	

1. *Prepare the koftas:* In a large bowl, using a fork, combine egg, oats, parsley, salt, garam masala and curry paste. Blend in ground beef. Form into 8 sausage-shaped logs, each about 5 inches (12.5 cm) long, pinching into points at each end. Place in prepared baking dish, leaving as much space as possible between each kofta.

2. Bake in preheated oven until firm and starting to brown, about 20 minutes.

3. *Meanwhile, prepare the curry:* In a saucepan, heat oil over medium heat. Add carrots, onion and curry leaves; cook, stirring, until onion is softened and starting to brown, about 5 minutes. Add chile peppers, cumin and curry paste; cook, stirring, until blended and fragrant, about 1 minute. Add eggplant and salt; stir until eggplant is coated in spices.

4. Add tomatoes and stock; bring to a boil, scraping up bits stuck to pan. Reduce heat, cover and simmer, stirring occasionally, until sauce is flavorful and carrots are almost tender, about 5 minutes. Season to taste with salt.

5. Pour sauce over koftas and bake until sauce is bubbling and koftas are no longer pink inside, about 15 minutes. Serve sprinkled with garam masala and parsley.

Serving Suggestion

To complete this nutritious all-in-one-meal, serve with basmati rice, Spinach Rice Pilau (page 255) or Dry Curry of Potatoes and Onions (page 242) and Naan (page 268 or store-bought).

Tips

If curry leaves aren't available, substitute 4 bay leaves and discard before serving.

Any Asian- or Italian-style eggplant will work well in this recipe. When purchasing an eggplant, choose one that is shiny and firm without any blemishes and with a fresh-looking green stem.

If the skin seems thick, you may want to peel the eggplant; if the skin is tender, leave it on.

Jamaican Curried Beef Patties

Makes 10 patties

Nothing says "I care" as much as a properly turned out pie or patty. It is the crust that always gets them, because it's so much fun to eat something crispy. Make a batch of these patties one afternoon when you have time, and whip them out of the freezer to bake fresh at just the right moment.

Tips

Lean ground beef is preferred for this recipe. Extra-lean tends to be too dry, and medium or regular will have too much fat, making the patties soggy.

Be very cautious when chopping Scotch bonnet peppers. Wear disposable gloves and wash all utensils and cutting boards well.

Beef patties can be prepared to the end of step 5 and frozen on baking sheets until solid. Transfer to an airtight container for up to 2 months. Return to prepared baking sheets and bake directly from frozen, increasing baking time to 25 to 30 minutes.

• Large baking sheets, lined with parchment paper

Pastry

2 cups	all-purpose flour	500 mL
1 tsp	salt	5 mL
¼ tsp	curry powder, preferably Jamaican- or other Caribbean-style	1 mL
⅓ cup	cold butter, cut into cubes	75 mL
3 tbsp	vegetable oil	45 mL
¼ cup	cold water (approx.)	50 mL
1	egg, beaten	1

Curry Beef Filling

1 lb	lean ground beef	500 g
1 tbsp	minced gingerroot	15 mL
2 tsp	curry powder, preferably Jamaican- or other Caribbean-style	10 mL
1 tsp	dried thyme	5 mL
½ tsp	salt	2 mL
4	green onions, finely chopped	4
4	cloves garlic, minced	4
1	Scotch bonnet pepper, minced	1
½ cup	beef stock or water	125 mL
¼ cup	dry bread crumbs	50 mL

1. *Prepare the pastry:* In a bowl, combine flour, salt and curry powder. Using a pastry blender or two knives, cut in butter until crumbly. Using a fork, stir in oil until evenly blended. Stir in enough of the water to make a soft, not sticky dough. Gather dough with your hands and squeeze into a ball. Press into a disk and wrap in plastic. Refrigerate for at least 30 minutes or for up to 2 days.

2. *Prepare the filling:* In a large skillet over medium-high heat, brown ground beef, ginger, curry powder, thyme and salt, breaking up beef with a spoon, until beef is no longer pink, about 7 minutes. Add green onions, garlic and Scotch bonnet pepper; cook, stirring, until onions are softened, about 2 minutes.

3. Stir in stock, reduce heat and simmer, stirring often, until most of the liquid is absorbed and mixture is starting to brown, about 5 minutes. Remove from heat and stir in bread crumbs. Season to taste with salt. Let cool completely.

4. Preheat oven to 400°F (200°C).

5. Divide dough into 10 equal balls, squeezing until pliable. On a floured surface or a large piece of parchment paper, roll out each ball to a 6-inch (15 cm) circle, keeping surface well floured. Spoon about 1/4 cup (50 mL) of the filling onto one half of each circle. Brush edge of circle with egg. Fold other side of circle over filling into a half-moon shape, pinching edge to seal. Trim edges to neaten, if desired. Place on prepared baking sheets, at least 2 inches (5 cm) apart. Brush top of each pastry with egg.

6. Bake, in batches as necessary, until pastry is golden brown and crispy, about 20 minutes. Serve hot.

Variations

For appetizer-size patties, divide the dough into 20 balls and roll each into a 3-inch (7.5 cm) circle. Fill with about 2 tbsp (25 mL) of the filling. Reduce baking time to about 15 minutes.

Make a selection of different patties (the regular size or the appetizer size) for a Global Curry Party. Use this dough recipe with any of the samosa filling recipes (pages 284–290). Be sure to mark the pastry or add some decoration so you can identify which filling is inside. Serve different chutneys on the side to really liven up the flavors.

Meatballs in Tangy Goan-Style Curry

Serves 4

This meatball dish draws from the vinegar-tart cuisine left over in Goa from their erstwhile Portuguese colonizers. Serve it with rice or potatoes for a family dinner, or on a buffet as a secondary meat curry. It'll become your sleeper hit.

Tip

This version is warmly spiced and tangy. If you like it tangy and hot, use a hot curry paste.

Meatballs

1	egg	1
1/2 cup	fresh bread crumbs	125 mL
1/4 tsp	salt	1 mL
1/4 tsp	ground cinnamon	1 mL
Pinch	ground cloves	Pinch
2 tsp	vindaloo or Indian yellow curry paste	10 mL
1 lb	lean ground beef	500 g

Tangy Curry Sauce

1 tbsp	vegetable oil	15 mL
2	cloves garlic, minced	2
1	onion, finely chopped	1
1/4 tsp	ground cinnamon	1 mL
Pinch	ground cardamom	Pinch
Pinch	ground cloves	Pinch
1 tbsp	vindaloo or Indian yellow curry paste	15 mL
1/4 cup	red wine vinegar	50 mL
1 1/2 cups	beef stock	375 mL
1/4 cup	tomato paste	50 mL
	Salt	
	Chopped fresh cilantro	

1. *Prepare the meatballs:* In a large bowl, using a fork, combine egg, bread crumbs, salt, cinnamon, cloves and curry paste. Blend in ground beef. Form into twenty 1 1/2-inch (4 cm) balls.

2. In a large nonstick skillet over medium heat, brown meatballs on all sides, about 8 minutes. Transfer to a bowl.

3. *Prepare the sauce:* Wipe out skillet. Return to medium heat and heat oil. Add garlic, onion, cinnamon, cardamom, cloves and curry paste; cook, stirring, until onion is softened and starting to brown, about 3 minutes. Add vinegar and bring to a boil, stirring. Add stock and tomato paste; bring to a boil, stirring until blended.

4. Add meatballs and any accumulated juices and stir gently to coat in sauce. Reduce heat and simmer, stirring gently and turning meatballs occasionally, until meatballs are no longer pink inside and sauce is slightly thickened, about 10 minutes. Season to taste with salt. Serve sprinkled with cilantro.

Pork

Tandoori Pork Loin Roast

Serves 8

A pork roast with a difference, this loin is long-marinated in a spiced tandoori-style yogurt coating and slow-baked or grilled for juicy and flavorful succulence. Leftovers, thinly sliced and dabbed with a fruit chutney, make a cheerful sandwich.

• ◆ •

Tips

Be sure to use a single loin roast. If you purchase a roast that is two pieces tied together (a double loin), cut the strings and use the two pieces separately to get the most flavor and so that the cooking is even and takes the recommended time.

A lower-fat yogurt can be used, but make sure it does not contain gelatin. When cooked, gelatin in yogurt can cause the yogurt to split and create a curdled texture.

If you prefer the traditional bright red color of tandoori that you often see in restaurants, add red and yellow food coloring to the yogurt marinade.

• *Roasting pan with rack (for oven method)*
• *Meat thermometer*

2 lb	boneless single pork loin roast	1 kg
½ tsp	salt	2 mL
2 tbsp	freshly squeezed lemon juice	25 mL
2 tsp	garam masala	10 mL
1½ tsp	ground cumin	7 mL
1 tsp	ground coriander	5 mL
¼ tsp	ground cardamom	1 mL
1	clove garlic, minced	1
1	hot green chile pepper, minced	1
2 tsp	minced gingerroot	10 mL
2 tsp	paprika	10 mL
¾ cup	plain yogurt, preferably full-fat (see tip, at left)	175 mL
	Lemon wedges	

1. Place pork roast in a shallow dish and sprinkle with salt and lemon juice. Rub with your hands or toss to coat evenly. Let stand at room temperature for 15 minutes. Drain off excess juice.

2. Meanwhile, in a dry small skillet over medium heat, toast garam masala, cumin, coriander and cardamom, stirring constantly, just until spices have a toasted aroma and are starting to darken, 1 to 2 minutes. Transfer immediately to a small bowl. Stir in garlic, chile pepper, ginger, paprika and yogurt. Spread over pork roast, coating evenly. Cover and refrigerate for at least 4 hours or for up to 1 day. Let stand at room temperature for 30 minutes before cooking.

3. *To grill:* Preheat barbecue to high (see tip, opposite). Turn off one burner and reduce remaining burner(s) to medium. Remove roast from marinade, leaving a layer of marinade on roast. Discard any excess marinade. Place roast on grill over unlit side and close lid. Grill, maintaining heat at 325°F (160°C) or as close as possible, until thermometer inserted in center of roast reaches 155°F (68°C) for medium, about 2 hours. Without turning, place roast over hot side of grill and cook just until grill marks appear on bottom, about 3 minutes.

4. *To bake in oven:* Preheat oven to 325°F (160°C). Remove roast from marinade, leaving a layer of marinade on roast. Discard any excess marinade. Place roast on rack in roasting pan and roast until thermometer inserted in center of roast reaches 155°F (68°C) for medium, about 2 hours.

5. *For both methods:* Transfer to a cutting board and tent with foil. Let stand for 10 minutes before slicing. Serve with lemon wedges to squeeze over top.

Serving Suggestion

Serve with Major Grey–Style Mango Chutney (page 36 or store-bought), Fresh Cilantro Mint Chutney (page 39), Dal Curry with Chiles and Coconut (page 187) and Cauliflower and Potato Curry (page 243).

Tips

To barbecue, you need a gas grill with at least 2 burners. If using a charcoal barbecue, use your favorite method of indirect cooking. If you don't have a working thermometer on your barbecue, place an oven thermometer beside the roast.

If making the oven version, give the roast a smoky flavor by adding $\frac{1}{4}$ tsp (1 mL) smoked paprika with the regular paprika.

Cilantro Mint Curry–Crusted Pork Loin Roast

Serves 8

Moist and tender, this pork loin is crusted with herbs and spices to maximize its natural flavors. Excellent as a Sunday roast, it works with Asian rices or noodles, but also with oven-roasted potatoes (from the same oven as the pork), as well as steamed buttered vegetables and salad.

Tips

Be sure to use a single loin roast. If you purchase a roast that is two pieces tied together (a double loin), cut the strings and use the two pieces separately to get the most flavor and so that the cooking is even and takes the recommended time.

After washing the herbs, pat dry well so the paste doesn't get watered down and slide off the meat.

- Preheat oven to 325°F (160°C)
- Roasting pan with rack
- Meat thermometer

2 lb	boneless single pork loin roast	1 kg
3	cloves garlic, slivered	3
1 or 2	hot green chile peppers, chopped	1 or 2
1 cup	packed fresh cilantro leaves	250 mL
¼ cup	packed fresh mint leaves	50 mL
1 tsp	granulated sugar	5 mL
½ tsp	ground cumin	2 mL
¼ tsp	salt	1 mL
2 tbsp	freshly squeezed lime juice	25 mL
2 tsp	Indian yellow curry paste or masala blend	10 mL
2 tbsp	olive or vegetable oil (approx.)	25 mL
	Lime wedges	

1. Cut several slits in pork roast and insert a sliver of garlic into each slit. Place on rack in roasting pan and set aside.

2. In a food processor or blender, combine chile peppers, cilantro, mint, sugar, cumin, salt, lime juice and curry paste. Purée, adding just enough of the oil as necessary to make a thick, smooth paste. Scrape sides of the bowl or jug as necessary to incorporate the ingredients.

3. Spread herb paste evenly over roast. Bake in preheated oven until thermometer inserted in center of roast reaches 155°F (68°C) for medium, 1½ to 2 hours. Transfer to a cutting board and tent with foil. Let stand for 10 minutes before slicing. Serve with lime wedges to squeeze over top.

Braised Pork with Caribbean Coconut Lime Curry

Serves 8 to 10

With obligatory sunshiny elements such as ginger, allspice, powerhouse chiles and thyme, this affordable island-style pork shoulder will please when it's fresh out of the oven at supper and, just as tastily, cold in the next day's lunch sandwich.

Tip

It is mush easier to grate the zest from the lime before squeezing it. Since it isn't added to the pan until the end, wrap zest in a small piece of plastic wrap or waxed paper and refrigerate until using.

Variation

To cook on the barbecue, use a foil roasting pan and cook over indirect heat (see instructions in Tandoori Pork Loin Roast, page 112), maintaining temperature at 350°F (180°C). If desired, brown roast over medium heat on grill after removing from the juices.

• *Roasting pan*

4 lb	boneless pork shoulder blade (butt) roast, tied	2 kg
4	cloves garlic, minced	4
1 or 2	Scotch bonnet peppers, minced	1 or 2
2 tbsp	minced gingerroot	25 mL
2 tbsp	packed brown sugar	25 mL
1 tbsp	dried thyme	15 mL
1 tsp	salt	5 mL
1 tsp	ground allspice	5 mL
½ tsp	ground cinnamon	2 mL
1 cup	coconut milk, divided	250 mL
1 tsp	finely grated lime zest (see tip, at left)	5 mL
¼ cup	freshly squeezed lime juice	50 mL
	Fresh Mango Pineapple Relish (page 47) or Caramelized Mango Relish (page 46)	
	Lime wedges	

1. Place pork in roasting pan. In a bowl, combine garlic, Scotch bonnet peppers, ginger, brown sugar, thyme, salt, allspice, cinnamon and 1 tbsp (15 mL) of the coconut milk. Spread all over roast. Let stand at room temperature for 30 minutes, or cover and refrigerate for up to 1 day (if refrigerated, let stand at room temperature for 30 minutes before cooking).

2. Preheat oven to 350°F (180°C).

3. In a bowl, combine remaining coconut milk, lime zest and lime juice. Pour around roast in pan. Cover pan with foil, sealing tightly around pan but not touching roast. Bake for 2½ hours.

4. Uncover and baste roast with pan juices. Bake, uncovered, for 30 to 45 minutes, basting twice more, until fork-tender and a meat thermometer inserted in center reads 170°F (75°C).

5. Transfer roast to a cutting board and tent with foil. Discard pan juices. Let roast stand for 15 minutes before slicing. Cut off strings and cut roast into thin slices. Serve with relish and lime wedges to squeeze over top.

Sweet Mango Curry of Pork Medallions

Serves 4

With the sweetness of its mango as a counterpoint, this pork curry is as elegant as only the best party recipes know how to be. Accompanied with a crisp vegetable curry such as Cashew Green Beans with Mustard Seeds (page 218) and rice, it's suitable for the most fancy of dinners.

Tips

This recipe is mild, but you can use a medium or hot curry paste if you want to turn up the fire.

Be sure the mango is sweet and ripe but not too soft, or it will break up in the sauce and get mucky. If your mango is soft, add after the pork is cooked and just heat through.

2 tbsp	vegetable oil or butter, divided	25 mL
1 lb	pork tenderloin, cut into 1-inch (2.5 cm) thick medallions	500 g
3	cloves garlic, minced	3
2 tbsp	minced gingerroot	25 mL
½ tsp	salt	2 mL
Pinch	ground cinnamon	Pinch
1 tbsp	Indian yellow curry paste or masala blend	15 mL
1	large tomato, diced	1
1	ripe but firm sweet mango, peeled and sliced	1
¼ cup	water	50 mL
½ cup	plain yogurt	125 mL
	Chopped fresh cilantro or mint	

1. In a large skillet, heat half the oil over medium-high heat until hot but not smoking. Brown pork medallions, turning once, for about 2 minutes per side. Transfer to a plate.

2. Reduce heat to medium-low and add remaining oil. Add garlic, ginger, salt, cinnamon and curry paste; cook, stirring, until softened and fragrant, about 1 minute. Add tomato and cook, stirring, until softened, about 2 minutes. Stir in mango and water.

3. Return pork and any accumulated juices to pan and turn to coat in sauce. Bring to a simmer, stirring gently. Cook, turning pork once and stirring sauce gently, until just a hint of pink remains in pork, about 4 minutes. Season to taste with salt. Serve topped with yogurt and sprinkled with cilantro.

Curried Pork Chops with Crispy Sweet Potatoes

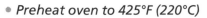

Serves 4

Here's a meat-and-potatoes recipe that turns the notion upside down. Sweet potato and pork in an aromatic curry sauce team up to nourish like any other plate of pork chop and spuds, but do it in a way that will add sunshine to dinner on the bleakest winter's eve.

Tips

If you don't have parchment paper, you can line the baking sheet with foil and grease the foil — or use nonstick foil.

If lime leaves aren't available, substitute ½ tsp (2 mL) finely grated lime zest and stir into sauce before adding pork chops in step 6.

To get a nice brown crust, be sure the pan and oil are well heated before adding the pork. Don't try to turn the pork too soon, or it will stick and tear.

- Preheat oven to 425°F (220°C)
- Rimmed baking sheet, lined with parchment paper

2	sweet potatoes	2
1½ tsp	curry powder, divided	7 mL
½ tsp	salt, divided	2 mL
4	boneless pork chops, about ¾-inch (2 cm) thick	4
2 tbsp	vegetable oil	25 mL
2	wild lime leaves (see tip, at left)	2
1 cup	Basic Gravy (see recipe, page 7)	250 mL
½ cup	chicken stock	125 mL
2 tbsp	chopped fresh Thai or sweet basil	25 mL

1. Peel sweet potatoes, if desired, and cut into ½-inch (1 cm) thick slices. Sprinkle with 1 tsp (5 mL) of the curry powder and about three-quarters of the salt. Set aside. Sprinkle pork chops with remaining curry powder and salt. Set aside separately.

2. In a large skillet, heat half the oil over medium heat. Add sweet potatoes, in batches as necessary, and cook, turning once, until well browned on both sides, about 5 minutes per batch. Transfer to prepared baking sheet. Add more of the oil between batches as necessary.

3. Bake potatoes in preheated oven until tender, about 10 minutes.

4. Meanwhile, increase heat to medium-high, add remaining oil to pan and heat for 15 seconds. Add pork chops and cook, turning once, until well browned, 1 to 2 minutes per side. Transfer to a plate and set aside.

5. Add lime leaves and gravy to pan and cook, stirring, for 2 minutes. Stir in stock and bring to a boil, scraping up bits stuck to pan. Boil for 3 minutes or until thickened.

6. Return pork chops and any accumulated juices to pan, turning to coat in sauce. Reduce heat and simmer, turning pork once, until just a hint of pink remains in pork, about 5 minutes. Serve pork and sauce over sweet potatoes and sprinkle with basil.

Quick Pork Vindaloo Curry

Serves 4

Pork vindaloo is traditionally made with pork shoulder, which requires a long braise, but this pork loin is ready quickly. If you like your vindaloo to be fiery, use a hot curry paste. Either way, you'll please fans of this Portuguese-invented pork curry.

Tip

Be sure not to overcook the pork, or it will become dry and leathery.

2 tbsp	all-purpose flour	25 mL
1 tbsp	vindaloo or Indian yellow curry paste or masala blend	15 mL
¼ tsp	ground cinnamon	1 mL
Pinch	ground cardamom	Pinch
Pinch	ground cloves	Pinch
1 lb	boneless pork loin rib chops, cut into thin strips	500 g
2 tbsp	vegetable oil, divided	25 mL
1	onion, finely chopped	1
3 tbsp	white vinegar	45 mL
1 cup	chicken stock	250 mL
2 tbsp	tomato paste	25 mL
½ tsp	salt, or to taste	2 mL
1 tbsp	chopped fresh cilantro	15 mL

1. In a bowl, combine flour, curry paste, cinnamon, cardamom and cloves; add pork and toss to coat. Let stand at room temperature for 15 minutes.

2. In a large skillet, heat half the oil over medium-high heat until hot but not smoking. Add pork, in two batches, and cook, turning once, until browned on both sides, adding more of the oil between batches as necessary. Transfer to a clean bowl.

3. Reduce heat to medium-low and add any remaining oil to pan. Add onion and cook, stirring, until softened, about 3 minutes. Stir in vinegar, scraping up any bits stuck to pan. Stir in stock and tomato paste. Increase heat to medium and bring to a boil, stirring. Boil until slightly thickened, about 2 minutes.

4. Return pork and any accumulated juices to pan. Cook, stirring, until pork is heated through and just a hint of pink remains inside, about 2 minutes. Season with salt and stir in cilantro.

Slow-Simmered Pork Vindaloo Curry

Serves 8

Meals in one dish don't come much more comforting than this slow-simmered pork and potato vindaloo. Nor are any of them more meaningfully spiced. This one definitely qualifies as fiery, for fans of the mighty chile.

Serving Suggestion

Serve topped with Cucumber Raita (page 45) or Fresh Mint Raita (page 44) and your favorite chutney.

6	cloves garlic	6
5	dried red chile peppers	5
1	large onion, cut into 8 pieces	1
1/4 cup	chopped gingerroot	50 mL
1 tbsp	mustard seeds, preferably black	15 mL
2 tsp	cumin seeds	10 mL
1 tsp	fenugreek seeds	5 mL
1/2 tsp	whole black peppercorns	2 mL
1 cup	water, divided	250 mL
2 tbsp	vegetable oil, divided (approx.)	25 mL
2 lbs	trimmed boneless pork shoulder blade (butt), cut into 1-inch (2.5 cm) pieces	1 kg
1 1/2 tsp	salt	7 mL
1/2 tsp	ground turmeric	2 mL
1/4 tsp	ground cloves	1 mL
1/2 cup	dry white wine	125 mL
4	boiling or all-purpose potatoes, cut into 1-inch (2.5 cm) chunks	4

1. In a blender or food processor, purée garlic, chile peppers, onion, ginger, mustard seeds, cumin seeds, fenugreek seeds, peppercorns and 1/2 cup (125 mL) of the water until fairly smooth, adding a little more water if necessary to blend. Set aside.

2. In a large, deep pot, heat half the oil over medium-high heat. Add pork, in two or three batches, and cook, turning to brown all sides, adding more of the oil as necessary between batches. Transfer to a bowl.

3. Reduce heat to medium-low. Carefully add puréed garlic mixture (it will splatter), salt, turmeric and cloves; cook, stirring often, until fragrant and thickened, about 5 minutes. Pour in wine. Increase heat to medium-high and bring to a boil, scraping up bits stuck to pot.

4. Stir in remaining water and potatoes and return pork and any accumulated juices to pot. Reduce heat to medium-low, cover and simmer, stirring occasionally, until pork and potatoes are fork-tender, about 1 hour. Season to taste with salt.

Tamarind Ginger Curried Pork

Serves 4

Packed with flavor and tartly exotic with tamarind and ginger, this slow-simmered pork melts in the mouth while it excites the palate. The squash adds the necessary textural counterpoint to keep things interesting.

Tip

This curry doesn't have much chile heat at all; rather, it is laced with warm spices. If you like a hotter curry, increase the chile peppers to 2 or 3.

2 lbs	trimmed boneless pork shoulder blade (butt), cut into 1-inch (2.5 cm) pieces	1 kg
½ cup	Basic Gravy (see recipe, page 7)	125 mL
2 tbsp	vegetable oil	25 mL
6	whole cloves	6
1	stick cinnamon, about 2 inches (5 cm) long	1
1 tbsp	mustard seeds	15 mL
2 tsp	cumin seeds	10 mL
½ tsp	fenugreek seeds	2 mL
1	hot green chile pepper, minced	1
⅓ cup	finely chopped gingerroot	75 mL
¼ tsp	ground cardamom	1 mL
2 tbsp	packed brown or palm sugar	25 mL
1 cup	tamarind water (see tip, page 94)	250 mL
1 cup	water	250 mL
4 cups	cubed peeled butternut or other winter squash (¾-inch/2 cm cubes)	1 L
	Salt	
2 tbsp	chopped fresh cilantro or basil	25 mL

1. In a large bowl, combine pork and gravy. Toss to coat evenly. Let stand at room temperature for 30 minutes.

2. In a large pot, heat oil over medium heat until hot but not smoking. Add cloves, cinnamon, mustard seeds, cumin seeds and fenugreek seeds; cook, stirring, until seeds are toasted but not yet popping, about 30 seconds. Reduce heat to medium-low. Add chile pepper, ginger and cardamom; cook, stirring, until pepper is softened but not browned, 1 to 2 minutes.

3. Add pork mixture and stir until coated in spices. Stir in brown sugar, tamarind water and water. Increase heat to medium-high and bring to a simmer. Reduce heat to medium-low, cover and simmer, stirring occasionally, for 45 minutes. Stir in squash, cover and simmer, stirring occasionally, until pork is fork-tender and squash is just tender, about 30 minutes.

4. Uncover, increase heat to medium and boil gently until squash is tender and sauce is slightly thickened, about 10 minutes. Discard cloves and cinnamon stick, if desired. Season to taste with salt and serve sprinkled with cilantro.

Filipino Pork Adobo

Serves 8

Slow-simmered and vinegar-tart, this lively but mild pork curry represents culinary fusion between Asia and Europe, but its taste appeal is universal.

Tip

For the best flavor and color, use a high-quality naturally brewed reduced-sodium soy sauce. Check the label carefully, as some products sold as soy sauce have very little soy and loads of salt and coloring. If reduced-sodium soy sauce is not available, use water instead of chicken stock; otherwise, the dish will be too salty.

2 tbsp	vegetable oil, divided	25 mL
2 lbs	trimmed boneless pork shoulder blade (butt), cut into 1½-inch (4 cm) pieces	1 kg
2	large onions, chopped	2
8	cloves garlic, chopped	8
4	bay leaves	4
1½ tsp	paprika	7 mL
½ tsp	ground turmeric	2 mL
¼ tsp	freshly ground black pepper	1 mL
1 cup	chicken stock or water	250 mL
⅔ cup	rice vinegar or white vinegar	150 mL
½ cup	soy sauce, preferably reduced-sodium	125 mL
	Salt, optional	

1. In a large, deep pot, heat half the oil over medium-high heat until hot but not smoking. Add pork, in two or three batches, and cook, turning to brown all sides, adding more of the oil as necessary between batches. Transfer to a plate.

2. Reduce heat to medium-low and add any remaining oil to pot. Add onions and cook, stirring often, until very soft and golden brown, about 8 minutes. Add garlic, bay leaves, paprika, turmeric and pepper; cook, stirring, until fragrant, about 1 minute.

3. Pour in stock, vinegar and soy sauce. Increase heat to medium-high and bring to a simmer, scraping up bits stuck to pot. Return pork and any accumulated juices to pot. Reduce heat to medium-low, cover and simmer, stirring occasionally, until pork is fork-tender, 1 to 1½ hours.

4. Uncover, increase heat to medium and boil gently, stirring occasionally, until sauce is slightly thickened, about 5 minutes. Discard bay leaves. Season to taste with salt.

Serving Suggestion

Serve with Cilantro Lime Sweet Potatoes (page 246), Spinach Rice Pilau (page 255) or good old-fashioned mashed potatoes.

Spicy Pork Curry with Ginger

Serves 8

Fairly fiery and supremely oniony, this tender pork curry will do wonders for your well-being on a frigid winter evening. Throw a log in the fireplace and load up your plate with rice and curry for some instant happiness.

Tip

The onions can be chopped in a food processor; just be sure not to purée them to the point that they become juicy.

5	dried red chile peppers, crumbled	5
¼ cup	white wine vinegar or rice vinegar	50 mL
2 lbs	trimmed boneless pork shoulder blade (butt), cut into 1-inch (2.5 cm) pieces	1 kg
2 tbsp	Madras curry paste, divided	25 mL
2 tbsp	vegetable oil	25 mL
1	stick cinnamon, broken in half	1
1 tbsp	mustard seeds	15 mL
2	large onions, finely chopped	2
¼ cup	finely chopped gingerroot	50 mL
1 cup	chicken stock	250 mL
	Salt	
	Chopped fresh cilantro	

1. In a microwave-safe bowl or a small saucepan, combine chile peppers and vinegar. Bring just to a boil in microwave on High, about 1 minute, or in saucepan over high heat. Remove from heat, cover and let stand until peppers are soft, about 15 minutes, or for up to 1 day.

2. In a large bowl, combine vinegar mixture, pork and half the curry paste. Toss to coat evenly. Let stand at room temperature for 15 minutes.

3. Meanwhile, in a large pot, heat oil over medium heat until hot but not smoking. Add cinnamon and mustard seeds; cook, stirring, until slightly toasted but not yet popping, about 15 seconds. Add onions and cook, stirring, until starting to soften, about 2 minutes.

4. Stir in ginger. Reduce heat to medium-low and cook, stirring often, until onion is very soft and deep golden brown, 10 to 15 minutes. Add remaining curry paste and cook, stirring, until blended and fragrant, about 1 minute.

5. Add pork mixture and stir until coated in onions. Pour in stock. Increase heat to medium-high and bring to a simmer, scraping up bits stuck to pot. Reduce heat to medium-low, cover and simmer, stirring occasionally, until pork is fork-tender, about 1 hour.

6. Uncover, increase heat to medium and boil gently, stirring occasionally, until sauce is slightly thickened, about 10 minutes. Discard cinnamon stick, if desired. Season to taste with salt and serve sprinkled with cilantro.

Red Curry Pork with Green Mango

Serves 4

Inspired by little-known Burmese cuisine, this curried pork is luxuriously sauced with layers of flavors, and partnered to sweetly tart green mango for a nice contrast. Though quick and easy to make, it's a celebratory dish that is sure to delight.

Tips

This dish has a nice kick of heat. If you like a fiery curry, increase the curry paste by ½ to 1 tsp (2 to 5 mL), adding the extra amount in step 2.

Green mangoes are firm enough to peel with a sharp vegetable peeler or paring knife. Peel off skin and cut flesh away from the pit in slices. Cut each slice crosswise into thin strips.

2 tbsp	vegetable oil, divided	25 mL
2 tsp	Thai red curry paste, divided	10 mL
1 lb	boneless pork loin or tenderloin, cut into thin strips	500 g
1	onion, sliced lengthwise	1
3	cloves garlic, minced	3
1 tbsp	minced gingerroot	15 mL
1	large green mango (or 2 small), peeled and thinly sliced	1
¾ cup	chicken stock or water	175 mL
2 tbsp	freshly squeezed lime juice	25 mL
1 tbsp	fish sauce (nam pla)	15 mL
	Salt, optional	
	Chopped fresh mint or cilantro	

1. In a bowl, combine 1 tbsp (15 mL) of the oil and 1 tsp (5 mL) of the curry paste. Add pork and toss to evenly coat. Let stand at room temperature for 15 minutes.

2. In a large skillet, heat remaining oil over medium-high heat. Add onion and cook, stirring, until softened and starting to brown, about 3 minutes. Add remaining curry paste, garlic and ginger; cook, stirring, until well blended and fragrant, about 1 minute.

3. Add pork mixture and cook, stirring, until pork starts to turn white, about 1 minute. Stir in mango. Add stock, lime juice and fish sauce; bring to a simmer, scraping up bits stuck to pan. Reduce heat and simmer gently, stirring often, until just a hint of pink remains in pork and mango is tender, about 5 minutes. Season to taste with salt, if using, and serve sprinkled with mint.

Thai Sweet-and-Sour Curried Pork

Serves 4

Quickly sautéed and perky, this Thai-inspired combination of aromatic vegetables, pork and sweet-sour condiments is a natural partner for rice or noodles and makes for a lively meal.

Tips

This dish is moderately spicy. If you want more heat, add Asian chili sauce to taste with the salt. For a milder dish, reduce the amount of curry paste to 1 tsp (5 mL), adding half with the pork and half with ginger in step 2.

If using pork tenderloin, cut it in half crosswise where it starts to thicken. Cut the thick end in half lengthwise, then cut crosswise into thin slices. Cut the thin end crosswise into thin slices.

2 tbsp	vegetable oil, divided	25 mL
2 tsp	Thai red curry paste, divided	10 mL
1 lb	boneless pork loin or tenderloin, cut into thin strips	500 g
1	onion, sliced lengthwise	1
1 tbsp	minced gingerroot	15 mL
1	large tomato, chopped	1
1	green or red bell pepper, chopped	1
1	tart apple, diced (peeled if desired), optional	1
2 tbsp	packed brown or palm sugar	25 mL
¼ cup	rice vinegar	50 mL
2 tbsp	fish sauce (nam pla)	25 mL
	Salt, optional	
	Chopped fresh Thai or sweet basil or cilantro	

1. In a bowl, combine 1 tbsp (15 mL) of the oil and 1 tsp (5 mL) of the curry paste. Add pork and toss to coat evenly. Let stand at room temperature for 15 minutes.

2. In a wok or large skillet, heat remaining oil over medium-high heat. Add onion and cook, stirring, until softened and starting to brown, about 3 minutes. Add remaining curry paste and ginger; cook, stirring, until well blended and fragrant, about 30 seconds. Add tomato and cook, stirring, until starting to soften, about 2 minutes.

3. Add pork mixture, green pepper and apple, if using; cook, stirring, for 1 minute. Add brown sugar, vinegar and fish sauce; bring to a simmer, scraping up bits stuck to pan. Reduce heat and simmer gently, stirring often, until just a hint of pink remains in pork and green pepper is tender, about 5 minutes. Season to taste with salt, if using, and serve sprinkled with basil.

Lemongrass Coconut Curried Pork with Zucchini

Serves 4

The smooth texture and subtle taste of zucchini transform this mild Thai-style pork curry into a soothing dish, especially if served with lightly sautéed rice noodles.

Tips

To prepare lemongrass, trim off tough outer layers. Cut remaining stalk into 2-inch (5 cm) sections. Smash each piece with the broad side of a knife to bruise; this will help release the flavor when the lemongrass is cooked.

If lime leaves aren't available, substitute ½ tsp (2 mL) finely grated lime zest and add with the lime juice in step 2.

1 tbsp	vegetable oil	15 mL
1	onion, sliced lengthwise	1
3	cloves garlic, minced	3
2	stalks lemongrass, chopped and bruised (see tip, at left)	2
2	wild lime leaves (see tip, at left)	2
½ tsp	salt	2 mL
1 tbsp	Thai yellow curry paste	15 mL
1	zucchini, halved and thinly sliced	1
1 lb	boneless pork loin or tenderloin, cut into thin strips	500 g
1 cup	coconut milk	250 mL
½ cup	chicken stock, vegetable stock or water	125 mL
1 tbsp	freshly squeezed lime juice	15 mL
¼ cup	thin strips red bell pepper	50 mL
	Chopped fresh Thai or sweet basil	

1. In a large skillet or wok, heat oil over medium heat. Add onion and cook, stirring, until softened and starting to turn golden, about 3 minutes. Stir in garlic, lemongrass, lime leaves, salt and curry paste; cook, stirring, until fragrant, about 1 minute. Add zucchini and cook, stirring, for 1 minute.

2. Stir in pork until well coated in spices. Add coconut milk and bring to a simmer, scraping up bits stuck to pan. Reduce heat and simmer gently, stirring often, until just a hint of pink remains in pork and zucchini is tender, about 5 minutes. Discard lemongrass and lime leaves, if desired. Stir in lime juice and season to taste with salt. Serve sprinkled with red pepper and basil.

Curried Pork with Sweet Peppers, Carrots and Coconut

Serves 4

This sensibly balanced dish combines the pleasures of fragrant pork with the goodness of carrots and peppers. Easy to make, it's a quick one-dish weekday dinner. Serve over rice or noodles.

◆

Tips

Use Indian- or Thai-style yellow curry in this recipe. Each gives a different flavor, so you can try both and decide which you like best.

If using pork tenderloin, cut it in half crosswise where it starts to thicken. Cut the thick end in half lengthwise, then cut crosswise into thin slices. Cut the thin end crosswise into thin slices.

1 tbsp	vegetable oil	15 mL
2	carrots, thinly sliced on the diagonal	2
1	onion, sliced lengthwise	1
1 tbsp	minced gingerroot	15 mL
½ tsp	salt	2 mL
1 tbsp	Indian or Thai yellow curry paste or masala blend (see tip, at left)	15 mL
1 lb	boneless pork loin or tenderloin, cut into thin strips	500 g
2	bell peppers (any color), chopped	1
1 cup	coconut milk	250 mL
¼ cup	chicken stock or water	50 mL
	Chopped fresh mint or cilantro	

1. In a large skillet or wok, heat oil over medium heat. Add carrots and onion; cook, stirring, until softened, about 5 minutes. Stir in ginger, salt and curry paste; cook, stirring, until fragrant, about 2 minutes.

2. Stir in pork and bell peppers until well coated in spices. Stir in coconut milk and stock; bring to a simmer, scraping up bits stuck to pan. Reduce heat and simmer until just a hint of pink remains in pork and peppers are tender-crisp, about 3 minutes. Season to taste with salt. Serve sprinkled with mint.

Serving Suggestions

If using Indian curry paste, serve with Peanut and Cucumber Salad (page 23), basmati rice and Dal Fry (page 186).

If using Thai curry paste, expand on the theme by serving with Thai Basil Sticky Rice (page 261) or over cooked rice noodles, with Marinated Cucumber Carrot Salad (page 22) on the side (omit the carrots, if desired).

Cashew Basil Pork, Eggplant and Snow Peas in Green Curry

Serves 4

Smooth eggplant and crisp snow peas with tender pork in a sauce that is zesty-hot and also rich with cashews — a feast for the palate that will uplift the spirits and earn serious kudos for the chef. Serve over jasmine rice or wide rice noodles.

Tips

If lime leaves aren't available, substitute ½ tsp (2 mL) finely grated lime zest and add with the lime juice in step 2.

One chile pepper perks it up, and 2 will get you sweating. If you really dare, use 3!

The cashews give the best texture to the sauce if pulsed in a food processor to a coarse meal (without processing too much into butter). You may need to do more than ¼ cup (50 mL), depending on the size of your food processor. Extra ground nuts can be frozen for future use.

1 tbsp	vegetable oil	15 mL
1	Japanese eggplant, halved lengthwise and sliced	1
2	wild lime leaves (see tip, at left)	2
1 to 3	Thai bird chile peppers, minced	1 to 3
1 tbsp	minced gingerroot	15 mL
4 tsp	Thai green curry paste	20 mL
1 lb	boneless pork loin or tenderloin, cut into thin strips	500 g
¼ cup	salted roasted cashews, ground or finely chopped (see tip, at left)	50 mL
1 tbsp	packed brown or palm sugar	15 mL
1	can (14 oz/400 mL) coconut milk	1
2 tbsp	fish sauce (nam pla)	25 mL
1 cup	snow peas, trimmed and halved diagonally	250 mL
2 tbsp	freshly squeezed lime juice	25 mL
	Salt	
2 tbsp	chopped fresh Thai or sweet basil	25 mL
	Salted roasted cashews	
	Lime wedges	

1. In a large skillet or wok, heat oil over medium-high heat. Add eggplant and lime leaves; cook, stirring, until eggplant starts to soften, about 2 minutes. Add chile peppers, ginger and curry paste; cook, stirring, until fragrant and blended, about 30 seconds.

2. Stir in pork until well coated in spices. Add ground cashews, brown sugar, coconut milk and fish sauce; bring to a simmer, stirring until blended. Stir in snow peas. Reduce heat and simmer gently, stirring often, until just a hint of pink remains in pork and snow peas are tender-crisp, about 5 minutes. Discard lime leaves, if desired. Stir in lime juice and season to taste with salt. Serve sprinkled with basil and cashews and garnished with lime wedges to squeeze over top.

Yellow Curry Pork with Pineapple

Serves 4

A tart sauce adds substance to tender pork topped with roasted cashews. Exotic and luxurious, this dish works well on a party buffet alongside other curries and a pilaf or two.

Tips

If fresh pineapple isn't available, substitute one 19-oz (540 mL) can pineapple chunks, drained; add in step 3 for the last 5 minutes of cooking.

This dish is definitely on the fiery side. For a milder version, decrease the curry paste to 1 to 2 tsp (5 to 10 mL).

1 tbsp	vegetable oil	15 mL
¼ cup	raw cashews	50 mL
1	onion, sliced lengthwise	1
1½ cups	chopped fresh pineapple	375 mL
1 tbsp	Thai yellow curry paste	15 mL
1 lb	boneless pork loin or tenderloin, cut into thin strips	500 g
1 cup	drained canned diced tomatoes	250 mL
1 tbsp	packed brown or palm sugar	15 mL
½ cup	tamarind water (see tip, page 94)	125 mL
1 tbsp	soy sauce (approx.)	15 mL
2 tbsp	chopped fresh Thai or sweet basil	25 mL
2 tsp	chopped fresh mint, optional	10 mL

1. In a large skillet, heat oil over medium heat until hot but not smoking. Add cashews and cook, stirring, until toasted, about 2 minutes. Using a slotted spoon, transfer to a bowl, leaving as much oil in the pan as possible. Set aside.

2. Add onion to pan and cook, stirring, until softened and starting to turn golden, about 3 minutes. Add pineapple and curry paste; cook, stirring, until fragrant and pineapple starts to release its juices, about 1 minute.

3. Stir in pork until well coated in spices. Stir in tomatoes, brown sugar, tamarind water and soy sauce; bring to a simmer. Reduce heat and simmer gently, stirring often, until just a hint of pink remains in pork, about 5 minutes. Season to taste with soy sauce. Serve sprinkled with reserved cashews, basil and mint, if using.

Beef Korma Curry with Almonds (page 93)

Meatballs in Zesty Coconut Curry (page 105)

Curried Pork with Sweet Peppers, Carrots and Coconut (page 126)

Thai Curry Pork Ribs (page 131)

Tomato Curry Pork with Spinach

Serves 4

Saucy and tastily nutritious with its generous spinach content, this quick pork curry will enliven any family dinner.

◆

Tips

A deep skillet helps to prevent too much splatter while the tomatoes and gravy simmer.

Prewashed baby spinach is terrific for this dish, and in most cases only the very large stems need to be trimmed off. If using large-leaf spinach, wash well and dry in a salad spinner or blot between tea towels. Trim off tough stems and tear any very large leaves into smaller pieces.

1 tbsp	vegetable oil	15 mL
½ tsp	cumin seeds	2 mL
½ tsp	fenugreek seeds	2 mL
1 cup	chopped tomatoes	250 mL
10	curry leaves	10
1 lb	boneless pork loin or tenderloin, cut into thin strips	500 g
½ tsp	salt	2 mL
½ cup	Basic Gravy (see recipe, page 7)	125 mL
⅓ cup	chicken stock or water	75 mL
4 cups	lightly packed fresh spinach (about 4 oz/125 g), trimmed	1 L
	Chopped fresh cilantro	

1. In a large, deep skillet, heat oil over medium heat until hot but not smoking. Add cumin seeds and fenugreek seeds; cook, stirring, until seeds start to pop, about 1 minute. Add tomatoes and curry leaves; cook, stirring, until tomatoes start to soften, about 2 minutes.

2. Stir in pork and salt until pork is well coated in spices. Pour in gravy and stock; bring to a simmer. Reduce heat and simmer, stirring often, until just a hint of pink remains in pork and sauce is slightly thickened, about 5 minutes.

3. Gradually add spinach, a handful at a time, stirring just until wilted. Season to taste with salt. Serve sprinkled with cilantro.

Serving Suggestion

Serve with Curried Cauliflower and Sweet Corn with Yogurt (page 223), Red Lentil Curry with Coconut and Cilantro (page 190) and basmati rice.

Laos-Style Red Curry Pork with Spinach

Serves 4

A blend of Thai and Vietnamese influences, this Laotian pork curry is loaded with beneficial spinach as well as the perky tastes of its two curry pastes. Rice is all you need as an accompaniment.

• ◆ •

Tip

Dried shrimp are available at Asian specialty stores and some well-stocked grocery stores. They add saltiness and depth to curries. If they're not available, use an additional 1 tbsp (15 mL) fish sauce or add ¼ tsp (1 mL) salt.

• ◆ •

Variation

For a milder version of this dish, decrease the Thai red curry paste to 2 tsp (10 mL).

1 tbsp	vegetable oil	15 mL
4	green onions, sliced	4
1 tbsp	minced gingerroot	15 mL
1 tbsp	dried shrimp, optional (see tip, at left)	15 mL
1 tbsp	Thai red curry paste	15 mL
1 tsp	Indian yellow curry paste or masala blend	5 mL
1 lb	boneless pork loin or tenderloin, cut into ¾-inch (2 cm) pieces	500 g
1	can (8 oz/227 mL) sliced bamboo shoots, drained	1
1 tbsp	packed brown or palm sugar	15 mL
1 cup	coconut milk	250 mL
1 tbsp	fish sauce (nam pla)	15 mL
4 cups	lightly packed spinach (about 4 oz/125 g), trimmed	1 L
	Chopped fresh cilantro and/or mint	

1. In a large skillet or wok, heat oil over medium heat. Add green onions, ginger, shrimp, if using, red curry paste and yellow curry paste; cook, stirring, until onions are softened and spices are fragrant, about 2 minutes.

2. Stir in pork and bamboo shoots until well coated in spices. Add brown sugar, coconut milk and fish sauce; bring to a simmer, scraping up bits stuck to pan. Reduce heat and simmer gently, stirring often, until just a hint of pink remains in pork, about 3 minutes.

3. Gradually add spinach, a handful at a time, stirring just until wilted. Serve sprinkled with cilantro and/or mint.

Thai Curry Pork Ribs

Serves 4 to 6

Ribs can be prepared a thousand different ways, but this one just might become your favorite. Nicely glazed and deeply aromatic, the ribs practically levitate off the plate and melt in your mouth. Serve with ice-cold beer to create an instant party mood.

Tips

The wild lime leaves add a wonderful flavor to the braising liquid that can't be replicated with lime zest, so it's worth seeking them out. If the leaves aren't available, serve the ribs with lime wedges to squeeze over top.

This glaze has a bit of a fiery kick. For a milder version, reduce the curry paste to 2 tsp (10 mL).

- Preheat oven to 325°F (160°C)
- 13- by 9-inch (3 L) glass baking dish

2	racks pork back ribs (about 3 lbs/1.5 kg)	2
4	wild lime leaves (see tip, at left)	4
2	stalks lemongrass, chopped and bruised (see tip, page 125)	2
½ cup	water	125 mL
½ cup	coconut milk, divided	125 mL
2	cloves garlic, minced	2
1 tbsp	minced gingerroot	15 mL
1 tbsp	Thai red curry paste	15 mL
⅓ cup	packed brown or palm sugar	75 mL
1 cup	tamarind water (see tip, page 94)	250 mL
2 tbsp	fish sauce (nam pla)	25 mL

1. Using the tip of a knife, lift one end of the thin membrane on underside of ribs. Gripping membrane with a paper towel, carefully peel off and discard. Cut ribs into 2- or 3-rib portions.

2. Place ribs in baking dish with lime leaves and lemongrass. Pour in water and cover with foil. Bake in preheated oven until ribs are almost tender, about 1 hour.

3. Meanwhile, in a small saucepan, heat 2 tbsp (25 mL) of the coconut milk over medium heat until bubbling. Add garlic, ginger and curry paste; cook, stirring, until softened and fragrant, about 1 minute. Add remaining coconut milk, brown sugar, tamarind water and fish sauce; bring to a boil, stirring until sugar is dissolved. Reduce heat and boil gently until reduced by about one-third, about 20 minutes.

4. Transfer ribs to a bowl. Drain off liquid from baking dish and discard lime leaves and lemongrass. Return ribs to dish and pour in sauce, turning ribs to coat. Bake, uncovered, turning and basting ribs occasionally, until ribs are fork-tender and glazed, about 30 minutes. Broil until glaze is browned and bubbly, about 3 minutes. Serve ribs with any sauce from the dish spooned over top.

Pork Meatballs with Red Curry Peanut Sauce

Serves 4

There are meatballs, and then there are meatballs. These can be as proudly served to guests at a party as to the family on a weekday. Baked rather than fried, the meatballs nestle in a rich coconut milk and peanut sauce, tart from a drizzle of lime juice.

Tip

The meatballs and sauce can be made ahead, cooled and refrigerated separately for up to 2 days or frozen for up to 3 months (thaw overnight in the refrigerator). To reheat, combine meatballs and sauce in a skillet over medium heat and heat until meatballs are hot inside, then proceed with step 3.

Serving Suggestion

Serve spooned over fluffy jasmine rice, with stir-fried broccoli and red bell peppers on the side.

- Preheat oven to 450°F (230°C)
- Large rimmed baking sheet, lined with foil and greased

Meatballs

1	egg	1
½ cup	fresh bread crumbs	125 mL
1 tbsp	chopped fresh basil	15 mL
1 tbsp	freshly squeezed lime juice	15 mL
1 tsp	Thai red curry paste	5 mL
1 lb	lean ground pork	500 g

Red Curry Peanut Sauce

½ cup	salted roasted peanuts, finely chopped	125 mL
2 tbsp	packed brown or palm sugar	25 mL
1	can (14 oz/400 mL) coconut milk	1
2 tsp	Thai red curry paste	10 mL
1 tsp	finely grated lime zest	5 mL
1 tbsp	freshly squeezed lime juice	15 mL
2 tbsp	sweetened flaked coconut	25 mL
	Chopped fresh basil and/or mint	
	Lime wedges	

1. *Prepare the meatballs:* In a large bowl, using a fork, combine egg, bread crumbs, basil, lime juice and curry paste. Blend in ground pork. Form into twenty 1½-inch (4 cm) balls and place on prepared baking sheet, at least 1 inch (2.5 cm) apart. Bake in preheated oven until no longer pink inside, about 15 minutes.

2. *Meanwhile, prepare the sauce:* In a skillet, combine peanuts, brown sugar, coconut milk and curry paste. Bring to a boil over medium-high heat, stirring until blended. Reduce heat and boil gently, stirring often, until slightly thickened, about 5 minutes.

3. Stir meatballs, lime zest and lime juice into sauce and stir gently until meatballs are well coated with sauce. Serve sprinkled with coconut, basil and/or mint and garnished with lime wedges to squeeze over top.

Lamb & Goat

•◆•

Curry Mint–Crusted Rack of Lamb

Serves 8

The most courtly of all cuts of lamb, the rack deserves a special occasion and this recipe does it proud. Spiced just right and baked to juicy tenderness, it is quick to assemble, making it perfect for small, elegant dinner parties.

Tip

The mint paste can be made ahead, covered and refrigerated for up to 8 hours.

- *Preheat oven to 425°F (220°C)*
- *Large rimmed baking sheet, lined with foil*

1 cup	fresh bread crumbs	250 mL
¼ tsp	freshly ground black pepper	1 mL
½ cup	packed fresh mint leaves	125 mL
¼ cup	olive oil, divided	50 mL
1 tbsp	Indian yellow curry paste or masala blend	15 mL
4	lamb racks (each about 1 lb/500 g)	4
	Salt	

1. In a shallow dish, combine bread crumbs and pepper.
2. In a food processor, purée mint, 2 tbsp (30 mL) of the olive oil and the curry paste until smooth. Transfer to a bowl.
3. Sprinkle lamb with salt. In a large skillet, heat half the remaining oil over high heat until hot but not smoking. In batches, sear lamb on all sides, adding more oil as necessary. Transfer to a plate.
4. Spread one-quarter of the mint paste evenly over each lamb rack, then roll in bread crumb mixture. Place on prepared baking sheet, leaving as much room between racks as possible. Discard any excess crumbs.
5. Roast in preheated oven until a thermometer inserted in the thickest part of meat reaches 140°F (60°C) for medium, about 17 minutes, or until desired doneness. Transfer to a cutting board and tent with foil for 5 minutes before slicing into chops.

> ### Serving Suggestion
>
> Serve with a curried lentil dish, such as Dal Curry with Chiles and Coconut (page 187), and Rhubarb Chutney (page 41).

Curried Lamb with Sweet Corn and Spinach

Serves 8

With its wintry deep greens and browns and sunny speckles of golden corn, this recipe is as ideal for the cold months in the Himalayan foothills as it is in similar terrains of Montana and Quebec. All it needs to complete its wholesome comfort is some rice on the side and a log in the dining-room fireplace.

Tips

Reduced-sodium stock works best in this recipe. If it is not available, use 1½ cups (375 mL) stock and ½ cup (125 mL) water.

Any type of corn will work in this recipe. If using fresh, cook 2 large cobs and cut off kernels. If using canned, drain well. If using frozen, measure then thaw and drain.

2 tbsp	vegetable oil	25 mL
1	stick cinnamon, broken in half	1
2 tsp	mustard seeds	10 mL
1 tsp	cumin seeds	5 mL
1	onion, chopped	1
1 or 2	hot green chile peppers, minced	1 or 2
2 tbsp	minced gingerroot	25 mL
2 tbsp	Indian yellow curry paste or masala blend	25 mL
2 lbs	boneless lamb for stew, cut into 1-inch (2.5 cm) pieces	1 kg
2 cups	beef stock (see tip, at left)	500 mL
1½ cups	corn kernels (see tip, at left)	375 mL
6 cups	fresh spinach (about 6 oz/175 g), torn	1.5 L
	Salt	
	Chopped fresh cilantro or basil	

1. In a large, deep pot, heat oil over medium heat until hot but not smoking. Add cinnamon stick, mustard seeds and cumin seeds; cook, stirring, until toasted and fragrant but not yet popping, about 1 minute. Add onion and cook, stirring, until softened and starting to brown, about 5 minutes. Add chile peppers, ginger and curry paste; cook, stirring, until softened and fragrant, about 1 minute.

2. Stir in lamb until well coated with spices, about 2 minutes. Stir in stock and bring to a boil, scraping up any bits stuck to pan. Reduce heat to medium-low, cover and simmer, stirring often, until lamb is fork-tender, 1½ to 2 hours.

3. If desired, uncover, increase heat to medium and simmer until sauce is slightly thickened, about 10 minutes.

4. Stir in corn. Gradually stir in spinach by handfuls, just until wilted. Discard cinnamon stick, if desired. Season to taste with salt. Serve sprinkled with cilantro.

Thai Tamarind Curry–Braised Lamb Shanks

Serves 8

For fans of lamb, there is no greater happiness than a properly baked lamb shank whose tender nuggets fall off the bone and melt in the mouth. To enhance that prandial pleasure, this recipe dresses the meat in exotic perfumes and meaningful spices. It takes a while to cook, but it does so all by itself in the oven while it suffuses the air with its exciting promise.

Tip

To prepare lemongrass, trim off tough outer layers. Cut remaining stalk into 2-inch (5 cm) sections. Smash each piece with the broad side of a knife to bruise; this will help release the flavor when the lemongrass is cooked.

Serving Suggestion

Serve with Cilantro Lime Sweet Potatoes (page 246) and Sweet Onion and Date Chutney (page 43).

- Preheat oven to 325°F (160°C)
- Large roasting pan

8	lamb shanks (about 4 lbs/2 kg), trimmed	8
	Salt and freshly ground black pepper	
2 tbsp	vegetable oil (approx.), divided	25 mL
6	wild lime leaves	6
4	stalks lemongrass, chopped and bruised	4
4	cloves garlic, chopped	4
1/4 cup	minced gingerroot	50 mL
2 tbsp	Thai red curry paste	25 mL
1	can (28 oz/796 mL) diced tomatoes with juice	1
1/4 cup	packed brown or palm sugar	50 mL
1 cup	tamarind water (see tip, page 94)	250 mL
2 tbsp	fish sauce (nam pla)	25 mL
	Chopped fresh Thai or sweet basil	

1. Sprinkle lamb shanks with salt and pepper. In a large skillet, heat half the oil over medium-high heat until hot but not smoking. Add lamb shanks, in batches, and brown on all sides, turning often, about 5 minutes per batch, adding more oil between batches as necessary. Transfer to roasting pan.

2. Drain all but 1 tbsp (15 mL) of the fat from skillet and return to medium heat. Add lime leaves, lemongrass, garlic, ginger and curry paste; cook, stirring, until softened and fragrant, about 2 minutes. Add tomatoes with juice, brown sugar, tamarind water and fish sauce; bring to a boil, stirring until sugar is dissolved. Reduce heat and boil gently for 5 minutes.

3. Pour sauce over lamb shanks, turning to coat. Cover and bake in preheated oven, turning shanks and stirring sauce occasionally, until lamb is fork-tender, 2 to 2 1/2 hours. Uncover and bake until meat is slightly glazed, about 30 minutes. Discard lime leaves and lemongrass, if desired. Transfer lamb shanks to serving plates. Season sauce to taste with salt, spoon over lamb shanks and serve sprinkled with basil.

Red Curry Lamb Rogan Josh

Serves 8

A curry-house staple, the textures and flavors of this lamb curry define the notion for most of us outside India. The yogurt topping adds the necessary sweetness to complement the spice-explosive sauce and very tender meat.

Tips

Five dried red chiles provide a detectable but pleasant heat. Add more if you like your curry more fiery.

Grate whole nutmeg on a fine grater for the freshest, most delicate nutmeg flavor. Whole nutmeg is available in some bulk food stores and specialty stores. If using preground nutmeg, you may want to use a little less, as it can be quite strong.

6	cloves garlic	6
5 to 10	dried red chile peppers, crumbled	5 to 10
1	large onion, cut into 8 pieces	1
1/4 cup	chopped gingerroot	50 mL
1/2 cup	water (approx.)	125 mL
2 tbsp	vegetable oil	25 mL
4	whole cloves	4
2	bay leaves	2
1	stick cinnamon, broken in half	1
2 tsp	cumin seeds	10 mL
1/2 tsp	salt	2 mL
1/2 tsp	ground cardamom	2 mL
1/2 tsp	ground nutmeg, preferably freshly grated (see tip, at left)	2 mL
2 lbs	boneless lamb for stew, cut into 1-inch (2.5 cm) pieces	1 kg
1	can (28 oz/796 mL) tomatoes with juice, chopped	1
2 tbsp	chopped fresh cilantro	25 mL
	Plain yogurt	

1. In a blender or food processor, purée garlic, chile peppers, onion, ginger and water until smooth, adding a little more water if necessary. Set aside.

2. In a large, deep pot, heat oil over medium heat until hot but not smoking. Add cloves, bay leaves, cinnamon and cumin seeds; cook, stirring, until spices are toasted and fragrant, about 1 minute. Add puréed garlic mixture, salt, cardamom and nutmeg; cook, stirring, until fragrant and starting to thicken, about 5 minutes.

3. Stir in lamb until well coated with spices, about 2 minutes. Stir in tomatoes with juice and bring to a boil, scraping up any bits stuck to pan. Reduce heat to medium-low, cover and simmer, stirring often, until lamb is fork-tender, 1 1/2 to 2 hours.

4. Uncover, increase heat to medium and simmer until sauce is slightly thickened, about 10 minutes. Discard cloves, bay leaves and cinnamon stick. Stir in cilantro and season to taste with salt. Serve topped with yogurt.

Lucknow

I am in Raheem's "shop," a streetside kitchen with pots of nahari (lamb curry) simmering on a stove at one side, and browned, layered kulcha breads baking to steamy crispness in a clay tandoor oven at the other. The popular, ultra-affordable eatery is on the teeming market street of Akbar Gate, flanked by jewelry stores and attar-of-rose perfume counters and all-white mosques. This predominantly Moslem district in the old town of north-central India's regal Lucknow is renowned for its meat cookery, and Raheem's is its most venerable purveyor, now operated by the grandson of the original founder ("Raheem Junior Junior," he says and laughs).

Through the narrow entrance, between the stove and the tandoor, there are some slim wooden benches and rickety tables. I squeeze into one, taking up space normally allotted four people, and am served delicacies I shall never forget. And such simple fare. Meat and bread is all it is, but what meat and what bread! There are two lamb curries — one with cinnamon and cardamom, the other with cumin and chiles — and kulcha fresh from the oven, crusty outside and fluffy inside. Every bite is a delight, nothing short of miraculous.

At the end, I am too stunned to get up and leave, so I request a tea, which Raheem's doesn't make. They send a busboy to the chai-wallah next door, and I get a masala (spice) tea with which to chat up my fellow diner, a doctor of divinity who comes here once a week from his home 6 miles (10 km) away. He tells me that the kulcha, delicious as it is, is not properly digestible and advises me to eat it only on occasion. I disregard his warning and daily travel 7 miles (12 km) from my hotel for an entire week of Raheem's nahari and kulcha, braving suicidal traffic that would put anything in the Western world to shame.

In fact, I am in Akbar Gate so often that I first see Lucknow's famous sites — the Residency, doomed home of the besieged Brits during the 1857 Indian Mutiny, and the Bara Imambara, built in 1784 by Asaf-ud-Daula to house his 1,000 wives — sideways from the narrow wind vents of the autorickshaw on the way back and forth to Raheem's. Eventually, I find a few moments to visit the monuments themselves; splendid as they are, they cannot compete for personal satisfaction with my meals on those narrow tables. I therefore dedicate all the lamb dishes in this book to Raheem's.

But Lucknow's lamb curries are second in importance to the range of its legendary minced-meat kebabs (hamburgers). Also known as kakori, they are marinated in various combinations of tenderizing ingredients, such as fruits and spices and yogurt, overwrought by mighty kneading until all of the meat's fibers have relinquished their textures, left alone to ferment and then fried in butter. They turn out shiny and browned on the outside and unimaginably flavorful and tender inside. The connotation of their name is that they can be enjoyed without teeth and are therefore suitable for infants and very old people, as well as anyone in between.

I reluctantly venture away from Raheem's one evening to visit Tumde Nawab in the Amrigbad district of the old town for my kebab-tasting. This, too, is a streetside kitchen, with a tandoor for baking parotha and naan breads and a stove with countless kebabs sizzling in a pool of butter inside a gigantic frying pan. I sit on another skinny bench and soon my table is full of little burgers on shiny plates (four to an order) and plenty of excellent bread. A plateful of shaved onion and some cilantro chutney make the passage of the kebabs through my palate all that much more adventurous. The kebabs are succulent indeed, and so tender they literally melt on contact, but they take forever to digest, which for me nearly resulted in intestinal disaster. Because they are so difficult to digest, so relentlessly labor-intensive to prepare and require an unhealthy cooking method, I am excluding them from this book. But a visit to Lucknow wouldn't be complete without them. — B.A.

Raheem's Shop–Style Lucknow Lamb Curry

Serves 8

Deep in the heart of courtly Lucknow is the Akbar Gate market, home to attar of rose and to a treasure chest of jewelry stores, as well as to Raheem's shop, where this thin but flavorful lamb curry has been a staple for over a hundred years. It is easy to make but needs a long simmering time to be perfect. At Raheem's, they serve it with fluffy kulcha bread direct from the tandoor. Over here, it goes very well with buttered heated naan bread or rice.

Tips

If buying bone-in lamb, you'll need about 3½ lbs (1.75 kg) or more to make sure you get 2 lbs (1 kg) trimmed.

This is a good base to which you can add vegetables to make a one-pot meal. Add blanched vegetables for the last 10 minutes of cooking.

2 tbsp	vegetable oil	25 mL
4	bay leaves	4
4	whole cloves	4
1 tbsp	coriander seeds	15 mL
2 tsp	cumin seeds	10 mL
½ tsp	fennel seeds	2 mL
½ tsp	whole black peppercorns	2 mL
1	large onion, chopped	1
2 lbs	boneless lamb for stew, cut into 1-inch (2.5 cm) pieces	1 kg
2 or 3	hot green chile peppers, minced	2 or 3
2 tbsp	minced gingerroot	25 mL
½ tsp	ground turmeric	2 mL
¼ tsp	cayenne pepper	1 mL
1	can (28 oz/796 mL) tomatoes with juice	1
1 cup	chicken stock	250 mL
	Salt	
½ tsp	garam masala	2 mL
	Chopped fresh cilantro	

1. In a large, deep pot, heat oil over medium heat until hot but not smoking. Add bay leaves, cloves, coriander seeds, cumin seeds, fennel seeds and peppercorns; cook, stirring, until seeds start to pop, about 1 minute. Add onion and cook, stirring, until softened but not browned, about 4 minutes.

2. Stir in lamb, chile peppers, ginger, turmeric and cayenne until lamb is well coated with spices, about 2 minutes. Stir in tomatoes with juice and stock; bring to a simmer, scraping up any bits stuck to pan. Reduce heat to medium-low, cover and simmer, stirring occasionally and breaking up tomatoes with a spoon, until lamb is fork-tender, 1½ to 2 hours.

3. If desired, uncover, increase heat to medium and simmer until sauce is slightly thickened, about 5 minutes.

4. Discard bay leaves, cloves and peppercorns. Season to taste with salt. Serve sprinkled with garam masala and cilantro.

Gingery Lamb Curry

Serves 8

Intensely flavored with ginger, this lamb recipe is influenced by the cuisine of mysterious Burma, which combines culinary notions from neighboring Thailand and India. It is rich, lusty and saucy and will bring out smiles as naturally as if it were sunshine.

Tips

To julienne ginger, cut a 5-inch (12.5 cm) piece of gingerroot into thin slices. Working with 3 slices at a time, stack and cut across into thin strips.

If lime leaves are not available, substitute 1 tsp (5 mL) grated lime zest and stir in at the beginning of step 4.

The dried shrimp add depth and saltiness to the sauce. They can be omitted; just use more salt to bring out the other flavors.

2 tbsp	vegetable oil	25 mL
1	stick cinnamon, broken in half	1
1/3 cup	julienned gingerroot (see tip, at left)	75 mL
2	onions, chopped	2
4	wild lime leaves (see tip, at left)	4
2 or 3	hot green chile peppers, minced	2 or 3
2 tbsp	dried shrimp, optional (see tip, at left)	25 mL
2 tbsp	Indian yellow curry paste or masala blend	25 mL
2 lbs	boneless lamb for stew, cut into 1-inch (2.5 cm) pieces	1 kg
1	can (28 oz/796 mL) tomatoes with juice, chopped	1
1/2 cup	coconut milk	125 mL
	Salt	
	Chopped fresh basil	

1. In a large, deep pot, heat oil over medium heat until hot but not smoking. Add cinnamon and ginger; cook, stirring, until ginger is softened and fragrant, about 1 minute. Using a slotted spoon, transfer half the ginger to a bowl and set aside.

2. Add onions and lime leaves to pot and cook, stirring, until onions are softened, about 5 minutes. Add chile peppers, shrimp, if using, and curry paste; cook, stirring, until well blended and fragrant, about 1 minute.

3. Stir in lamb until well coated with spices, about 2 minutes. Stir in tomatoes with juice and coconut milk; bring to a boil, scraping up any bits stuck to pan. Reduce heat to medium-low, cover and simmer, stirring often, until lamb is fork-tender, 1 1/2 to 2 hours.

4. Uncover, increase heat to medium and simmer until sauce is slightly thickened, about 5 minutes. Discard cinnamon stick and lime leaves, if desired. Season to taste with salt. Serve sprinkled with reserved ginger and basil.

Kashmiri-Style Lamb and Root Vegetable Curry

Serves 8

This is a cold-weather favorite from the stunning mountain landscape of Kashmir, one of the most beautiful corners of India. With its earthy vegetables and long-simmered, tender lamb, it's comfort food all the way.

• ◆ •

Tips

If you have freshly harvested turnips with tender skins, there is no need to peel them. Just trim off the ends and give them a good scrub under running water.

Reduced-sodium stock works best in this recipe. If it is not available, use 2 cups (500 mL) stock and 1 cup (250 mL) water. If homemade lamb stock is available, by all means substitute it for the beef stock.

1 tbsp	vegetable oil	15 mL
15	curry leaves	15
1	stick cinnamon, broken in half	1
2 tsp	cumin seeds	10 mL
1	large onion, sliced lengthwise	1
1 cup	Basic Gravy (see recipe, page 7)	250 mL
4	small white turnips or parsnips (about 1 lb/500 g), peeled and cut into chunks	4
4	carrots, cut into chunks	4
2 or 3	hot green chile peppers, minced	2 or 3
2 lbs	boneless lamb for stew, cut into 1-inch (2.5 cm) pieces	1 kg
3 cups	beef or chicken stock (see tip, at left)	750 mL
4	boiling or all-purpose potatoes, cut into chunks	4
	Salt	
½ tsp	garam masala	2 mL
	Chopped fresh cilantro	

1. In a large, deep pot, heat oil over medium heat until hot but not smoking. Add curry leaves, cinnamon and cumin; cook, stirring, until seeds start to pop, about 1 minute. Add onion and cook, stirring, until it starts to soften, about 2 minutes. Reduce heat to medium-low and cook, stirring often, until very soft and golden brown, about 10 minutes.

2. Add gravy and cook, stirring, for 1 minute. Add turnips, carrots and chile peppers; cook, stirring, until well blended. Stir in lamb until coated with spices, about 2 minutes.

3. Stir in stock and bring to a simmer, scraping up any bits stuck to pan. Reduce heat to medium-low, cover and simmer, stirring occasionally, for 1 hour. Add potatoes, cover and simmer, stirring occasionally, until lamb and vegetables are fork-tender, about 1 hour.

4. Uncover, increase heat to medium and simmer until sauce is slightly thickened, about 5 minutes. Discard cinnamon stick, if desired. Season to taste with salt. Serve sprinkled with garam masala and cilantro.

Lamb Korma Curry

Serves 8

Deeply satisfying with its almonds and aromatic spices, this lamb recipe becomes airy and light once fresh mint and yogurt lace its collective tastes. It is a dish fit for royalty that will please everyone, especially since it has a mild finish and uses no chiles.

Tip

Full-fat yogurt provides the best texture. A lower-fat yogurt will work, but avoid fat-free yogurt and any with added gelatin. When cooked, gelatin in yogurt can cause the yogurt to split and create a curdled texture.

6	cloves garlic	6
⅓ cup	coarsely chopped gingerroot	75 mL
¾ cup	blanched almonds	175 mL
1½ cups	water, divided	375 mL
2 tbsp	vegetable oil (approx.), divided	25 mL
2 lbs	boneless lamb for stew, cut into 1-inch (2.5 cm) pieces	1 kg
1	stick cinnamon, broken in half	1
1 tbsp	coriander seeds, crushed	15 mL
2 tsp	cumin seeds	10 mL
2	onions, chopped	2
1½ tsp	salt	7 mL
½ tsp	ground cardamom	2 mL
2 tbsp	chopped fresh mint	25 mL
¾ cup	plain yogurt, preferably full-fat, at room temperature (see tip, at left)	175 mL
½ tsp	garam masala	2 mL

1. In a blender or food processor, purée garlic, ginger, almonds and ¾ cup (175 mL) of the water until smooth. Set aside.

2. In a large, deep pot, heat half the oil over medium-high heat until hot but not smoking. Add lamb, in three batches, and brown on all sides, adding more oil between batches as necessary. Transfer to a bowl.

3. Reduce heat to medium-low and add enough oil to pot to evenly coat in a thin layer. Add cinnamon, coriander seeds and cumin seeds; cook, stirring, until seeds start to pop, about 1 minute. Add onions, salt and cardamom; cook, stirring, until onions are softened and starting to brown, about 5 minutes. Add puréed garlic mixture and cook, stirring, until fragrant and starting to thicken, about 3 minutes.

4. Increase heat to medium-high. Add remaining water and bring to a boil, scraping up any bits stuck to pot. Return lamb and any accumulated juices to pot. Reduce heat to medium-low, cover and simmer, stirring occasionally, until lamb is fork-tender, 1½ to 2 hours.

5. Stir in mint and yogurt until blended and heated through, about 2 minutes. Discard cinnamon stick, if desired. Season to taste with salt. Serve sprinkled with garam masala.

Curried Lamb and Barley with Yogurt

Serves 8

The combination of barley and tender lamb is known to cure the blahs of any dark, cold winter evening. This recipe offers those ingredients in a sauce that sings with aromatic spices. It will almost make you wish for a blizzard so that you have an excuse to enjoy its delicious comforts. Serve extra yogurt on top for a delightful finish.

Tip

Full-fat yogurt provides the best texture. A lower-fat yogurt will work, but avoid fat-free yogurt and any with added gelatin. When cooked, gelatin in yogurt can cause the yogurt to split and create a curdled texture.

Variation

If you like heat in your curry, add 2 or 3 hot green chile peppers, minced, with the onion in step 2.

2 tbsp	vegetable oil (approx.), divided	25 mL
2 lbs	boneless lamb for stew, cut into 1-inch (2.5 cm) pieces	1 kg
2	bay leaves	2
2	sticks cinnamon, broken in half	2
2 tsp	cumin seeds	10 mL
1	large onion, finely chopped	1
½ tsp	ground ginger	2 mL
½ tsp	freshly ground black pepper	2 mL
½ tsp	ground cardamom	2 mL
¼ tsp	ground cloves	1 mL
3 cups	beef or chicken stock (see tip, page 142)	750 mL
½ cup	pot barley	125 mL
1 cup	frozen green peas	250 mL
½ cup	plain yogurt, preferably full-fat, at room temperature (see tip, at left)	125 mL
	Salt	
	Chopped fresh mint or cilantro	

1. In a large, deep pot, heat half the oil over medium-high heat until hot but not smoking. Add lamb, in three batches, and brown on all sides, adding more oil between batches as necessary. Transfer to a bowl.

2. Reduce heat to medium-low and add enough oil to pot to evenly coat in a thin layer. Add bay leaves, cinnamon and cumin seeds; cook, stirring, until seeds are toasted but not yet popping, about 1 minute. Add onion, ginger, pepper, cardamom and cloves; cook, stirring, until onion is softened and starting to brown, about 5 minutes.

3. Increase heat to medium-high. Add stock and bring to a boil, scraping up any bits stuck to pan. Stir in lamb and any accumulated juices. Reduce heat to medium-low, cover and simmer, stirring occasionally, for 1 hour. Stir in barley, cover and simmer, stirring occasionally, until lamb is fork-tender and barley is soft, about 1 hour.

4. Stir in peas and yogurt. Simmer, uncovered and stirring often, until sauce is slightly thickened and peas are hot, about 5 minutes. Discard bay leaves and cinnamon sticks. Season to taste with salt. Serve sprinkled with mint.

Lamb Curry with Chiles

Serves 4

The use of ground lamb and basic gravy makes this a quick recipe without losing any of the appeal of this particularly flavorful meat. With fewer (or no) chiles it could become child-friendly, as it is in countries where curry rules.

● ◆ ●

Tip

Made with 4 chiles, this dish is pleasantly hot; turn up the heat by using 6 chiles, or make a milder version by reducing them to 1 or 2.

● ◆ ●

Variation

Replace the green peas with diced zucchini or blanched chopped green beans.

1 tbsp	vegetable oil	15 mL
1	onion, chopped	1
1 lb	lean ground lamb	500 g
4 to 6	hot green chile peppers, sliced	4 to 6
10	curry leaves	10
1 tsp	cumin seeds	5 mL
1 cup	Basic Gravy (see recipe, page 7)	250 mL
1 cup	water	250 mL
1 cup	frozen green peas	250 mL
2 tbsp	chopped fresh cilantro	25 mL
	Salt	

1. In a large skillet, heat oil over medium-high heat. Add onion and cook, stirring, until it starts to soften, about 2 minutes. Reduce heat to medium-low and cook, stirring often, until very soft and golden brown, about 10 minutes.

2. Increase heat to high and add ground lamb. Brown, breaking up lamb with a spoon, until lamb is no longer pink, about 8 minutes. Drain all but 1 tbsp (15 mL) fat.

3. Reduce heat to medium. Add chile peppers, curry leaves and cumin seeds; cook, stirring, until fragrant, about 2 minutes. Add gravy and cook, stirring, for 1 minute. Stir in water and bring to a boil.

4. Reduce heat to medium-low, cover and simmer, stirring occasionally, until sauce is slightly thickened, about 15 minutes. Stir in peas, cover and simmer until peas are heated through and flavors are blended, about 5 minutes. Stir in cilantro and season to taste with salt.

> ### Serving Suggestion
>
> Serve with Dry Curry of Roasted Root Vegetables (page 247) and Chapati (page 270) or Zucchini Pancakes (page 273).

Baked Tomato Onion Curry Lamb Koftas

Serves 4

Meatloaf-like in concept, this recipe will turn that old standby on its head. The artfully combined spices in the sauce, added to the rich flavor of lamb, lend this dish a sense of luxury and pleasure that will make it a favorite weekday dinner in any home.

Tip

Be sure to mix the ground lamb with the seasonings just until blended, and handle gently when shaping. Overworking ground meat can make it tough and chewy.

- • Preheat oven to 400°F (200°C)
- • 13- by 9-inch (3 L) glass baking dish, greased

Koftas

1	egg	1
½ cup	fresh bread crumbs	125 mL
2 tbsp	chopped fresh cilantro	25 mL
½ tsp	salt	2 mL
¼ tsp	ground cinnamon	1 mL
1 tbsp	freshly squeezed lemon juice	15 mL
1 tbsp	Indian yellow curry paste or masala blend	15 mL
1 lb	lean ground lamb	500 g

Tomato Onion Curry

1 tbsp	vegetable oil	15 mL
1	onion, finely chopped	1
1 or 2	hot green chile peppers, minced, optional	1 or 2
½ tsp	ground cumin	2 mL
⅛ tsp	ground cinnamon	0.5 mL
2 tsp	Indian yellow curry paste or masala blend	10 mL
1½ cups	canned crushed (ground) tomatoes	375 mL
1 tsp	granulated sugar, or to taste	5 mL
½ tsp	salt, or to taste	2 mL
	Chopped fresh cilantro	
	Lemon wedges	

1. *Prepare the koftas:* In a large bowl, using a fork, combine egg, bread crumbs, cilantro, salt, cinnamon, lemon juice and curry paste. Blend in ground lamb. Form into eight sausage-shaped logs, each about 5 inches (12.5 cm) long, pinching into points at each end. Place in prepared baking dish, leaving as much space as possible between each kofta. Bake in preheated oven until firm and starting to brown, about 20 minutes.

2. *Meanwhile, prepare the curry:* In a saucepan, heat oil over medium heat. Add onion and cook, stirring, until softened and starting to brown, about 5 minutes. Add chile pepper, if using, cumin, cinnamon and curry paste; cook, stirring, until softened and fragrant, about 1 minute.

3. Stir in tomatoes and bring to a boil, scraping up any bits stuck to pan. Reduce heat, cover and simmer, stirring occasionally, until sauce is flavorful, about 10 minutes. Stir in sugar and salt.

4. Pour sauce over koftas and bake until sauce is bubbling and koftas are no longer pink inside, about 15 minutes. Serve sprinkled with cilantro and garnished with lemon wedges to squeeze over top.

Serving Suggestion

Serve with Roasted Bell Pepper Rice Pilau (page 254) or Potato and Spinach Curry (page 243) and with Naan (page 268 or store-bought) to sop up the sauce. A chutney topping is also a nice addition. Use Cold Coconut Chutney (page 34), Fresh Banana Mint Chutney (page 39) or Major Grey–Style Mango Chutney (page 36 or store-bought).

Tip

If canned crushed (ground) tomatoes are not available, purée whole canned tomatoes with juice and add 1 tbsp (15 mL) tomato paste.

Variation

In place of ground lamb, substitute ground beef or a blend of ground pork and veal.

Goat Curry with Pineapple

Serves 6 to 8

Pleasantly spiced, this long-simmered goat is further tenderized by the sweet-tart pineapple in the sauce. The yogurt enhancement at the end adds a satiny finish. This one is for celebratory dinners.

Tip

Full-fat yogurt provides the best texture. A lower-fat yogurt will work, but avoid fat-free yogurt and any with added gelatin. When cooked, gelatin in yogurt can cause the yogurt to split and create a curdled texture.

2 tbsp	vegetable oil, divided	25 mL
2 lbs	goat leg for stew, cut into 2-inch (5 cm) pieces (see tip, page 149)	1 kg
2	onions, chopped	2
2 or 3	hot green chile peppers, minced	2 or 3
2 tbsp	minced gingerroot	25 mL
2 tsp	garam masala	10 mL
2 tsp	ground turmeric	10 mL
1 tsp	salt	5 mL
1/4 cup	tandoori or tikka curry paste	50 mL
1 1/2 cups	chopped fresh pineapple	375 mL
1	can (28 oz/796 mL) diced tomatoes with juice	1
2 tsp	cornstarch	10 mL
1/2 cup	plain yogurt, preferably full-fat (see tip, at left)	125 mL
	Chopped fresh cilantro or mint	
	Toasted sliced almonds	

1. In a large, deep pot, heat half the oil over medium-high heat until hot but not smoking. Add goat, in three batches, and brown on all sides, adding more oil between batches as necessary. Transfer to a bowl.

2. Reduce heat to medium and add any remaining oil to pot. Add onions and cook, stirring, until softened, about 5 minutes. Add chile peppers, ginger, garam masala, turmeric, salt and curry paste; cook, stirring and adding up to 2 tbsp (25 mL) water if necessary to prevent burning, until spices are blended and fragrant, about 2 minutes.

3. Add pineapple and cook, stirring, until it starts to release its juices, about 2 minutes. Add tomatoes with juice and bring to a boil, scraping up any bits stuck to pot.

4. Return goat and any accumulated juices to pot. Reduce heat to medium-low, cover and simmer, stirring and mashing tomatoes occasionally, until goat is fork-tender, 2 to 2 1/2 hours.

5. In a bowl, stir cornstarch and yogurt until blended. Stir into pot. Simmer, uncovered and stirring often, until thickened, about 5 minutes. Season to taste with salt. Serve sprinkled with cilantro and almonds.

Auntie Norma's Jamaican Goat Curry

Serves 6 to 8

Sea breezes of Negril and Montego Bay permeate this deeply spiced curry. Though it takes a while to get ready, it does so practically by itself. All it needs on the side is some rice and a table on a Caribbean beach — or at least some reggae music on the stereo. The recipe comes to us courtesy of Jennifer's aunt, Norma MacKenzie, who learned it while growing up in Jamaica.

Tips

Goat leg meat for stew often comes with the bones cut up with the meat, and the bones lend extra flavor to the stew. Use boneless meat if you prefer.

When chopping Scotch bonnet peppers, wear gloves to prevent stinging and be sure to wash all utensils and your cutting board well when you're finished.

This curry doesn't have a lot of sauce. If you prefer a more saucy curry, increase the water in step 3 to 1½ cups (375 mL).

2 lbs	goat leg for stew, cut into 2-inch (5 cm) pieces (see tip, at left)	1 kg
	Juice of 1 lime	
2 tbsp	white vinegar	25 mL
	Cold water	
3	cloves garlic, minced	3
1	small onion, finely chopped	1
1	Scotch bonnet pepper, minced	1
2½ tbsp	curry powder, preferably Jamaican-style, divided	32 mL
1 tsp	dried thyme	5 mL
2 tbsp	olive oil	25 mL
1 tsp	salt	5 mL
½ tsp	freshly ground black pepper	2 mL

1. In a large bowl, combine goat, lime juice and vinegar. Add enough cold water to cover. Let soak at room temperature for 10 to 30 minutes. Drain, but do not pat meat dry. Return meat to bowl.

2. In a small bowl, combine garlic, onion, Scotch bonnet pepper, 2 tbsp (25 mL) of the curry powder and the thyme. Add to meat and rub to coat evenly. Cover and marinate at room temperature for 30 minutes or refrigerate overnight.

3. In a large, deep pot, heat oil over medium-high heat. Add remaining curry powder, salt and pepper; cook, stirring, for 30 seconds. Stir in goat mixture with marinade until well coated with spices, about 2 minutes. Stir in 1 cup (250 mL) water. Reduce heat to low, cover and simmer, stirring occasionally, until goat is fork-tender, 2 to 2½ hours. Season to taste with salt.

Serving Suggestion

Serve with plain white rice and a fruit chutney, such as Fruity Mango Papaya Chutney (page 37).

Guyanese Goat Curry

Serves 6 to 8

Mildly spiced but fragrant and saucy, this meat-and-potato recipe will bring the Caribbean into your dining room and please everyone, including children, with its familiar stew-like appeal. It keeps well in the fridge for a day or two, and actually improves in flavor.

Tips

Goat leg meat for stew often comes with the bones cut up with the meat, and the bones lend extra flavor to the stew. Use boneless meat if you prefer.

Guyanese-style garam masala is a blend of roasted spices. If you have unroasted garam masala, toast it in a dry small skillet over medium heat, stirring constantly, until the color darkens and spices smell toasted, about 2 minutes.

Reduced-sodium stock is best for this recipe. If it is not available, use 1½ cups (375 mL) stock and ½ cup (125 mL) water.

2 lbs	goat leg for stew, cut into 2-inch (5 cm) pieces (see tip, at left)	1 kg
¾ tsp	salt	3 mL
½ tsp	freshly ground black pepper	2 mL
6	cloves garlic	6
2	onions, each cut into 8 pieces	2
3 tbsp	curry powder, preferably Caribbean-style	45 mL
1 tbsp	garam masala, preferably Guyanese-style	15 mL
½ cup	water	125 mL
2 tbsp	vegetable oil	25 mL
2	large ripe tomatoes, chopped	2
2 cups	beef or chicken stock (see tip, at left)	500 mL
6	small boiling or all-purpose potatoes, cut into quarters	6

1. In a bowl, combine goat, salt and pepper. Toss to coat evenly. Let stand at room temperature for 15 minutes.

2. In a blender or food processor, purée garlic, onions, curry powder, garam masala and water until fairly smooth.

3. In a large, deep pot, heat oil over medium heat. Add puréed garlic mixture and cook, stirring, until softened and fragrant, about 5 minutes. Add goat mixture and cook, stirring, until most of the liquid has evaporated and outside of meat starts to turn white, about 8 minutes. Add tomatoes and stock; bring to a simmer, scraping up any bits stuck to pan.

4. Reduce heat to medium-low, cover and simmer, stirring occasionally, for 1½ hours. Stir in potatoes, cover and simmer, stirring occasionally, until goat and potatoes are fork-tender, about 1 hour.

5. Uncover, increase heat to medium and simmer until sauce is slightly thickened, about 5 minutes. Season to taste with salt.

Fish & Seafood

◆

Grilled Fish Tikka

Serves 4 to 6

Tender fish fingers, coated in a tandoori-like spiced yogurt marinade, come fresh from the grill or the oven. It makes for a light but meaningful opening course, even for your fanciest dinner party.

Tips

A lower-fat yogurt can be used, but make sure it does not contain gelatin. When cooked, gelatin in yogurt can cause the yogurt to split and create a curdled texture.

A large, thin metal spatula is very helpful for turning fish on the grill or lifting the cooked fish from the baking sheet.

• *Rimmed baking sheet, lined with greased foil (for oven version)*

1 tsp	hot pepper flakes	5 mL
1 tsp	ground cumin	5 mL
1 tsp	ground coriander	5 mL
1 tsp	ground turmeric	5 mL
½ tsp	ground cardamom	2 mL
½ tsp	ground cinnamon	2 mL
1 cup	plain yogurt, preferably full-fat (see tip, at left)	250 mL
1½ lbs	skinless fish fillet (swordfish, kingfish or other firm fish), cut into thin 4-inch (10 cm) long strips	750 g
½ tsp	salt	2 mL
	Thinly sliced onion	
	Chopped fresh cilantro	
	Lime wedges	

1. In a bowl, combine hot pepper flakes, cumin, coriander, turmeric, cardamom, cinnamon and yogurt. Add fish and toss to coat evenly. Let stand at room temperature for 15 minutes, or cover and refrigerate for up to 1 day.

2. *To grill:* Preheat barbecue to medium and grease grill rack. Remove fish from marinade, leaving a coating of marinade on fish. Discard excess marinade. Sprinkle fish with salt. Place fish on greased grill. Cover and grill, carefully turning once, just until coating is lightly browned and fish is firm and flakes easily with a fork, about 3 minutes per side.

3. *To bake in oven:* Preheat oven to 400°F (200°C). Remove fish from marinade, leaving a coating of marinade on fish. Discard excess marinade. Sprinkle fish with salt. Place fish on prepared baking sheet, leaving as much space between pieces as possible, and bake, without turning, just until coating is lightly browned and fish is firm and flakes easily with a fork, about 8 minutes.

4. *For both methods:* Transfer fish to a warmed platter and garnish with onion and cilantro and with lime wedges to squeeze over top.

Kerala Fish Fry

Serves 4 to 6

The long coast of Kerala is dotted with fishing villages where no day passes without a portion of just-caught fish fillets, dredged in spice and quick-fried in oil. In Kerala, a fish fry is not just delicious and nutritious, it's a way of life.

Tip

Be sure the oil does not get too hot while cooking subsequent batches of fish; otherwise, the coating may burn before the fish is cooked properly.

3 tbsp	chickpea flour (besan) or whole wheat flour	45 mL
1 tsp	hot pepper flakes	5 mL
1 tsp	ground cumin	5 mL
1 tsp	ground turmeric	5 mL
½ tsp	salt	2 mL
½ tsp	ground cardamom	2 mL
½ tsp	ground cinnamon	2 mL
1½ lbs	skinless fish fillet (swordfish, kingfish or other firm fish), cut into 2-inch (5 cm) pieces	750 g
½ cup	vegetable oil	125 mL
	Thinly sliced onion	
	Sliced tomatoes	
	Lime wedges	

1. In a shallow dish, combine flour, hot pepper flakes, cumin, turmeric, salt, cardamom and cinnamon. Dredge fish in the mixture, shaking off and discarding excess.

2. In a large skillet, heat oil over medium-high heat. Add fish, in batches as necessary, and cook, turning once, just until coating is browned and fish is firm and flakes easily with a fork, about 3 minutes per side, adjusting the heat as necessary between batches. Transfer to a paper towel–lined plate.

3. Transfer to a warmed platter and garnish with onion and tomatoes and with lime wedges to squeeze over top.

Spicy Kovalam Fish Curry

Serves 4 to 6

The official dish of Kovalam Beach, Kerala's best-known holiday destination, this fish curry is a natural in a place where there are endless fish and coconut trees everywhere you look. There are as many versions of this curry as there are cooks in Kovalam; we chose the easiest for this book.

Tips

If fresh or frozen unsweetened shredded coconut is available, substitute ⅓ cup (75 mL) for the dry coconut and water and skip the soaking in step 1. Thaw first and drain if using frozen.

This version is quite fiery. For a milder curry, reduce the cayenne pepper to ¼ or ½ tsp (1 or 2 mL).

¼ cup	unsweetened shredded coconut	50 mL
¼ cup	warm water	50 mL
1 tsp	cayenne pepper	5 mL
1 tsp	ground coriander	5 mL
2 tbsp	vegetable oil	25 mL
8	curry leaves	8
2	hot green chile peppers, minced	2
1 cup	diced tomato	250 mL
1 tbsp	minced gingerroot	15 mL
1 cup	water or fish stock	250 mL
1½ lbs	skinless fish fillet (swordfish, kingfish or other firm fish), cut into 2-inch (5 cm) pieces	750 g
1 cup	coconut milk	250 mL
2 tbsp	freshly squeezed lemon juice	25 mL
	Salt	
	Chopped fresh cilantro	

1. In a bowl, combine coconut and warm water. Let stand at room temperature until softened, about 30 minutes. Drain and squeeze out excess water and return to bowl. Stir in cayenne and coriander.

2. In a large skillet, heat oil over medium-high heat. Add coconut mixture and cook, stirring, until lightly toasted, about 1 minute. Add curry leaves, chile peppers, tomato and ginger; cook, stirring, until tomato starts to soften, about 2 minutes. Add water and bring to a boil.

3. Reduce heat to medium. Add fish and gently fold into sauce. Cook, stirring gently, for 3 minutes. Add coconut milk and cook, stirring gently occasionally, until sauce is bubbling and fish is firm and flakes easily with a fork, about 3 minutes. Stir in lemon juice and cook for 30 seconds. Season to taste with salt. Serve sprinkled with cilantro.

Curried Fish Malabari with Broccoli

Serves 4 to 6

A rich fish curry with the joint enhancements of coconut and cashews, this one is for those occasions when a bit of sin is actually good for soul and body. But it tastes so heavenly, it's almost like getting there.

Tip

If cashew butter or natural peanut butter are not available, substitute 3 tbsp (45 mL) ground or finely chopped cashews or peanuts.

2 tbsp	vegetable oil	25 mL
6	cloves garlic, thinly sliced	6
1	onion, thinly sliced into rings	1
2 tbsp	julienned gingerroot	25 mL
8	curry leaves	8
1 tbsp	finely grated lemon zest	15 mL
1 tsp	ground coriander	5 mL
½ tsp	ground turmeric	2 mL
½ tsp	cayenne pepper	2 mL
2 tbsp	cashew butter or natural peanut butter	25 mL
1 cup	water or fish stock	250 mL
1 cup	coconut milk	250 mL
½ tsp	salt	2 mL
1½ lbs	skinless fish fillet (swordfish, kingfish or other firm fish), cut into 2-inch (5 cm) pieces	750 g
2 cups	blanched broccoli florets	500 mL
2 tbsp	freshly squeezed lemon juice	25 mL
	Chopped fresh cilantro	

1. In a large skillet, heat oil over medium-high heat. Add garlic, onion and ginger; cook, stirring, until onion starts to soften, about 2 minutes. Reduce heat to medium and add curry leaves, lemon zest, coriander, turmeric and cayenne; cook, stirring, until blended and fragrant, about 30 seconds.

2. Stir in cashew butter and water; bring to a boil, stirring until cashew butter is well blended. Add coconut milk and salt; return to a boil, stirring often.

3. Add fish and gently fold into sauce. Cook, stirring gently, for 3 minutes. Stir in broccoli and simmer, stirring gently occasionally, just until fish is firm and flakes easily with a fork and broccoli is tender-crisp, 3 to 4 minutes. Stir in lemon juice and cook for 30 seconds. Season to taste with salt. Serve sprinkled with cilantro.

Serving Suggestion

Serve this rich fish curry topped with Green Mango Pickle (page 48) or another tangy chutney.

Tamarind Fish Curry

Serves 4 to 6

Tart and lively, this fish curry is as lean as it is appetizing. Rice is the only viable accompaniment, especially the plump short-grain variety from South India. In its homeland, this curry is reputed to be quite tasty served at room temperature the next day. If you do manage to salvage any leftovers from dinner, refrigerate and then let temper the next day for about an hour.

Tip

To make tamarind water, break a 2-oz (60 g) piece of block tamarind into small pieces and place in a heatproof bowl. Pour in 1 cup (250 mL) boiling water and let stand until very soft, about 30 minutes, or for up to 8 hours. Press through a fine-mesh sieve, discarding seeds and skins.

Variation

Add 1½ cups (375 mL) blanched chopped or frozen thawed green beans with the fish.

2 tbsp	vegetable oil	25 mL
1 tsp	mustard seeds	5 mL
½ tsp	fenugreek seeds	2 mL
2	hot green chile peppers, chopped	2
½ cup	Basic Gravy (see recipe, page 7)	125 mL
1 cup	tamarind water (see tip, at left)	250 mL
1½ lbs	skinless fish fillet (swordfish, kingfish or other firm fish), cut into 2-inch (5 cm) pieces	750 g
1	small tomato, cut into wedges	1
¼ tsp	salt, or to taste	1 mL
	Chopped fresh cilantro	

1. In a large skillet, heat oil over medium heat. Add mustard seeds and fenugreek seeds; cook, stirring, until starting to pop, about 1 minute. Add chile peppers and gravy; cook, stirring, for 1 minute. Stir in tamarind water and bring to a boil.

2. Add fish and gently fold into sauce. Cook, stirring gently, until almost firm, about 5 minutes. Add tomato and cook, stirring gently, just until tomato starts to soften and fish is firm and flakes easily with a fork, 1 to 2 minutes. Season to taste with salt. Serve sprinkled with cilantro.

Serving Suggestion

As part of a multi-curry feast, serve this fish curry with Chicken Korma Curry (page 60) or Indian-Style Butter Chicken (page 65), Yellow Lentil Curry with Vegetables (page 188), Cashew Green Beans with Mustard Seeds (page 218) and Lemon Coriander Rice (page 257).

Green Mango Fish Curry

Serves 4 to 6

The combination of the sweet-tart green mango and delicately cooked fish will transport your taste buds to sunnier climes. This ethereal dish practically levitates off the plate and into willing palates.

Tip

When cooking fragile fish, be sure to fold and stir enough that it cooks evenly but not so much that it breaks up and becomes mushy.

1 tbsp	vegetable oil, divided	15 mL
1	onion, sliced lengthwise	1
3	cloves garlic, minced	3
1 tbsp	minced gingerroot	15 mL
2 tsp	Thai yellow curry paste	10 mL
1	large green mango (or 2 small), peeled and thinly sliced	1
1	red bell pepper, sliced	1
½ tsp	packed brown or palm sugar	2 mL
½ cup	water or fish stock	125 mL
2 tbsp	fish sauce (nam pla)	25 mL
1 tbsp	freshly squeezed lime juice	15 mL
1½ lbs	skinless fish fillets (tilapia, snapper or other white fish), cut into 1½-inch (4 cm) pieces	750 g
	Salt, optional	
	Chopped fresh mint or cilantro	
	Lime wedges	

1. In a large skillet, heat oil over medium-high heat. Add onion and cook, stirring, until softened and starting to brown, about 3 minutes. Add garlic, ginger and curry paste; cook, stirring, until well blended and fragrant, about 1 minute.

2. Stir in mango and red pepper. Add brown sugar, water, fish sauce and lime juice; bring to a simmer, scraping up bits stuck to pan. Reduce heat and simmer gently, stirring often, until mango starts to soften, about 2 minutes.

3. Add fish and gently fold into sauce. Simmer, stirring gently once or twice, just until fish is firm and flakes easily with a fork and mango is tender, about 5 minutes. Season to taste with salt, if using. Serve sprinkled with mint and garnished with lime wedges to squeeze over top.

Red Curry Fish with Lemongrass

Serves 4 to 6

A refreshing combination of comforting zucchini and delicate fish, this curry offers gentle yet assertive excitement in its sauce. It is ready in minutes and will bring great joy to a weekday dinner.

Tips

To prepare lemongrass, trim off tough outer layers. Cut remaining stalk into 2-inch (5 cm) sections. Smash each piece with the broad side of a knife to bruise; this will help release the flavor when the lemongrass is cooked.

It is traditional to leave the pieces of lemongrass in when serving, but they are not meant to be eaten. You can discard them if you prefer.

1 tbsp	vegetable oil	15 mL
1	stalk lemongrass, chopped and bruised (see tip, at left)	1
1 tbsp	coriander seeds	15 mL
1	zucchini, halved lengthwise and thinly sliced on the diagonal	1
1 tbsp	packed brown or palm sugar	15 mL
½ tsp	salt	2 mL
1	can (14 oz/400 mL) coconut milk	1
¼ cup	water	50 mL
1 tbsp	Thai red curry paste	15 mL
1½ lbs	skinless fish fillets (tilapia, snapper or other white fish), cut into 1½-inch (4 cm) pieces	750 g
2 tbsp	freshly squeezed lemon juice	25 mL
1 tbsp	chopped fresh cilantro	15 mL

1. In a large skillet, heat oil over medium heat until hot but not smoking. Add lemongrass and coriander seeds; cook, stirring, until seeds start to pop, about 1 minute. Add zucchini and cook, stirring, until starting to soften, about 3 minutes. Add brown sugar, salt, coconut milk, water and curry paste; bring to a boil, stirring until blended.

2. Add fish and gently fold into sauce. Reduce heat and simmer, stirring gently occasionally, until fish is firm and flakes easily with a fork, about 5 minutes. Discard lemongrass, if desired. Stir in lemon juice and season to taste with salt. Serve sprinkled with cilantro.

Green Curry Snapper with Yogurt and Cilantro

Serves 4 to 6

A main course item for a special dinner, this recipe uses pricey snapper to excellent advantage. The fish comes out springy and fresh, and the yogurt-thickened, Thai-scented sauce is so flavorful you'll sop up every last drop with your rice.

Tips

A lower-fat yogurt will work, but avoid fat-free yogurt and any with added gelatin. When cooked, gelatin in yogurt can cause the yogurt to split and create a curdled texture.

If lime leaves are not available, add 1 tsp (5 mL) finely grated lime zest with the lime juice in step 5.

2 tbsp	chopped fresh cilantro	25 mL
2 tsp	cornstarch	10 mL
1 cup	plain yogurt (not fat-free, see tip, at left)	250 mL
2 tbsp	vegetable oil, divided	25 mL
1 tbsp	Thai green curry paste, divided	15 mL
1½ lbs	skinless snapper fillets (or other thin white fish), cut crosswise into ½-inch (1 cm) thick strips	750 g
4	wild lime leaves (see tip, at left)	4
2	carrots, thinly sliced on the diagonal	2
1	onion, sliced lengthwise	1
1 tsp	packed brown or palm sugar	5 mL
½ cup	water or fish stock	125 mL
1 tbsp	fish sauce (nam pla)	15 mL
2 tbsp	freshly squeezed lime juice	25 mL
	Fresh cilantro leaves	
	Lime wedges	

1. In a bowl, stir cilantro, cornstarch and yogurt until blended and smooth. Set aside at room temperature.

2. In another bowl, combine half each of the oil and curry paste. Add fish and toss to coat evenly. Set aside at room temperature.

3. In a large skillet, heat remaining oil over medium-high heat until hot but not smoking. Add lime leaves and cook, stirring, until fragrant, about 30 seconds. Add carrots and onion; cook, stirring, until softened and onions start to brown, about 3 minutes. Add remaining curry paste and cook, stirring, until blended and fragrant, about 30 seconds.

4. Stir in fish mixture. Add brown sugar, water and fish sauce; bring to a simmer, scraping up bits stuck to pan. Reduce heat and simmer gently, stirring often, just until fish starts to firm up, about 3 minutes.

5. Stir in yogurt mixture and simmer, stirring gently, until sauce is thickened and fish is firm and flakes easily with a fork, about 2 minutes. Stir in lime juice just until heated through. Serve sprinkled with cilantro leaves and garnished with lime wedges to squeeze over top.

Tikka Fish Curry with Tomatoes

Serves 4 to 6

These succulent, pleasantly spice-crusted fish fingers come with a zesty sauce for a lovely party dish. You can make the sauce and marinate the fish in advance. Bake the fish while reheating your sauce, proceed with step 6, and it's ready for your buffet within 10 minutes.

Tips

Full-fat yogurt provides the best texture. A lower-fat yogurt will work, but avoid fat-free yogurt and any with added gelatin. When cooked, gelatin in yogurt can cause the yogurt to split and create a curdled texture.

Use a delicate white fish such as snapper, tilapia or other thin fillets.

If ripe tomatoes aren't available, substitute 1½ cups (375 mL) drained canned diced tomatoes and decrease salt in step 5 to ¼ tsp (1 mL), adding more to taste, if necessary, in step 6.

• Rimmed baking sheet, lined with greased foil

2 tsp	cornstarch	10 mL
½ cup	plain yogurt, preferably full-fat	125 mL
3 tbsp	tikka curry paste or masala blend, divided	45 mL
1½ lbs	skinless fish fillets, cut into 1½-inch (4 cm) pieces	750 g
1 tbsp	vegetable oil	15 mL
1 tbsp	coriander seeds	15 mL
½ tsp	cumin seeds	2 mL
1	onion, finely chopped	1
2	large ripe tomatoes, chopped	2
¾ tsp	salt	3 mL
½ cup	water	125 mL
2 tbsp	freshly squeezed lemon juice	25 mL
2 tbsp	chopped fresh cilantro	25 mL

1. In a bowl, stir cornstarch, yogurt and 1 tbsp (25 mL) of the curry paste until blended and smooth. Add fish and toss to coat evenly. Let stand at room temperature for 15 minutes.

2. Preheat oven to 450°F (230°C).

3. Spread fish pieces with marinade on prepared baking sheet. Bake until starting to brown, about 5 minutes. Set aside.

4. Meanwhile, in a large skillet, heat oil over medium heat until hot but not smoking. Add coriander seeds and cumin seeds; cook, stirring, until toasted and fragrant but not yet popping, about 1 minute. Add onion and cook, stirring, until softened and golden brown, about 5 minutes. Add remaining curry paste and cook, stirring, until blended and fragrant, about 1 minute.

5. Add tomatoes and salt; cook, stirring, until starting to soften, about 2 minutes. Add water and bring to a simmer, stirring occasionally. Reduce heat and simmer, stirring often, until tomatoes are soft, about 5 minutes.

6. Using a slotted spatula, transfer fish to sauce, discarding excess juice. Gently stir fish to coat in sauce and simmer, stirring gently occasionally, just until fish is firm and flakes easily with a fork, about 5 minutes. Stir in lemon juice and season to taste with salt. Serve sprinkled with cilantro.

Grilled Tilapia in Jamaican Curry

Serves 4

When the tropical sun dips into its fiery horizon and Jamaica's beaches become a postcard of Caribbean bliss, it's time to sit back and enjoy spicy grilled fish that has been well earned from a day's worth of sun and surf. With this recipe, you can have the same repast, whatever the view from your dinner table.

Tip

This works best with fish fillets that are about $\frac{1}{2}$ inch (1 cm) thick or slightly thicker. If fillets are too thin, the fish will cook too quickly and the flavor of the spices won't develop as well. Also, for the grill version, thin fish tends to stick, since it isn't on the grill long enough to get crispy.

• Rimmed baking sheet, lined with greased foil (for broiler method)

4	skinless tilapia fillets or other mild white fish, about $\frac{1}{2}$ inch (1 cm) thick (see tip, at left)	4
2 tsp	curry powder, preferably Jamaican- or other Caribbean-style	10 mL
1 tsp	finely chopped fresh thyme (or $\frac{1}{4}$ tsp/1 mL dried)	5 mL
2 tbsp	vegetable oil	25 mL
1 tsp	hot pepper sauce, preferably Caribbean-style	5 mL
	Salt	
2	green onions, thinly sliced	2
	Lime or lemon wedges	
	Hot pepper sauce	

1. Rinse fish fillets and pat dry.

2. In a shallow dish, combine curry powder, thyme, oil and hot pepper sauce. Add fish fillets and turn to coat. Cover and refrigerate for at least 1 hour or for up to 1 day.

3. *To grill:* Preheat barbecue to medium-high and grease grill rack. Remove fish from marinade, discarding any excess marinade. Season with salt. Place on greased grill and sprinkle with green onions. Reduce heat to medium, cover and cook, without turning, just until fish is opaque, flakes easily with a fork and is crispy on the bottom, 4 to 5 minutes.

4. *To broil:* Preheat broiler and place rack about 6 inches (15 cm) from the heat. Remove fish from marinade, discarding any excess marinade. Season with salt. Place on prepared baking sheet. Broil just until fish is opaque around the edges, 2 to 3 minutes. Turn pieces over and sprinkle with green onions. Broil just until fish is opaque and flakes easily with a fork, about 2 minutes.

5. *For both methods:* Using a large spatula, carefully lift fish off grill or baking sheet and transfer to a serving plate. Garnish with lime wedges to squeeze over top and pass the hot pepper sauce at the table.

Tandoori Grilled Calamari

Serves 4

An excellent appetizer for a party dinner, these spiced calamari turn out so light they melt on contact with the palate, so long as they are not overcooked. They can be marinated and then refrigerated until you're ready to serve them to your guests. Once you place them on the grill or broiler, they are ready within 5 minutes.

Tips

Full-fat yogurt provides the best texture. A lower-fat yogurt will work, but avoid fat-free yogurt and any with added gelatin. When cooked, gelatin in yogurt can cause the yogurt to split and create a curdled texture.

If you prefer the traditional bright red color of tandoori chicken that you often see in restaurants, add red and yellow food coloring to the yogurt marinade.

If making the oven version, add a little smoky flavor by adding ⅛ tsp (0.5 mL) smoked paprika with the regular paprika.

• *Rimmed baking sheet, lined with greased foil (for broiler method)*

1½ lbs	small squid (calamari)	750 g
1 tsp	garam masala	5 mL
1 tsp	ground coriander	5 mL
½ tsp	ground cumin	2 mL
1	clove garlic, minced	1
1	small hot green chile pepper, minced	1
2 tsp	minced gingerroot	10 mL
½ tsp	paprika	2 mL
½ cup	plain yogurt, preferably full-fat (see tip, at left)	50 mL
	Salt	
	Lemon wedges	

1. Remove cartilage from cavity of squid. Rinse and pat dry inside and out. Using a sharp paring knife, lightly score bodies in a cross-hatch pattern. Set aside.

2. In a dry small skillet over medium heat, toast garam masala, coriander and cumin, stirring constantly, just until spices have a toasted aroma and are starting to darken, 1 to 2 minutes. Transfer immediately to a bowl. Stir in garlic, chile pepper, ginger, paprika and yogurt. Add squid and toss to coat evenly. Let stand at room temperature for 15 minutes, or cover and refrigerate for up to 1 day.

3. *To grill:* Preheat barbecue to high and grease grill rack. Remove squid from marinade, leaving a thin coating of marinade on squid. Discard any excess marinade. Season with salt. Place on greased grill, cover and cook, turning once, just until squid are firm and grill marks appear, about 2 minutes per side.

4. *To broil:* Preheat broiler and place rack about 6 inches (15 cm) from the heat. Remove squid from marinade, leaving a thin coating of marinade on squid. Discard any excess marinade. Season with salt. Place on prepared baking sheet, leaving as much space between pieces as possible. Broil, turning once, just until coating is lightly browned and squid is firm, about 2 minutes per side.

5. *For both methods:* Using tongs, carefully lift squid off grill or baking sheet and transfer to a serving plate. Serve garnished with lemon wedges to squeeze over top.

Serving Suggestion

Serve with Peanut and Cucumber Salad (page 23) and Tomato and Onion Rice Pilau (page 256).

Tips

Be sure the grill or broiler is very hot before cooking the calamari. It is essential to cook it very quickly on high heat to prevent a rubbery texture.

Some squid will have the tentacles attached when purchased. It's your choice to use or discard them. If using, cut the tentacles from the body piece before marinating.

Calamari in Tomato Onion Curry

Serves 4

Calamari has been fashionable long enough that it's universally available. It is loved for its delicate texture, so it's imperative to avoid overcooking it, as that would turn it rubbery. This simple, aromatic recipe will join your lexicon of favorite seafood dishes.

Tip

When buying whole and ground spices, purchase from a source that has a high turnover to make sure you are getting fresh spices with maximum flavor. Purchase small amounts at a time and store in an airtight jar or container in a cool, dark place for up to 1 year.

Variation

Substitute a bag of frozen mixed seafood, peeled and deveined shrimp or small sea scallops for the calamari rings.

2 tbsp	vegetable oil	25 mL
2	bay leaves	2
1 tbsp	coriander seeds, crushed	15 mL
1 tsp	cumin seeds	5 mL
1/2 tsp	fennel seeds	2 mL
1/2 tsp	fenugreek seeds	2 mL
1	large red onion, finely chopped	1
4	cloves garlic, minced	4
1 or 2	hot green chile peppers, minced	1 or 2
2 tbsp	minced gingerroot	25 mL
1/2 tsp	ground turmeric	2 mL
1	can (28 oz/796 mL) diced tomatoes with juice	1
1	green bell pepper, finely chopped	1
1 lb	frozen calamari rings, thawed, drained and patted dry	500 g
	Salt	
2	green onions, thinly sliced	2

1. In a large skillet, heat oil over medium heat until hot but not smoking. Add bay leaves, coriander seeds, cumin seeds, fennel seeds and fenugreek seeds; cook, stirring, just until seeds are slightly darker but not yet popping, about 1 minute.

2. Add onion and cook, stirring, until starting to soften, about 2 minutes. Reduce heat to medium-low and cook, stirring, until onion is very soft and starting to brown, about 8 minutes. Add garlic, chile peppers, ginger and turmeric; cook, stirring, until softened and fragrant, about 1 minute.

3. Add tomatoes with juice and bring to a boil, scraping up bits stuck to pan. Reduce heat and boil gently, stirring often, until sauce is flavorful and slightly thickened, about 5 minutes. Stir in green pepper and simmer for 3 minutes.

4. Stir in calamari and cook, stirring often, just until calamari start to firm up, about 3 minutes. Discard bay leaves. Season to taste with salt. Serve sprinkled with green onions.

Curry Lime Bay Scallops with Papaya

Serves 4

Bay scallops are an affordable way to enjoy the sweetly fragrant luxury of scallops. Here, they are gently simmered in an aromatic sauce, their appeal bolstered by the exotic taste and silken texture of papaya. Serve with chilled white wine to give even a weekday dinner a celebratory feel.

Tips

If lime leaves are not available, substitute 1 tsp (5 mL) finely grated lime zest and add with the lime juice in step 5.

Removing the small connecter muscle attached to the scallops is tedious, but it really improves the texture of the dish. Use a sharp paring knife to carefully slice off just the muscle portion.

Be sure to just barely cook the scallops so they don't get tough and rubbery.

2 tsp	cornstarch	10 mL
1 cup	plain yogurt (not fat-free)	250 mL
1 lb	bay scallops	500 g
2 tbsp	vegetable oil, divided	25 mL
1 tbsp	Indian yellow curry paste, divided	15 mL
4	wild lime leaves (see tip, at left)	4
2 tsp	mustard seeds	10 mL
1 tsp	coriander seeds	5 mL
1	onion, finely chopped	1
1 tbsp	packed brown or palm sugar	15 mL
1/2 tsp	salt	2 mL
1/2 cup	water or fish stock	125 mL
1 cup	thinly sliced peeled papaya	250 mL
2 tbsp	freshly squeezed lime juice	25 mL
	Chopped fresh mint or cilantro	
	Lime wedges	

1. In a bowl, stir cornstarch and yogurt until blended and smooth. Set aside at room temperature.

2. Drain scallops in a colander and rinse with cool water. Drain well. Remove the small white muscle from each scallop. Place scallops on a paper towel–lined plate and pat dry.

3. In another bowl, combine half each of the oil and curry paste. Add scallops and toss to coat evenly. Set aside.

4. In a large skillet, heat remaining oil over medium-high heat until hot but not smoking. Add lime leaves, mustard seeds and coriander seeds; cook, stirring, just until seeds start to pop, about 30 seconds. Add onion, brown sugar and salt. Reduce heat to medium-low and cook, stirring, until onions are deep golden brown, about 8 minutes. Add remaining curry paste and cook, stirring, until blended and fragrant, about 1 minute.

5. Stir in scallop mixture. Add water and bring to a simmer, scraping up bits stuck to pan. Simmer gently, stirring often, just until scallops start to firm up, about 2 minutes. Add yogurt mixture and cook, stirring, until sauce is thickened, about 2 minutes. Stir in papaya and lime juice just until heated through. Season to taste with salt. Serve sprinkled with mint and garnished with lime wedges to squeeze over top.

Green Curry Mussels with Lime and Basil

Serves 2 to 4

Mussels are a bit of a bother to clean and beard, but they reward mightily with the juicy texture of their sweet flesh. Plus, they provide a party atmosphere of hands-on abandon, what with pulling them off their shells. The attendant fragrances of this sauce add even more levels of enjoyment.

Tip
If lime leaves are not available, substitute 1 tsp (5 mL) finely grated lime zest and add with the lime juice in step 4.

2 lbs	fresh mussels	1 kg
1	can (14 oz/400 mL) coconut milk, divided	1
2	slices gingerroot, each about 1/4 inch (0.5 cm) thick	2
2	wild lime leaves (see tip, at left)	2
1	onion, thinly sliced lengthwise	1
1 tsp	packed brown or palm sugar	5 mL
1/2 cup	water	125 mL
4 tsp	Thai green curry paste	20 mL
1 tbsp	fish sauce (nam pla)	15 mL
2 tbsp	shredded fresh Thai or sweet basil	25 mL
2 tbsp	freshly squeezed lime juice	25 mL

1. Gently scrub mussels and remove beards, if necessary. If any mussels are open, tap to close. Discard any that do not close. Drain well and set aside.

2. In a large, deep skillet, heat 1/2 cup (125 mL) of the coconut milk over medium-low heat until bubbling. Add ginger and lime leaves; cook, stirring, until fragrant, about 1 minute.

3. Increase heat to medium. Add onion and cook, stirring, until softened, about 3 minutes. Add brown sugar, remaining coconut milk, water, curry paste and fish sauce. Increase heat to medium-high and bring to a boil, stirring until curry paste is blended and sugar is dissolved. Boil, stirring occasionally, until slightly reduced, about 3 minutes.

4. Stir in mussels. Cover and boil gently, shaking pan occasionally, until mussels are open, about 10 minutes. Discard any that do not open. Using a slotted spoon, transfer mussels to warmed serving bowls. Discard lime leaves and ginger. Stir basil and lime juice into sauce and ladle over mussels.

Bengal Coconut Curry Shrimp

Serves 4

Bengal is renowned for its literary and cinematic arts, for eternally fascinating Calcutta, for Mother Teresa, and for its seaside villages, where fishermen reward their day's labors with a curry of these signature shrimp. Now you can enjoy them in the comfort of your home, and you don't even have to scamper out and fish for them all day.

Tips

The onions can be chopped in a food processor; just be sure not to purée them to the point where they become juicy.

This recipe can be doubled easily; just cook the shrimp in two batches in step 2.

1 lb	large or jumbo shrimp, peeled, deveined and patted dry	500 g
1 tsp	salt, or to taste, divided	5 mL
¼ tsp	ground turmeric	1 mL
2 tbsp	vegetable oil, divided	25 mL
2	bay leaves	2
1	stick cinnamon, about 2 inches (5 cm) long	1
2 tsp	cumin seeds	10 mL
4	cloves garlic, minced	4
2	onions, finely chopped	2
2	hot green chile peppers, minced, or to taste	2
2 tbsp	minced gingerroot	25 mL
Pinch	ground cardamom	Pinch
1	can (14 oz/400 mL) coconut milk	1

1. In a bowl, combine shrimp, ½ tsp (2 mL) of the salt and the turmeric. Toss to coat evenly and let stand for 15 minutes.

2. In a large skillet, heat half the oil over medium-high heat until hot but not smoking. Add shrimp and cook, turning once, just until starting to curl and turn pink, about 2 minutes. Transfer to a bowl.

3. Reduce heat to medium-low and add remaining oil to skillet. Add bay leaves, cinnamon and cumin seeds; cook, stirring, until seeds start to pop, about 1 minute. Add garlic, onions, chile peppers, ginger and cardamom; cook, stirring, until onions are deep golden brown, about 10 minutes.

4. Increase heat to medium-high. Add coconut milk and bring to a boil, scraping up bits stuck to pan. Reduce heat and boil gently until slightly thickened, about 3 minutes. Stir in shrimp and cook, stirring, just until shrimp are pink and opaque, about 2 minutes. Discard bay leaves and cinnamon stick, if desired. Season to taste with remaining salt.

Shrimp Butter Curry

Serves 4

Butter endows sauces with such splendid smoothness and satisfaction that, once in a while, it's essential for the well-being of one's spirit. If you're fat-shy, try a small portion of these delightful shrimp alongside other, leaner curries. But do try them — they'll make you happy!

Tips

A lower-fat yogurt will work, but avoid fat-free yogurt and any with added gelatin. When cooked, gelatin in yogurt can cause the yogurt to split and create a curdled texture.

Large or jumbo shrimp work best for this recipe. Medium or small shrimp will cook too quickly in the oven, and the flavor of the spices won't develop as well.

To avoid a rubbery texture, be sure not to overcook the shrimp.

• Rimmed baking sheet, lined with parchment paper or greased foil

½ tsp	garam masala	2 mL
½ tsp	ground coriander	2 mL
¼ tsp	ground cumin	1 mL
1	clove garlic, minced	1
1 tsp	minced gingerroot	5 mL
⅛ tsp	paprika	0.5 mL
¼ cup	plain yogurt, preferably full-fat (see tip, at left)	50 mL
1 lb	large shrimp, peeled, deveined and patted dry	500 g

Butter Curry Sauce

3 tbsp	butter, divided	45 mL
1	hot green chile pepper, chopped	1
1 tbsp	minced gingerroot	15 mL
1 tsp	ground cumin	5 mL
1 tsp	ground coriander	5 mL
½ tsp	salt	2 mL
½ tsp	paprika	2 mL
⅛ tsp	ground cardamom	0.5 mL
1 cup	canned crushed (ground) tomatoes	250 mL
¾ cup	water	175 mL
½ cup	whipping (35%) cream	125 mL
	Chopped fresh cilantro	
	Lemon wedges	

1. In a dry small skillet over medium heat, toast garam masala, coriander and cumin, stirring constantly, just until spices have a toasted aroma and are starting to darken, 1 to 2 minutes. Transfer immediately to a bowl. Stir in garlic, ginger, paprika and yogurt. Add shrimp and toss to coat evenly. Let stand at room temperature for 15 minutes, or cover and refrigerate for up to 1 day.

2. *Prepare the sauce:* In a large skillet, melt half the butter over medium heat. Add chile pepper, ginger, cumin, coriander, salt, paprika and cardamom; cook, stirring, until softened and fragrant, about 2 minutes. Carefully pour in tomatoes and water (it will splatter); cook, scraping up bits stuck to pan, for 2 minutes. Stir in cream. Reduce heat and simmer, stirring occasionally, until thickened and flavorful, about 10 minutes.

3. Meanwhile, preheat oven to 450°F (230°C).

4. Spread shrimp with marinade in a single layer on prepared baking sheet. Bake just until starting to curl, about 5 minutes.

5. Transfer shrimp and any accumulated juices to sauce and stir until coated. Reduce heat and simmer gently, stirring often, until shrimp are pink and opaque and flavors are blended, about 3 minutes. Remove from heat.

6. Cut remaining butter into small pieces and stir into sauce until melted. Season to taste with salt. Serve sprinkled with cilantro and garnished with lemon wedges to squeeze over top.

Serving Suggestions

Serve with Spinach Rice Pilau (page 255) or Lemon Coriander Rice (page 257), or with plain basmati rice and Spinach Potato Fry with Curried Yellow Lentils (page 245).

Other complementary curries for a multi-course meal include Quick Pork Vindaloo Curry (page 118), Green Mango Curry Chicken with Basil (page 74), Curried Plantain with Raisins and Pecans (page 215) and Golden Curried Cauliflower with Green Peas (page 222).

Tip

To make ahead, prepare the sauce in step 2. Cool, cover and refrigerate for up to 2 days or freeze for up to 1 month. Marinate the shrimp overnight. To serve, thaw sauce, if necessary, and reheat over medium heat until bubbling, then proceed with step 3.

Variation

Scallops in Butter Curry: Substitute 1 lb (500 g) large sea scallops for the shrimp. In step 4, cook just until scallops start to firm up, 3 to 5 minutes. In step 5, cook just until scallops are somewhat firm, about 3 minutes.

Shrimp in Coconut Red Curry with Peanuts

Serves 4

These luscious, confection-like shrimp luxuriate in a rich, lustrous sauce that only the Thai affinity to sweetly tart heat could have created. They can be made hotter by increasing the amount of red curry paste, but they attain an exquisite balance with the amount suggested. It's essential to avoid overcooking the shrimp, especially if using the more affordable medium size.

Tips

If lime leaves aren't available, substitute ½ tsp (2 mL) finely grated lime zest and stir in with the lime juice in step 2.

The peanuts give the best texture to the sauce if pulsed in a food processor to a coarse meal (without processing too much into peanut butter). You may need to do more than ¼ cup (50 mL), depending on the size of your food processor. Extra ground nuts can be frozen for future use.

1 tbsp	vegetable oil	15 mL
1	red bell pepper, thinly sliced	1
2	wild lime leaves (see tip, at left)	2
¼ cup	salted roasted peanuts, ground or finely chopped (see tip, at left)	50 mL
1 tbsp	packed brown or palm sugar	15 mL
1	can (14 oz/400 mL) coconut milk	1
¼ cup	water	50 mL
2 tsp	Thai red curry paste	10 mL
1 lb	medium or large shrimp, peeled, deveined and patted dry	500 g
2 tbsp	freshly squeezed lime juice	25 mL
	Salt	
	Chopped fresh mint and/or basil	
	Lime wedges	

1. In a skillet, heat oil over medium heat. Add red pepper and lime leaves; cook, stirring, until starting to soften, about 1 minute. Add peanuts, brown sugar, coconut milk, water and curry paste; bring to a boil, stirring until blended. Reduce heat and boil gently, stirring often, until sauce is flavorful and slightly thickened, about 5 minutes.

2. Stir in shrimp and simmer gently, stirring often, just until shrimp are pink and opaque, 2 to 3 minutes. Stir in lime juice and season to taste with salt. Serve sprinkled with mint and/or basil and garnished with lime wedges to squeeze over top.

Caribbean-Style Shrimp Curry with Pineapple

Serves 4

Plump shrimp are gently poached in a joyful sauce of spiked coconut and pineapple, almost begging to be cooked up in an outdoor kitchen on an island beach. Failing that, they'll taste just as good coming out of your home kitchen, especially in winter when every bit of joy is welcome.

Tips

If a very ripe tomato is not available, substitute 1 cup (250 mL) drained canned diced tomatoes.

In place of fresh pineapple, substitute 1 can (14 oz/ 398 mL) pineapple tidbits, drained, and add with the shrimp in step 3.

1 tbsp	vegetable oil	15 mL
1	onion, sliced lengthwise	1
1 tbsp	minced gingerroot	15 mL
1 tbsp	curry powder, preferably Caribbean-style	15 mL
1 tsp	chopped fresh thyme (or $1/4$ tsp/1 mL dried)	5 mL
$3/4$ tsp	salt	3 mL
Pinch	ground allspice	Pinch
1	very ripe large tomato, chopped	1
$1/2$	Scotch bonnet pepper, minced, or to taste	$1/2$
1 cup	chopped fresh pineapple	250 mL
1	can (14 oz/400 mL) coconut milk	1
1 lb	large shrimp, peeled, deveined and patted dry	500 g
2 tbsp	freshly squeezed lime juice	25 mL
	Fresh thyme sprigs	

1. In a large skillet, heat oil over medium heat. Add onion and cook, stirring, until starting to soften, about 3 minutes. Add ginger, curry powder, thyme, salt and allspice; cook, stirring, until onion is soft and spices are fragrant, about 2 minutes.

2. Stir in tomato, Scotch bonnet pepper and pineapple; cook, stirring, until tomato starts to soften, about 2 minutes. Add coconut milk and bring to a simmer, scraping up bits stuck to pan. Reduce heat and boil gently, stirring often, until pineapple is almost tender, about 3 minutes.

3. Stir in shrimp. Reduce heat and simmer gently, stirring often, just until shrimp are pink and opaque, 2 to 3 minutes. Stir in lime juice and season to taste with salt. Serve garnished with thyme.

Grilled Shrimp Masala

Serves 4

Whether grilled or roasted, these zesty shrimp skewers will be a huge hit with the grateful guests of any patio barbecue. The skewers can be prepared through step 5 and cooked up in minutes when you're ready to serve them.

• ◆ •

Tips

Disposable latex or rubber gloves are handy not only for chopping hot chile peppers, but also to prevent the curry from staining your hands while you're skewering the shrimp.

Using 2 skewers for each kabob helps prevent shrimp from flipping around the skewer when you turn them. If you have flat metal or bamboo skewers, one is enough.

• Sixteen 6-inch (15 cm) metal or bamboo skewers
• Rimmed baking sheet, lined with greased foil (for broiler version)

3 tbsp	vegetable oil	45 mL
1	hot green chile pepper, minced	1
2 tsp	minced gingerroot	10 mL
5	curry leaves	5
1 tsp	Indian yellow curry paste or masala blend	5 mL
1 lb	jumbo shrimp, peeled, deveined and patted dry	500 g
1/4 tsp	salt, or to taste	1 mL
2 tbsp	chopped fresh cilantro	25 mL
	Garam masala	
	Lemon wedges	

1. In a small skillet, heat oil over medium heat until hot but not smoking. Reduce heat to medium-low. Add chile pepper, ginger, curry leaves and curry paste; cook, stirring, until softened and fragrant, about 2 minutes. Transfer to a shallow dish and let cool completely.

2. Add shrimp to spice mixture, turning to coat evenly. Let stand at room temperature for 15 minutes, or cover and refrigerate for up to 8 hours.

3. If using bamboo skewers, soak in another shallow dish for at least 30 minutes or for up to 4 hours.

4. Preheat barbecue to medium-high and grease grill rack, or preheat broiler with rack placed 6 inches (15 cm) from burner.

5. Remove shrimp from marinade, discarding remaining marinade. Sprinkle shrimp with salt. Using 2 skewers held parallel to each other about 1/4 inch (0.5 cm) apart, thread shrimp onto skewers. Place on greased grill or on prepared baking sheet, if broiling. Grill or broil, turning skewers once, until shrimp are pink and opaque, about 2 minutes per side. Serve sprinkled with cilantro and garam masala and garnished with lemon wedges to squeeze over top.

Shrimp Curry with Mushrooms and Green Pepper

Serves 4

Shrimp go well with a number of vegetables, but especially mushrooms and green peppers. This works very well alongside other dishes at a dinner party, or accompanied simply with rice at a family dinner.

Serving Suggestion

Serve with Roasted Bell Pepper Rice Pilau (page 254), Lemon Coriander Rice (page 257) or plain basmati rice.

2 tbsp	vegetable oil	25 mL
10	curry leaves	10
1 tbsp	coriander seeds, crushed	15 mL
1 tsp	cumin seeds	5 mL
1	large onion, sliced lengthwise	1
8 oz	mushrooms, sliced	250 g
4	cloves garlic, minced	4
1 or 2	hot green chile peppers, minced	1 or 2
2 tbsp	Indian yellow curry paste or masala blend	25 mL
1	can (28 oz/796 mL) diced tomatoes with juice	1
1	green or red bell pepper, halved crosswise and thinly sliced	1
1 lb	large shrimp, peeled, deveined and patted dry	500 g
	Salt	
¼ tsp	garam masala	1 mL
	Chopped fresh cilantro	

1. In a large skillet, heat oil over medium-high heat until hot but not smoking. Add curry leaves, coriander seeds and cumin seeds; cook, stirring, just until seeds are slightly darker but not yet popping, about 30 seconds.

2. Add onion and cook, stirring, until starting to soften, about 2 minutes. Add mushrooms and cook, stirring, until liquid is released and mushrooms are browned, about 8 minutes. Add garlic, chile peppers and curry paste; cook, stirring, until softened and fragrant, about 1 minute.

3. Add tomatoes with juice and bring to a boil, scraping up bits stuck to pan. Reduce heat and boil gently, stirring often, until sauce is flavorful and slightly thickened, about 5 minutes. Stir in green pepper and simmer for 3 minutes.

4. Stir in shrimp and cook, stirring often, just until shrimp are pink and opaque, 3 to 4 minutes. Season to taste with salt. Serve sprinkled with garam masala and cilantro.

Thai Green Curry Shrimp and Vegetables

Serves 4		

This perky shrimp dish from Phuket, Thailand's island paradise, is easy and fast, and will serve well for a family dinner if you use the more affordable medium shrimp. Remember the old shrimp proviso: don't overcook the little darlings.

Tip

This version is moderately spicy. You can adjust the heat by adding more or less green curry paste.

1 tbsp	vegetable oil	15 mL
1	onion, thinly sliced lengthwise	1
1	red bell pepper, chopped	1
1	zucchini, halved lengthwise and sliced	1
1 tsp	packed brown or palm sugar	5 mL
1	can (14 oz/400 mL) coconut milk	1
¼ cup	water	50 mL
4 tsp	Thai green curry paste	20 mL
1 tbsp	fish sauce (nam pla)	15 mL
1 lb	medium or large shrimp, peeled and deveined	500 g
1 tbsp	freshly squeezed lime juice	15 mL
	Salt, optional	
¼ cup	chopped fresh Thai or sweet basil	50 mL

1. In a large skillet or wok, heat oil over medium-high heat. Add onion, red pepper and zucchini; cook, stirring, until onion starts to soften, about 2 minutes.

2. Stir in brown sugar, coconut milk, water, curry paste and fish sauce. Bring to a boil, stirring until blended. Reduce heat and simmer, stirring often, until zucchini is slightly tender, about 3 minutes.

3. Stir in shrimp and simmer gently, stirring often, just until shrimp are pink and opaque, 2 to 3 minutes. Stir in lime juice and season to taste with salt, if using. Serve sprinkled with basil.

Serving Suggestion

Serve over Thai Basil Sticky Rice (page 261) or plain cooked jasmine rice.

Gingery Shrimp in Tomato Curry

Serves 4

Ginger is an all-time favorite spice, enhancing and redefining many different ingredients. These shrimp would have been delicious without ginger, but with it they achieve lightness, levitating on the palate in a burst of perfume.

• ◆ •

Tips

To julienne ginger, cut a 3-inch (7.5 cm) piece of gingerroot into thin slices. Working with 3 slices at a time, stack and cut across into thin strips.

If you prefer, you can replace the canned tomatoes with about 4 large fresh tomatoes. Peel tomatoes, if desired (see page 294). Chop, saving all juices, and measure 3½ cups (875 mL). For the most flavor, be sure the tomatoes are very ripe and flavorful.

1 tbsp	vegetable oil	15 mL
¼ cup	julienned gingerroot (see tip, at left)	50 mL
1	small red onion, thinly sliced lengthwise	1
1	red bell pepper, halved crosswise and thinly sliced	1
½ tsp	granulated sugar	2 mL
¼ tsp	salt	1 mL
Pinch	ground cinnamon	Pinch
Pinch	cayenne pepper	Pinch
½ cup	Basic Gravy (see recipe, page 7)	125 mL
1	can (28 oz/796 mL) diced tomatoes with juice	1
1 lb	medium or large shrimp, peeled, deveined and patted dry	500 g
1 tbsp	chopped fresh basil or mint Lime wedges	15 mL

1. In a large skillet, heat oil over medium heat until hot but not smoking. Add ginger and cook, stirring, until softened and fragrant, about 1 minute. Using a slotted spoon, transfer half the ginger to a bowl and set aside.

2. Add onion to ginger remaining in pan and cook, stirring, until softened and starting to brown, about 3 minutes. Add red pepper, sugar, salt, cinnamon and cayenne; cook, stirring, until pepper starts to soften, about 2 minutes. Add gravy and cook, stirring, for 1 minute.

3. Stir in tomatoes with juice and bring to a boil. Reduce heat and simmer, stirring often, until sauce is flavorful and slightly thickened, about 5 minutes.

4. Stir in shrimp and simmer gently, stirring often, just until shrimp are pink and opaque, 2 to 3 minutes. Stir in basil and season to taste with salt. Serve sprinkled with reserved ginger and garnished with lime wedges to squeeze over top.

Jumbo Shrimp and Snow Peas in Tamarind Curry

Serves 4 to 6

This simple curry features two favorite ingredients: the snap of snow peas and the springiness of just-poached shrimp. It must be served hot off the pan, and is ideally suited for a family dinner when everyone has been on good behavior and deserves the extra expense of shrimp this size.

• ❖ •

Tips

If you like a mild curry, omit the chile pepper; if you like it hotter, use 2.

To make tamarind water, break a 2-oz (60 g) piece of block tamarind into small pieces and place in a heatproof bowl. Pour in 1 cup (250 mL) boiling water and let stand until very soft, about 30 minutes, or for up to 8 hours. Press through a fine-mesh sieve, discarding seeds and skins.

2 tbsp	vegetable oil	25 mL
1	hot green chile pepper, minced	1
1 tsp	mustard seeds	5 mL
½ tsp	fenugreek seeds	2 mL
½ cup	Basic Gravy (see recipe, page 7)	125 mL
2 tbsp	packed brown or palm sugar	25 mL
1 cup	tamarind water (see tip, at left)	250 mL
½ cup	water	125 mL
1	large tomato, cut into wedges	1
2 cups	snow peas, trimmed and halved diagonally	500 mL
1 lb	jumbo shrimp, peeled, deveined and patted dry	500 g
	Salt	
	Chopped fresh cilantro	

1. In a large skillet, heat oil over medium heat until hot but not smoking. Add chile pepper, mustard seeds and fenugreek seeds; cook, stirring, until seeds start to pop, about 15 seconds. Add gravy and cook, stirring, for 1 minute.

2. Stir in brown sugar, tamarind water and water; bring to a boil. Reduce heat and simmer, stirring often, until sauce is flavorful and slightly thickened, about 5 minutes. Add tomato and snow peas; cook, stirring gently, until tomato starts to soften, about 3 minutes.

3. Add shrimp and simmer gently, stirring often, just until snow peas are tender-crisp and shrimp are pink and opaque, about 5 minutes. Season to taste with salt. Serve sprinkled with cilantro.

Serving Suggestion

Serve with Lemon Coriander Rice (page 257) or Golden Curried Pineapple Rice (page 259).

Curry Mint–Crusted Rack of Lamb (page 134)

Curried Lamb with Sweet Corn and Spinach (page 135)

Green Mango Fish Curry (page 157)

Curry Lime Bay Scallops with Papaya (page 165)

Kerala-Style Crab Curry

Serves 2 to 4

Saucy, spicy, sweet and uplifting, this crab curry is a lusty dining experience best shared by lovers. All you need on the side is candlelight, chilled white wine and lots of napkins.

Tips

This version is definitely fiery. For a milder version, decrease the cayenne and/or use just 1 chile pepper.

Have seafood shears and picks on hand to help diners cut open the crab shells and pick out the meat. It's not a tidy dining experience, but it is succulent!

Variation

Substitute 1 lb (500 g) large sea scallops for the crab. Skip steps 1 and 2 and cook scallops in step 5 just until opaque and slightly firm, 3 to 5 minutes.

2 lbs	fresh or frozen cooked crab legs, in shell (thawed if frozen)	1 kg
2 tbsp	vegetable oil	25 mL
1	onion, thinly sliced	1
6	cloves garlic, minced	6
2	hot green chile peppers, sliced	2
1 tbsp	minced gingerroot	15 mL
1 tbsp	ground coriander	15 mL
1 tsp	ground turmeric	5 mL
½ tsp	salt	2 mL
½ tsp	cayenne pepper	2 mL
1	large tomato, diced	1
8	curry leaves	8
1 cup	coconut milk	250 mL
2 tbsp	freshly squeezed lime juice	25 mL

1. If using fresh crab, in a large pot of boiling salted water, boil until shells are red and meat is firm and opaque, about 20 minutes. Drain and let cool. If using frozen, drain well.

2. Cut crab into 3-inch (7.5 cm) pieces. Set aside.

3. In a large skillet, heat oil over medium-high heat. Add onion and cook, stirring, until softened, about 3 minutes. Add garlic, chile peppers, ginger, coriander, turmeric, salt and cayenne; cook, stirring, until spices are softened and fragrant, about 2 minutes.

4. Add tomato and curry leaves; cook, stirring, until tomato is softened, about 2 minutes. Add coconut milk and bring to a boil, scraping up bits stuck to pan.

5. Add reserved crab and simmer, stirring often, until heated through and flavorful, 3 to 5 minutes. Served sprinkled with lime juice.

Kovalam Beach, Kerala

Some 30 years is all it took for this sleepiest of southern Indian fishing posts to become a medium-budget international beach destination, replete with luxury hotels alongside budget accommodations that sprang up to house the original hippie tourists who "discovered" Kovalam in the late 1960s. The resort that evolved is a long, beach-hugging corniche with an unbroken chain of shops, hotels and, of course, restaurants, mainly outdoor venues specializing in coconut-based curries, masalas and grills of seafood and fish fresh from the Arabian Sea. Of particular interest to fish lovers is searfish, a large beast with the flavor and texture of swordfish that is memorable whether cooked plump and juicy in sauce or brushed with spicy butter and grilled in a tandoor.

Directly behind the beach, along the watery byways of the palm forest, a whole other town has sprung up, with equally beautiful hotels that are much more peaceful than the ones on the beachfront, as well as another array of shops and restaurants. Charmingly located on the edge of a duck pond, I find Lonely Planet, Kovalam's oldest vegetarian, alternative-lifestyle eatery, a favorite to this day. This is the realm of Chef T. Siva Prasannan, a twinkly-eyed maestro who has put some 35 years into the craft of feeding the multitudes. He has encyclopedic knowledge of vegetarian Indian cuisine, the official diet of the huge Hindu or Buddhist majority, who abstain from eating all animal products except dairy.

Chef Prasannan gives very entertaining cooking classes, which I attended, and has published a comprehensive cookbook titled *Indian-Kerala Vegetarian Recipes*. I purchased the rights to adapt some of his recipes for this book. His most useful invention is a super-simple Basic Gravy, an all-purpose curry base that can be made in advance (see page 7). A small amount of this gravy will turn ordinary ingredients — say potato, cauliflower or spinach — into lovely spur-of-the-moment curries.

For seafood and fish cookery, Kerala-style, I turn to another long-standing establishment, the well-appointed Sea Rock Restaurant, situated on the beach-gazing patio of the eponymous hotel. Here, youthful chef Manju Nath graciously shares the recipes for my favorites from his menu, including the best and most sweetly meaty crab I've tasted in a lifetime of wandering the planet in search of the perfect crab recipe (see page 177 for our version of Chef Nath's crab specialty).

My relationship with Kovalam spans the same decades as its growth. We kind of grew up together. On my first visit, I camped here — well, "camp" being just an operative word. The beach had many helpful residents, and I was set up in a makeshift shelter of Rajasthani silk drapes with soft blankets for bedding. I was brought morning tea and fresh oranges at dawn, and a hearty breakfast of idli (lentil and rice dumplings) with a highly scented sambhar dipping sauce as well as a fresh coconut chutney. The rest of the day consisted of constant dips in the sea punctuated with heaping platefuls of peeled and sliced papaya and pineapple. In the evening, an addictively delicious fish curry or equally toothsome tandoori-grilled seafood (local giant prawns or lobsters) would be prepared for me.

That lifestyle, back in my wild traveler days, cost about $3 a day, all inclusive. Now, Kovalam offers all the same comforts and tastes, but in very civilized hotels and cheerful restaurants, for about $60 a day for two people, still a great bargain in a world whose beach destinations are getting less affordable by the minute. — B.A.

Curry-Crusted Broiled Lobster Tails

Serves 2

The ultimate luxury of the sea, lobster has no equal for a sense of occasion and obvious extravagance. But what the heck — life's short, and anniversaries, birthdays and Valentine's Days all require something special. Here's a recipe for the two of you, with flavorfully crusted, quick-roasted lobster to accompany the Champagne.

Tip

To make fresh bread crumbs: In a food processor fitted with a metal blade, pulse chunks of fresh bread just until crumbs form. Be sure not to overprocess. Extra bread crumbs can be frozen in a sealable freezer bag for up to 2 months.

- Preheat oven to 400°F (200°C)
- Rimmed baking sheet, ungreased

2	lobster tails, thawed if frozen	2
2 tbsp	butter	25 mL
1	clove garlic, minced	1
1 tsp	minced gingerroot	5 mL
1 tsp	minced hot green chile pepper	5 mL
½ tsp	curry powder	2 mL
¼ tsp	ground cumin	1 mL
¼ tsp	ground coriander	1 mL
2 tsp	chopped fresh cilantro	10 mL
¼ cup	fresh bread crumbs	50 mL
2 tbsp	freshly squeezed lemon juice	25 mL
	Lemon wedges	

1. Cut lobster tails in half lengthwise and remove the vein, if necessary. Place cut side down on paper towels to drain. Place cut side up on baking sheet. Set aside.

2. In a small skillet, melt butter over medium heat. Reduce heat to medium-low and add garlic, ginger, chile pepper, curry powder, cumin and coriander. Cook, stirring, until softened and fragrant, about 2 minutes. Transfer to a bowl and stir in cilantro, bread crumbs and lemon juice until blended. Press crumb mixture evenly over lobster meat.

3. Bake in preheated oven until lobster is just firm and opaque and crumbs are golden and fragrant, 10 to15 minutes. Broil until crumbs are browned, about 2 minutes. Serve with lemon wedges to squeeze over top.

Vegetarian Dishes

◆

Chickpeas in Tomato Curry (Channa Masala)

Serves 4

A very easy recipe for a rightfully popular legume, this chickpea dish works well as a simple lunch alongside rice or naan or as part of a complex meal. The meaty taste of the chickpea marries the tartness of tomato seamlessly.

Tip

If very ripe, flavorful fresh tomatoes aren't available, substitute drained canned diced tomatoes.

1 tbsp	vegetable oil	15 mL
½ tsp	cumin seeds	2 mL
1 cup	diced tomatoes	250 mL
8	curry leaves	8
½ cup	Basic Gravy (see recipe, page 7)	125 mL
¼ cup	water	50 mL
2 cups	cooked or canned chickpeas, drained and rinsed	500 mL

1. In a skillet, heat oil over medium heat until hot but not smoking. Add cumin seeds and cook, stirring, until starting to pop, about 1 minute. Add tomatoes and curry leaves; cook, stirring, until tomatoes are softened, about 2 minutes.

2. Add gravy and cook, stirring, for 1 minute. Add water and bring to a boil, stirring. Reduce heat and boil gently for 3 minutes. Add chickpeas and cook, stirring gently, until heated through and flavorful, about 5 minutes.

Serving Suggestion

Serve as a side dish with any creamy or coconut-based curry. For a hearty vegetarian meal, serve with Coconut Cashew Pumpkin Curry (page 234), Tofu with Lime, Lemongrass and Coconut Curry (page 198) or Curried Paneer with Mixed Peppers and Zucchini (page 209) and plain basmati rice.

Chickpeas and Cauliflower in Tomato Curry

Serves 4 to 6

This hearty dish with the protein of chickpeas and the appeal of al dente cauliflower is great with meat or chicken for a satisfying dinner or by itself with naan or rice for a breezy lunch.

Tips

If perfectly ripe fresh tomatoes are not available, substitute drained canned diced tomatoes.

If using dried chickpeas, soak and cook 1 cup (250 mL). One 19-oz (540 mL) can of chickpeas yields 2 cups (500 mL).

1 tbsp	vegetable oil	15 mL
1½ tsp	mustard seeds	7 mL
1 tsp	cumin seeds	5 mL
2 cups	small cauliflower florets	500 mL
¼ cup	water	50 mL
1½ cups	chopped tomatoes	375 mL
1 tsp	minced hot green chile pepper, or to taste	5 mL
8	curry leaves	8
½ cup	Basic Gravy (see recipe, page 7)	125 mL
2 cups	cooked or canned chickpeas, drained and rinsed	500 mL
½ tsp	salt, or to taste	2 mL

1. In a saucepan, heat oil over medium heat until hot but not smoking. Add mustard seeds and cumin seeds; cook, stirring, until starting to pop, about 1 minute. Add cauliflower and water; cover pan quickly. Cook, covered, until cauliflower starts to soften, about 5 minutes.

2. Uncover and add tomatoes, chile pepper and curry leaves. Cook, stirring, until tomatoes are softened, about 2 minutes. Add gravy and cook, stirring, for 1 minute. Stir in chickpeas until well coated. Cover and cook, stirring once, until cauliflower is tender, about 5 minutes. Season to taste with salt.

Caribbean Chickpea Curry with Potatoes

Serves 4 to 6

This is the official stuffing of meatless Caribbean roti. It is filling and tasty, and has nourished generations of Jamaicans in search of a satisfying snack. The recipe also works well as a side dish for meat or chicken.

Tips

If Scotch bonnet peppers are not available, substitute 1 tbsp (15 mL) minced jalapeño pepper (or to taste).

For the most authentic flavor, look for a Caribbean curry powder. Any Indian curry powder will work, but they tend to be hotter, so reduce the amount to 2 tsp (10 mL).

2 tbsp	vegetable oil	25 mL
1 tsp	cumin seeds	5 mL
1	onion, chopped	1
1	hot chile pepper, preferably Scotch bonnet, minced	1
1 tbsp	curry powder, preferably Caribbean-style (see tip, at left)	15 mL
1/2 tsp	salt	2 mL
1/4 tsp	dried thyme (or 1 tsp/5 mL chopped fresh)	1 mL
Pinch	ground allspice	Pinch
2	boiling or all-purpose potatoes, cut into 1/2-inch (1 cm) cubes	2
1	can (14 to 19 oz/398 to 540 mL) chickpeas, drained and rinsed	1
1/2 cup	water or vegetable stock	125 mL
1 tbsp	chopped fresh cilantro or green onion	15 mL

1. In a large skillet, heat oil over medium heat until hot but not smoking. Add cumin seeds and cook, stirring, until starting to pop, about 1 minute. Add onion and cook, stirring, until starting to soften, about 2 minutes. Add chile pepper, curry powder, salt, thyme and allspice; cook, stirring, until onion is softened and starting to brown, about 3 minutes.

2. Stir in potatoes and chickpeas until coated with spices. Pour in water and cover pan quickly. Reduce heat to medium-low and boil gently, stirring occasionally, until potatoes are tender, about 20 minutes. Season to taste with salt. Serve sprinkled with cilantro.

Serving Suggestion

To use for roti, spoon inside warmed Chickpea Flatbread (page 271), store-bought roti skins or whole wheat flour tortillas.

Caribbean Red Bean, Spinach and Potato Curry

Serves 4 to 6

To combine the Caribbean staples of beans, potato and greens is to invite the sunshine of the islands to dinner or lunch. This dish works hot as a vegetarian main course or cold as a salad alongside seafood or fish. Bring on the reggae!

• ◆ •

Tip

There are several varieties of curry powder from the Caribbean that vary in spices from island to island. Any will work nicely in this recipe. If using a stronger, Indian curry powder, reduce the amount to 1½ to 2 tsp (7 to 10 mL) or according to taste.

• ◆ •

Variation

Replace spinach with Swiss chard, callaloo or another hearty green. Add with beans in step 3, increasing time as necessary to make sure greens are tender.

2 lbs	baby new potatoes, halved (or quartered if large)	1 kg
	Cold water	
1 tsp	salt, divided	5 mL
2 tbsp	vegetable oil	25 mL
1	onion, sliced lengthwise	1
½	hot chile pepper, preferably Scotch bonnet, minced	½
1 tbsp	minced gingerroot	15 mL
1 tbsp	curry powder, preferably Caribbean-style (see tip, at left)	15 mL
1 tsp	ground coriander	5 mL
¼ tsp	ground allspice	1 mL
1	can (14 to 19 oz/398 to 540 mL) red kidney beans, drained and rinsed	1
½ cup	water or vegetable stock	125 mL
2 tbsp	freshly squeezed lemon juice	25 mL
2 cups	shredded fresh spinach	500 mL

1. In a pot, cover potatoes with cold water. Add ½ tsp (2 mL) of the salt and bring to a boil over high heat. Reduce heat and boil gently until potatoes are fork-tender, about 15 minutes. Drain well and transfer to a large bowl; set aside.

2. Meanwhile, in a skillet, heat oil over medium heat. Add onion, chile pepper, ginger, curry powder, coriander, allspice and remaining salt; cook, stirring, until onion is softened, about 3 minutes.

3. Stir in beans until coated with spices. Pour in water and bring to a boil, scraping up bits stuck to pan. Reduce heat and boil gently, stirring occasionally, until liquid is almost evaporated, about 5 minutes. Remove from heat and stir in lemon juice. Season to taste with salt. Pour over potatoes in bowl and stir in spinach just until wilted. Serve hot or let cool.

Dal Fry

Serves 4

❦

This is your basic yellow lentil (dal) concoction, served at just about every dinner all over India. It is nourishing and tasty, easy to digest and, most of all, essential for vegetarian diets because of the lentil's protein content.

◆

Tip

Rinse lentils well in a sieve under cool running water and pick through to remove any stones and foreign particles. Drain well.

1 cup	small yellow lentils (toor dal), rinsed	250 mL
1 tsp	ground turmeric	5 mL
½ tsp	salt	2 mL
3½ cups	water, divided (approx.)	875 mL
3 tbsp	vegetable oil	45 mL
8	curry leaves	8
1 tsp	mustard seeds	5 mL
1 tsp	aniseeds	5 mL
1 cup	diced onion	250 mL
1 cup	chopped tomatoes	250 mL
1 tbsp	chopped garlic	15 mL
1 tsp	minced gingerroot	5 mL
¼ tsp	cayenne pepper	1 mL

1. In a saucepan, combine lentils, turmeric, salt and 3 cups (750 mL) of the water. Bring to a boil over high heat. Reduce heat and simmer gently until lentils are slightly tender, about 15 minutes. Set aside in the cooking water.

2. In a skillet, heat oil over medium-high heat until hot but not smoking. Add curry leaves, mustard seeds and aniseeds; cook, stirring, until seeds start to pop, about 1 minute. Add onion and cook, stirring, until starting to soften, about 2 minutes. Add tomatoes, garlic, ginger and cayenne; cook, stirring, until tomatoes are softened, about 2 minutes.

3. Add reserved lentils with cooking water and remaining water; bring to a simmer, stirring often. Reduce heat to medium-low and simmer, stirring often and adding more water as necessary to keep mixture from getting dry, until lentils are softened and flavorful, 10 to 15 minutes.

Serving Suggestion

Serve with a saucy curry, such as Fiery Pineapple Chicken Curry (page 75), Tofu, Eggplant and Basil in Tamarind Curry (page 199) or Beef Curry with Green Beans and Yogurt (page 96).

Dal Curry with Chiles and Coconut

Serves 4 to 6

This deluxe version of dal with added chilies and fresh coconut turns the vegetarian staple into a rich and sensuous experience.

Tips

To shred fresh coconut, peel off brown outer layer and use the coarse side of a box cheese grater or pulse in a food processor until finely chopped but not smooth. Frozen coconut is available at Asian specialty stores; thaw and drain well before using.

In a pinch, packaged dried shredded unsweetened coconut can be used. Soak about ⅓ cup (75 mL) in boiling water for 1 hour, drain well and measure ½ cup (125 mL).

1 cup	small yellow lentils (toor dal), rinsed	250 mL
½ tsp	salt	2 mL
3½ cups	water, divided	875 mL
2 tbsp	vegetable oil	25 mL
2	whole dried red chile peppers	2
1	dried red chile pepper, crumbled	1
2 tsp	coriander seeds	10 mL
1 tsp	cumin seeds	5 mL
½ cup	fresh or frozen unsweetened shredded coconut (see tips, at left)	125 mL
¼ tsp	ground turmeric	1 mL
⅛ tsp	ground cloves	0.5 mL
2 tbsp	freshly squeezed lemon juice	25 mL
2 tbsp	chopped fresh cilantro	25 mL

1. In a saucepan, combine lentils, salt and 3 cups (750 mL) of the water. Bring to a boil over high heat. Reduce heat and simmer gently until lentils are slightly tender, about 15 minutes. Set aside in the cooking water.

2. In a skillet, heat oil over medium heat until hot but not smoking. Add whole and crumbled chile peppers, coriander seeds and cumin seeds; cook, stirring, until seeds are toasted and fragrant but not yet popping, about 30 seconds. Add coconut, turmeric and cloves; cook, stirring, until blended and fragrant, about 1 minute.

3. Add reserved lentils with cooking water and remaining water; bring to a simmer, stirring often. Reduce heat to medium-low and cook, stirring often, until lentils are softened and flavorful, 10 to 15 minutes. Discard whole chile peppers. Stir in lemon juice and season to taste with salt. Serve sprinkled with cilantro.

Yellow Lentil Curry with Vegetables (Dhansak)

Serves 4

This meal-in-one-dish combines the protein of lentils with the comfort of flavorful vegetables. Add some rice, and you're all set for a casual but enjoyable lunch or dinner.

Tip

Simmering the lentils slowly and uncovered allows them to hold their shape and soften nicely, but be sure not to let them dry out.

1 cup	small yellow lentils (toor dal), rinsed	250 mL
½ tsp	salt	2 mL
	Cold water	
2 tbsp	vegetable oil	25 mL
1 cup	diced onion	250 mL
½ cup	chopped green bell pepper	125 mL
½ cup	small cauliflower florets	125 mL
½ cup	cubed eggplant (½-inch/1 cm cubes)	125 mL
½ cup	thinly sliced carrot	125 mL
1	hot green chile pepper, minced	1
½ cup	chopped tomato	125 mL
1 tbsp	minced gingerroot	15 mL
1 tbsp	minced garlic	15 mL
1 tsp	ground cumin	5 mL
1 tsp	garam masala	5 mL
2½ cups	boiling water, divided (approx.)	625 mL

1. In a bowl, combine lentils and salt. Add enough cold water to cover by about 1 inch (2.5 cm). Let stand at room temperature for 1 hour.

2. In a skillet, heat oil over medium-high heat. Add onion, green pepper, cauliflower, eggplant and carrot; cook, stirring, until starting to brown, about 5 minutes. Add chile pepper, tomato, ginger, garlic, cumin and garam masala; cook, stirring, until tomato is softened, about 2 minutes.

3. Drain lentils and add to skillet. Add 1 cup (250 mL) of the boiling water. Reduce heat and simmer, stirring occasionally and adding more of the boiling water, about ½ cup (125 mL) at a time, as mixture becomes dry, until lentils are very soft, about 20 minutes.

Tomato Onion Curry of Brown Lentils

Serves 4 to 6

❧

An alternative to the more popular split yellow lentils, this brown version has a nuttier taste and a more substantial texture. It goes very well with creamy curries, providing a meaningful contrast.

•—◆—•

Tip

If ripe fresh tomatoes aren't available, substitute 1½ cups (375 mL) drained canned diced tomatoes and reduce salt to ¼ tsp (1 mL), adding more to taste at the end if necessary.

1 cup	whole brown lentils (masoor dal), rinsed	250 mL
5 cups	water, divided	1.25 L
2 tbsp	vegetable oil	25 mL
2	bay leaves	2
½ tsp	cumin seeds	2 mL
1	large onion, finely chopped	1
2	cloves garlic, minced	2
1	hot green chile pepper, minced	1
1 tbsp	minced gingerroot	15 mL
1 tsp	salt	5 mL
½ tsp	ground turmeric	2 mL
2	tomatoes, diced	2

1. In a saucepan, combine lentils and 4 cups (1 L) of the water. Bring to a boil over high heat. Reduce heat and simmer until lentils are almost tender, about 25 minutes. Drain and set aside.

2. In a skillet, heat oil over medium-high heat until hot but not smoking. Add bay leaves and cumin seeds; cook, stirring, until seeds are toasted but not yet popping, about 30 seconds. Add onion and cook, stirring, until starting to soften, about 2 minutes. Reduce heat to medium-low and cook, stirring often, until onions are very soft and golden brown, about 10 minutes.

3. Add garlic, chile pepper, ginger, salt and turmeric; cook, stirring, until softened and fragrant, about 2 minutes. Increase heat to medium and add tomatoes. Cook, stirring, until tomatoes are softened, about 2 minutes.

4. Add reserved lentils and remaining water; bring to a boil, stirring often. Reduce heat and boil gently, stirring often, until lentils are tender and most of the liquid is absorbed, 10 to 15 minutes. Discard bay leaves and season to taste with salt.

Red Lentil Curry with Coconut and Cilantro

Serves 4 to 6

Easy to make, these red lentils have a luxurious coconut finish and a lovely, bright yellow color. They partner any curry of your choice — vegetable or meat — as well as rice, for a complete and satisfying meal.

Tips

Traditionally, Indian lentil dishes such as this one are served very loose and almost soupy. You can adjust the texture to your taste by adding more water or simmering longer to thicken in step 2.

Leftovers will thicken considerably upon cooling. If reheating in the microwave or a saucepan, add boiling water before heating to return to desired consistency.

Variation

To add some heat to this dish, add 1 or 2 hot red or green chile peppers, minced, with the garlic.

2 tbsp	vegetable oil	25 mL
1	small onion, finely chopped	1
2	cloves garlic, minced	2
1 tbsp	minced gingerroot	15 mL
1 tsp	salt	5 mL
1 tsp	ground coriander	5 mL
1 tsp	ground cumin	5 mL
1/4 tsp	ground turmeric	1 mL
1 cup	red lentils (masoor dal), rinsed	250 mL
1	can (14 oz/400 mL) coconut milk	1
1 cup	water	250 mL
1/4 cup	torn cilantro leaves	50 mL
	Garam masala	

1. In a saucepan, heat oil over medium heat. Add onion and cook, stirring, until softened and starting to brown, about 5 minutes. Add garlic, ginger, salt, coriander, cumin and turmeric; cook, stirring, until softened and fragrant, about 2 minutes.

2. Stir in lentils until coated with spices. Stir in coconut milk and water; bring to a boil, scraping up bits stuck to pan and stirring to prevent lumps. Reduce heat to low, partially cover and simmer, stirring often, until lentils are very soft and mixture is thick, about 15 minutes.

3. Remove from heat, cover and let stand for 5 minutes. Season to taste with salt. Stir in all but a few leaves of cilantro. Serve sprinkled with remaining cilantro and garam masala.

Butter Curry Black Lentils

Serves 6 to 8

Rajasthan, a fabled land of red headdresses, embroidered shawls, palaces in desert oases and erstwhile maharajas, is also the home of black lentils cooked in butter. They are as smooth as a night breeze under a million stars.

Tip

Rinse lentils well in a sieve under cool running water and pick through to remove any stones and foreign particles. Drain well.

Variation

If black lentils are not available, substitute whole brown lentils (masoor dal) and reduce the cooking time in step 2 to about 8 minutes.

1 cup	whole black lentils (urad dal), rinsed	250 mL
	Water	
2 tbsp	butter	25 mL
1	small onion, finely chopped	1
1	hot green chile pepper, minced	1
½ tsp	ground cumin	2 mL
½ tsp	paprika	2 mL
Pinch	ground cardamom	Pinch
Pinch	ground cloves	Pinch
½ cup	Basic Gravy (see recipe, page 7)	125 mL
1½ cups	canned crushed (ground) tomatoes	375 mL
¾ cup	whipping (35%) cream	175 mL
	Salt	
	Chopped fresh cilantro	

1. Place lentils in a bowl and add enough water to cover by about 2 inches (5 cm). Let soak at room temperature for at least 4 hours or for up to 1 day.

2. Drain lentils and transfer to a saucepan. Add 4 cups (1 L) fresh water and bring to a boil over high heat. Reduce heat and boil gently until lentils are almost tender, about 30 minutes. Drain well.

3. Meanwhile, in a deep saucepan, melt butter over medium heat. Add onion and cook, stirring, until softened and starting to brown, about 5 minutes. Add chile pepper, cumin, paprika, cardamom and cloves; cook, stirring, until blended and fragrant, about 1 minute. Add gravy and cook, stirring, for 1 minute. Stir in tomatoes and ½ cup (125 mL) water; bring to a boil.

4. Stir in drained lentils and cream. Reduce heat and simmer, stirring occasionally, until sauce is slightly thickened and lentils are tender, about 10 minutes. Season to taste with salt. Serve sprinkled with cilantro.

Serving Suggestion

Serve over brown rice or with Chapati (page 270) to scoop up the luxurious sauce.

African Curried Kidney Beans with Ginger

Serves 4 to 8

This simple curried bean stew makes for an excellent side course. On its own, it can be wrapped in a Chapati (page 270) and topped with Fruity Mango Papaya Chutney (page 37) for a sensational lunch.

• ◆ •

Tips

To julienne ginger, cut a 2½-inch (6 cm) piece of gingerroot into thin slices. Working with 3 slices at a time, stack and cut across into thin strips.

If a 19-oz (540 mL) can of diced tomatoes isn't available, use 2⅓ cups (575 mL) from a 28-oz (796 mL) can and reserve the remainder for another use.

2 tbsp	vegetable oil	25 mL
2	dried red chile peppers	2
1	onion, finely chopped	1
2	cloves garlic, minced	2
3 tbsp	julienned gingerroot (see tip, at left)	45 mL
10	curry leaves	10
1 tsp	garam masala	5 mL
¼ tsp	ground cinnamon	1 mL
¼ tsp	ground turmeric	1 mL
2	cans (each 14 to 19 oz/398 to 540 mL) red kidney beans, drained and rinsed	2
1	can (19 oz/540 mL) diced tomatoes with juice	1
½ cup	water	125 mL
	Salt	
2 tbsp	chopped fresh cilantro	25 mL

1. In a large skillet, heat oil over medium heat. Add chile peppers and onion; cook, stirring, until starting to soften, about 2 minutes. Reduce heat to medium-low and add garlic, ginger, curry leaves, garam masala, cinnamon and turmeric; cook, stirring often, until onion is very soft, about 7 minutes.

2. Stir in beans until coated with spices. Add tomatoes with juice and water. Increase heat to medium-high and bring to a boil, scraping up bits stuck to pan. Reduce heat and boil gently, stirring occasionally, until sauce is thick and beans are flavorful, 10 to 15 minutes. Discard chile peppers. Season to taste with salt. Serve sprinkled with cilantro.

Baked Curried Tofu with Tomato Masala

Serves 4 to 6

Two stages of cooking infuse the tofu with deep flavor and a jammy-textured curry coating. They also make it look very appetizing, elevating humble tofu into a dish fit for company.

Tip

The tofu and sauce can be made ahead through step 3, covered and refrigerated for up to 2 days.

Variations

Add shredded mozzarella cheese on top of tofu for the last 5 minutes of baking in step 5.

To grill tofu instead of baking, preheat grill to medium. Place tofu and sauce on a large piece of greased foil on grill. Cover and grill until sauce is lightly browned, about 10 minutes.

• *Baking sheet, lined with parchment paper*

12 oz	firm or extra-firm tofu, drained	375 g
1 tbsp	vegetable oil	15 mL
1 or 2	hot green chile peppers, minced	1 or 2
10	curry leaves	10
½ tsp	garam masala	2 mL
1 cup	Basic Gravy (see recipe, page 7)	250 mL
1 cup	canned crushed (ground) tomatoes	250 mL
½ cup	water	125 mL
1 tbsp	soy sauce	15 mL
	Chopped fresh cilantro	
	Plain yogurt, optional	

1. On a cutting board, stand block of tofu on one long, narrow side. Cut lengthwise into 3 slices. Cut each slice in half to make 2 squares and cut each square diagonally to make triangles. Set aside.

2. In a large nonstick skillet, heat oil over medium heat until hot but not smoking. Add chile peppers, curry leaves and garam masala; cook, stirring, until fragrant, about 1 minute. Add gravy and cook, stirring, for 1 minute. Add tomatoes, water and soy sauce; bring to a boil, stirring.

3. Add tofu and turn to coat in sauce. Reduce heat and simmer, turning tofu once, until sauce is very thick, about 15 minutes. Discard curry leaves, if desired.

4. Meanwhile, preheat oven to 400°F (200°C).

5. Using a slotted spatula, transfer tofu pieces, with sauce clinging to them, to prepared baking sheet, placing them at least 1 inch (2.5 cm) apart. Set any remaining sauce aside. Bake until tofu is glazed and sauce is lightly browned, about 15 minutes. Serve sprinkled with cilantro and with reserved sauce and topped with yogurt, if using.

Tofu and Snow Peas in Tamarind Ginger Curry

Serves 4

Here's a springtime dish for when snow peas are in season and winter's heavy meat-eating can give way to far gentler, though equally nutritious, tofu. The combination of tangy Thai and Indian spices is an added bonus.

•—◆—•

Tips

To julienne ginger, cut a 3-inch (7.5 cm) piece of gingerroot into thin slices. Working with 3 slices at a time, stack and cut across into thin strips.

Thai and Indian curry pastes will give very different flavors, but either works nicely in this recipe.

1 tbsp	vegetable oil	15 mL
¼ cup	julienned gingerroot (see tip, at left)	50 mL
1	onion, sliced lengthwise	1
¼ tsp	ground cinnamon	1 mL
Pinch	ground cardamom	Pinch
1 tbsp	Thai or Indian yellow curry paste or masala blend	15 mL
12 oz	firm or extra-firm tofu, drained and cut into ½-inch (1 cm) cubes	375 g
2 tsp	packed brown or palm sugar	10 mL
1 cup	coconut milk	250 mL
½ cup	tamarind water (see tip, page 199)	125 mL
¼ cup	water	50 mL
1 tbsp	fish sauce (nam pla) or ½ tsp (2 mL) salt	15 mL
1½ cups	trimmed snow peas, halved diagonally	375 mL
	Salt, optional	
	Chopped fresh mint	

1. In a large skillet, heat oil over medium heat until hot but not smoking. Add ginger and cook, stirring, until softened and fragrant, about 1 minute. Using a slotted spoon, transfer half to a bowl and set aside.

2. Add onion, cinnamon, cardamom and curry paste to pan; cook, stirring, until onion is softened and starting to brown, about 5 minutes.

3. Stir in tofu until coated with spices. Stir in brown sugar, coconut milk, tamarind water, water and fish sauce; bring to a simmer, scraping up bits stuck to pan. Reduce heat and simmer, stirring occasionally, until sauce is slightly thickened, about 10 minutes.

4. Stir in snow peas, cover and simmer until snow peas are tender-crisp, about 5 minutes. Season to taste with salt, if using, and serve sprinkled with reserved ginger and mint.

Tofu in Red Curry with Zucchini

Serves 4

Thai-inspired flavors add gustatory excitement to the easygoing tastes and soft texture of tofu and zucchini. Easy and fast, this recipe will become a favorite for a casual lunch or dinner with family.

Tips

If very ripe, flavorful tomatoes are not available, substitute 1 cup (250 mL) drained canned diced tomatoes.

If you wish, prepare the tofu through step 2, cover loosely with foil and let stand for up to 2 hours.

3 tbsp	cornstarch	45 mL
1 lb	medium tofu, drained and patted dry	500 g
2 tbsp	vegetable oil	25 mL
1	onion, chopped	1
1	zucchini, halved lengthwise and sliced diagonally	1
1 tbsp	Thai red curry paste	15 mL
2	tomatoes, diced	2
1 tsp	packed brown or palm sugar	5 mL
½ tsp	salt	2 mL
2 tbsp	chopped fresh cilantro	25 mL

1. Sift cornstarch into a shallow dish. Cut tofu into 1-inch (2.5 cm) cubes. Place on a paper towel–lined tray and blot all sides of each cube dry.

2. In a large nonstick skillet, heat oil over medium-high heat until hot but not smoking. Working in batches as necessary, roll tofu cubes in cornstarch, turning to coat all sides and dusting off excess. Immediately place in hot oil. Cook, turning carefully to brown all sides, and transfer to a dry paper towel–lined plate. Set aside. Discard any excess cornstarch.

3. Reduce heat to medium. Add onion to pan and cook, stirring, until softened and starting to brown, about 3 minutes. Add zucchini and curry paste; cook, stirring, until zucchini starts to wilt, about 1 minute. Stir in tomatoes, brown sugar and salt; cook, stirring, until tomatoes are starting to soften, about 2 minutes.

4. Return browned tofu to pan and gently fold into vegetables. Cook, without stirring, until tofu is heated through and tomatoes are saucy, about 3 minutes. Season to taste with salt. Serve sprinkled with cilantro.

Thai Green Curry with Tofu

Serves 4

Explosive green curry always works well to highlight the flavor of eggplant. Here, it's partnered with tofu instead of the better-known version with chicken, making it easier on the constitution without sacrificing any of the pleasure.

Tips

In this recipe, high-quality coconut milk will make all the difference. Be sure to buy one with minimal added water.

This is moderately spicy, but you can adjust the heat to your taste by adding more or less green curry paste.

1 tsp	packed brown or palm sugar	5 mL
1	can (14 oz/400 mL) coconut milk	1
½ cup	water	125 mL
1 tbsp	Thai green curry paste	15 mL
1 tbsp	fish sauce (nam pla) or ½ tsp (2 mL) salt	15 mL
12 oz	firm or extra-firm tofu, drained and cut into ½-inch (1 cm) cubes	375 g
1	onion, thinly sliced lengthwise	1
1	red bell pepper, chopped	1
2 cups	thinly sliced Japanese eggplant	500 mL
2 cups	snow peas, trimmed and halved diagonally	500 mL
2 tbsp	freshly squeezed lime juice	25 mL
	Salt, optional	
2 tbsp	shredded fresh Thai or sweet basil	25 mL

1. In a large skillet, combine brown sugar, coconut milk, water, curry paste and fish sauce. Bring to a boil over medium-high heat, stirring until curry paste is blended and sugar is dissolved. Boil for 1 minute.

2. Stir in tofu, onion, red pepper and eggplant. Reduce heat and simmer, stirring often, until eggplant is tender, about 10 minutes. Stir in snow peas and simmer until snow peas are tender-crisp, about 3 minutes. Stir in lime juice and season to taste with salt, if using. Serve sprinkled with basil.

Serving Suggestion

The thin, spicy sauce makes this a natural to serve over jasmine rice, sticky rice or thin rice noodles.

Thai Red Curry Tofu with Sweet Mango and Basil

Serves 4

Mango and tofu combine their charms in this Thai-inspired recipe. The sauce complements them without overpowering. It would make a lovely introduction to curry for uninitiated palates.

Tip

This is flavorful and spicy, but not fiery hot. For more heat and spice, increase the curry paste to 4 tsp (20 mL).

1 tbsp	vegetable oil	15 mL
1	onion, sliced lengthwise	1
1	red bell pepper, thinly sliced	1
2 tbsp	minced gingerroot	25 mL
½ tsp	salt	2 mL
1 tbsp	Thai red curry paste	15 mL
12 oz	extra-firm or firm tofu, drained and cut into ½-inch (1 cm) cubes	375 g
2 tsp	packed brown or palm sugar	10 mL
1 cup	coconut milk	250 mL
¾ cup	water	175 mL
1	firm ripe sweet mango, peeled and sliced	1
2 tbsp	freshly squeezed lime juice	25 mL
¼ cup	shredded fresh Thai or sweet basil	50 mL

1. In a large skillet, heat oil over medium heat. Add onion and cook, stirring, until softened and starting to turn golden, about 3 minutes. Stir in red pepper, ginger, salt and curry paste; cook, stirring, until spices are fragrant, about 1 minute.

2. Stir in tofu until coated with spices. Stir in brown sugar, coconut milk and water; bring to a simmer, scraping up bits stuck to pan. Reduce heat and simmer, stirring occasionally, until tofu is flavorful and sauce is slightly thickened, about 10 minutes.

3. Stir in mango. Increase heat to medium and cook, stirring gently, just until starting to soften, about 3 minutes. Stir in lime juice and season to taste with salt. Serve sprinkled with basil.

Tofu with Lime, Lemongrass and Coconut Curry

Serves 4

Vietnamese cuisine blends the flavors and textures of Thai and Chinese cookery in this sublimely aromatic tofu and eggplant dish that allows each ingredient to assert its own flavor while linking to the other in the lovely sauce.

Tips

To prepare lemongrass, trim off tough outer layers. Cut remaining stalk into 2-inch (5 cm) sections. Smash each piece with the broad side of a knife to bruise; this will help release the flavor when the lemongrass is cooked.

If lime leaves are not available, add ½ tsp (2 mL) finely grated lime zest with the lime juice in step 3.

1 tbsp	vegetable oil	15 mL
1	onion, sliced lengthwise	1
3	cloves garlic, minced	3
2	stalks lemongrass, chopped and bruised (see tip, at left)	2
2	wild lime leaves (see tip, at left)	2
½ tsp	salt	2 mL
1 tbsp	Indian yellow curry paste or masala blend	15 mL
2 cups	cubed eggplant (½-inch/1 cm cubes)	500 mL
1 cup	coconut milk	250 mL
½ cup	vegetable stock or water	125 mL
12 oz	firm or extra-firm tofu, drained and cut into ¾-inch (2 cm) cubes	375 g
2 tbsp	freshly squeezed lime juice	25 mL
2	green onions, thinly sliced	2
¼ cup	thin strips red bell pepper	50 mL

1. In a large skillet, heat oil over medium heat. Add onion and cook, stirring, until softened and starting to turn golden, about 3 minutes. Stir in garlic, lemongrass, lime leaves, salt and curry paste; cook, stirring, until softened and fragrant, about 1 minute.

2. Stir in eggplant until coated with spices. Add coconut milk and stock; bring to a simmer, scraping up bits stuck to pan.

3. Stir in tofu. Reduce heat and simmer, stirring often, until eggplant is tender and sauce is slightly thickened, about 10 minutes. Discard lemongrass and lime leaves, if desired. Stir in lime juice and season to taste with salt. Serve sprinkled with green onions and red pepper.

Tofu, Eggplant and Basil in Tamarind Curry

Serves 4

This tangy and pleasant vegetarian dish has a trace of heat that is softened by the soothing tofu and the creamy eggplant. It is saucy, which makes it a good partner for rice, and has a well-balanced list of ingredients that nourish as they tease the palate.

Tips

If you like a mild curry, omit the chile pepper; if you like it hotter, use 2.

To make tamarind water, break a 2-oz (60 g) piece of block tamarind into small pieces and place in a heatproof bowl. Pour in 1 cup (250 mL) boiling water and let stand until very soft, about 30 minutes, or for up to 8 hours. Press through a fine-mesh sieve, discarding seeds and skins.

2 tbsp	vegetable oil	25 mL
1 tsp	mustard seeds	5 mL
1/2 tsp	fenugreek seeds	2 mL
1	hot green chile pepper, chopped	1
2 cups	diced eggplant (peeled, if desired)	500 mL
1/2 tsp	salt	2 mL
1/2 cup	Basic Gravy (see recipe, page 7)	125 mL
2 tbsp	packed brown or palm sugar	25 mL
1 cup	tamarind water (see tip, at left)	250 mL
1/2 cup	water	125 mL
12 oz	firm or extra-firm tofu, drained and cut into 3/4-inch (2 cm) cubes	375 g
1	tomato, chopped	1
1/4 cup	chopped fresh basil	50 mL

1. In a large skillet, heat oil over medium heat until hot but not smoking. Add mustard seeds and fenugreek seeds; cook, stirring, until slightly darker but not yet popping, about 30 seconds.

2. Add chile pepper, eggplant and salt; cook, stirring, until eggplant starts to soften, about 2 minutes. Add gravy and cook, stirring, for 1 minute. Stir in brown sugar, tamarind water and water; bring to a boil.

3. Stir in tofu. Reduce heat and simmer, stirring often, until sauce is slightly thickened, about 3 minutes. Add tomato and cook, stirring gently, until eggplant is tender and tofu is heated through, about 5 minutes. Season to taste with salt. Serve sprinkled with basil.

Tofu and Spinach in Tomato Curry

Serves 4

Tofu and spinach in the same dish — lunch does not get much healthier, or easier to prepare, than this. And just for good measure, there is a pleasantly spiced sauce to make it attractive. Add some rice or noodles on the side, and you're all set.

Tip

A deep skillet helps to prevent too much splatter while the tomatoes and gravy simmer.

Variation

For some punch, add 1 hot chile pepper, minced, with the curry leaves and substitute torn arugula for half the spinach.

1 tbsp	vegetable oil, divided	15 mL
2 tsp	mustard seeds	10 mL
½ tsp	cumin seeds	2 mL
½ tsp	fenugreek seeds	2 mL
10	curry leaves	10
½ cup	Basic Gravy (see recipe, page 7)	125 mL
1½ cups	canned diced tomatoes with juice	375 mL
12 oz	extra-firm tofu, drained and cut into sticks	500 g
¼ tsp	salt	1 mL
6 cups	fresh spinach (about 6 oz/175 g), trimmed	1.5 L
	Chopped fresh cilantro	

1. In a large, deep skillet, heat oil over medium heat until hot but not smoking. Add mustard seeds, cumin seeds and fenugreek seeds; cook, stirring, until slightly darker but not yet popping, about 30 seconds. Add curry leaves and gravy; cook, stirring, for 1 minute. Stir in tomatoes and bring to a boil, stirring. Boil for 1 minute.

2. Gently fold in tofu and salt. Reduce heat and simmer, stirring gently once, until tofu is hot and flavorful and sauce is slightly thickened, about 5 minutes. Gradually add spinach, one handful at a time, folding just until wilted. Season to taste with salt. Serve sprinkled with cilantro.

Serving Suggestion

For a vegetarian feast, serve with Dal Fry (page 186), Eggplant (Brinjal) Coconut Curry (page 226) and Potato and Green Peas Rice Biryani (page 252).

Saffron Curry Mushrooms and Tofu

Serves 4 to 6

Saffron, exotic mushrooms and calorific cream turn this recipe into a luxury, yet an affordable and relatively sinless one, as tofu itself is inexpensive and easy on the calories. This one is for a special occasion or an elegant dinner party.

Tips

Avoid very dark mushrooms, such as portobello, as they will discolor the sauce.

The whipping cream is essential to accent the flavor of the saffron and create a velvety texture. Don't be tempted to substitute a lower-fat cream in this one.

Medium tofu lends a soft texture to this dish that matches the mushrooms. For a contrasting texture, use firm tofu. If using medium, pat it dry after draining and avoid stirring too much, as this will cause it to break up.

1/8 tsp	saffron threads	0.5 mL
3/4 cup	vegetable stock, heated	175 mL
1 tsp	cumin seeds	5 mL
1/2 tsp	fennel seeds	2 mL
2 tbsp	butter or vegetable oil	25 mL
2	cloves garlic, minced	2
1	onion, chopped	1
1 tsp	garam masala	5 mL
1/2 tsp	ground coriander	2 mL
1/4 tsp	salt	1 mL
1/4 tsp	hot pepper flakes	1 mL
12 oz	exotic mushrooms (shiitake, cremini, oyster, king, etc.), trimmed and sliced	375 g
1/4 cup	dry white wine	50 mL
1/2 cup	whipping (35%) cream	125 mL
12 oz	medium or firm tofu, drained and cut into 1/2-inch (1 cm) cubes	375 g
	Chopped fresh cilantro	

1. In a measuring cup or bowl, combine saffron and stock; let stand for 15 minutes.

2. In a dry large skillet over medium-high heat, toast cumin seeds and fennel seeds, stirring constantly, until slightly darker and fragrant, about 30 seconds.

3. Add butter and swirl to coat pan. Add garlic, onion, garam masala, coriander, salt and hot pepper flakes; cook, stirring, until onion starts to soften, about 2 minutes. Add mushrooms and cook, stirring often, until liquid is released and mushrooms are browned, about 8 minutes.

4. Add wine and bring to a boil, scraping up bits stuck to pan. Stir in stock mixture and cream; bring to a boil. Boil for 2 minutes.

5. Gently stir in tofu. Reduce heat and simmer gently, stirring occasionally, until tofu is flavorful and sauce is slightly thickened, about 10 minutes. Season to taste with salt. Serve sprinkled with cilantro.

Curry Scrambled Eggs and Mushrooms

Serves 4 to 6

Scrambled eggs are a universal favorite, and here they become gourmet with added mushrooms and an interesting mix of spices. Good for brunch, good anytime.

Tip

Use any type of mushrooms you like, the more flavorful, the better. Do steer clear of the very dark portobellos, as they will discolor the eggs.

8	eggs	8
2 tbsp	butter or vegetable oil	25 mL
2 cups	sliced mushrooms	500 mL
½ tsp	salt	2 mL
¼ tsp	ground cumin	1 mL
⅛ tsp	ground turmeric	0.5 mL
2	cloves garlic, minced	2
1	hot green chile pepper, minced	1
1 tsp	minced gingerroot	5 mL
2 tbsp	chopped fresh cilantro or parsley	25 mL
	Lemon wedges	

1. In a bowl, whisk eggs until blended, but not foamy. Set aside.
2. In a large nonstick skillet, melt butter over medium-high heat. Add mushrooms, salt, cumin and turmeric; cook, stirring, until mushrooms have released their liquid and are starting to brown, about 5 minutes. Add garlic, chile pepper and ginger; cook, stirring, until softened and fragrant, about 1 minute.
3. Reduce heat to medium-low and stir in eggs. Cook, stirring gently, until just set, about 2 minutes. Serve sprinkled with cilantro and garnished with lemon wedges to squeeze over top.

Serving Suggestion

Serve with Tomato Chutney (page 42) or Cucumber Raita (page 45), or with sliced fresh tomatoes on the side.

Egg Vindaloo Curry

Serves 4 to 8

Tart and aromatic, this hard-cooked egg recipe will redefine that lowly ingredient. It sits well on a brunch buffet, as it actually improves in taste at room temperature.

• ◆ •

Tip

This method outlines how to properly hard-cook eggs. "Hard-boiled" is in fact a misnomer, as boiling eggs in the shell leads to rubbery, tough eggs with that dreadful gray ring around the yolk.

8	eggs	8
	Cold water	
1 tbsp	vegetable oil	15 mL
1	small onion, finely chopped	1
2	cloves garlic, minced	2
1/4 tsp	ground cinnamon	1 mL
Pinch	ground cardamom	Pinch
Pinch	ground cloves	Pinch
1 tsp	vindaloo or Indian yellow curry paste or masala blend	5 mL
2 tbsp	red or white wine vinegar	25 mL
1 cup	vegetable or chicken stock	250 mL
1/4 cup	tomato paste	50 mL

1. Place eggs in a large saucepan and add enough cold water to cover by about 1 inch (2.5 cm). Bring to a boil over high heat. Remove from heat, cover and let stand for 15 minutes. Place pan in the sink and run cold water into pan until water is completely cold. Let eggs stand in cold water, refreshing as necessary, until chilled. Drain and peel off shells. Cut eggs in half lengthwise and set aside.

2. In a large saucepan, heat oil over medium heat. Add onion and cook, stirring, until starting to soften, about 2 minutes. Add garlic, cinnamon, cardamom, cloves and curry paste; cook, stirring, until onion is softened and starting to brown, about 3 minutes.

3. Stir in vinegar and bring to a boil, stirring. Stir in stock and tomato paste; bring to a boil, stirring until blended. Reduce heat and simmer gently until flavors are blended, about 5 minutes.

4. Add eggs, cut side up, and spoon sauce over top. Simmer, basting eggs often with sauce, until eggs are heated through and sauce is slightly thickened, about 10 minutes.

Nepalese Potato, Cauliflower and Egg Curry

Serves 4

An excellent lunch or light dinner item, this recipe combines potato and cauliflower with boiled eggs. It is easy to make and can be prepared in advance through step 2, allowing for a last-minute finish simply by reheating and proceeding with step 3. It comes to us from Jennifer's friend Annie Scherz.

Tips

To hard-cook eggs, follow step 1 on page 203.

Once added to the potato mixture, the yolks will fall out of the whites and blend in, creating a bit of a creamy texture.

2 tbsp	vegetable oil	25 mL
1 tsp	fenugreek seeds	5 mL
1 tsp	fennel seeds	5 mL
4	cloves garlic, minced	4
2 tsp	curry powder	10 mL
3/4 tsp	salt	3 mL
1/4 tsp	cayenne pepper, or to taste	1 mL
2	boiling or all-purpose potatoes, cut into 1/2-inch (1 cm) cubes	2
1/2 cup	water	125 mL
2 cups	small cauliflower florets	500 mL
4	hard-cooked eggs, peeled and quartered lengthwise	4

1. In a large skillet, heat oil over medium heat until hot but not smoking. Add fenugreek seeds and fennel seeds; cook, stirring, until starting to pop, about 1 minute. Add garlic, curry powder, salt and cayenne; cook, stirring, until blended and fragrant, about 1 minute.

2. Stir in potatoes until coated in spices. Add water and cover quickly. Reduce heat to medium-low and simmer, stirring once, until potatoes are slightly tender, about 10 minutes. Stir in cauliflower, cover and simmer until potatoes and cauliflower are almost tender, about 7 minutes.

3. Uncover and increase heat to medium. Stir in eggs and simmer, stirring gently, just until liquid evaporates, potatoes start to brown and eggs are heated through, about 5 minutes. Season to taste with salt.

Serving Suggestion

Serve on its own or wrapped in Chickpea Flatbread (page 271), as a filling in Easy Masala Dosa (page 276) or in store-bought roti skins or flour tortillas with a raita of your choice (see pages 44–45).

Spicy Tomato Curry with Poached Eggs

Serves 2 to 4

Here's *huevos rancheros,* curry-style. The eggs are poached in a flavorful, juicy sauce and topped with yogurt for a finish that is lustrous and slurpable. It's a superb egg dish that works with toast for a festive breakfast or as part of a multi-dish Indian meal.

Tips

If a flavorful, ripe tomato is not available, substitute 1½ cups (375 mL) canned diced tomatoes with juice and omit the water. Add the canned tomatoes after the gravy.

Cracking each egg into a separate bowl may seem tedious, but it helps you get them into the sauce quickly, allowing them to cook at the same time.

1 tbsp	vegetable oil	15 mL
1	small onion, finely chopped	1
2 or 3	hot green chile peppers, minced	2 or 3
1	large ripe tomato, chopped	1
1 cup	Basic Gravy (see recipe, page 7)	250 mL
½ cup	water	125 mL
4	eggs	4
	Salt	
	Chopped fresh cilantro	
¼ tsp	garam masala	1 mL
	Plain yogurt	

1. In a nonstick skillet, heat oil over medium heat. Add onion and cook, stirring, until starting to soften, about 2 minutes. Reduce heat to medium-low and cook, stirring often, until very soft and golden brown, about 5 minutes.

2. Increase heat to medium and add chile peppers and tomato. Cook, stirring, until tomato is starting to soften, about 2 minutes. Add gravy and cook, stirring, for 2 minutes. Stir in water and bring to a boil. Reduce heat and boil gently, stirring often, until slightly thickened and flavorful, about 5 minutes.

3. Crack each egg into a separate small bowl. Carefully drop eggs into simmering sauce, leaving as much space as possible between each. Reduce heat to low, cover and simmer just until whites are set and yolks are cooked to desired doneness, 5 to 8 minutes. Season to taste with salt. Serve sprinkled with cilantro and garam masala and topped with yogurt.

Lorraine's Spicy Curry Omelet

Serves 2

Jennifer's friend Lorraine Collaço cooked up this zingy omelet for breakfast on a weekend visit. Lorraine is such a terrific houseguest that not only did she cook breakfast, she brought her own chiles and curry leaves. Lorraine suggests that you enjoy this with a hot cup of tea.

1 tbsp	butter or vegetable oil	15 mL
1 to 3	hot green chile peppers, minced	1 to 3
2 tbsp	diced onion	25 mL
5	curry leaves, minced	5
1	small tomato, diced	1
1 tbsp	minced fresh cilantro	15 mL
1/4 tsp	salt	1 mL
4	eggs, beaten	4

1. In a small nonstick skillet, melt butter over medium heat. Add chile peppers, onion and curry leaves; cook, stirring, until onion is soft, about 1 minute. Add tomato and cook, stirring, until softened, about 2 minutes. Add cilantro and salt; cook, stirring, for 15 seconds.

2. Reduce heat to low. Add eggs and cook, stirring gently with a rubber spatula, until eggs are about half set, about 2 minutes. Cook, without stirring, just until eggs are set, about 3 minutes. Flip omelet into a roll or divide in half and slide flat onto a plate.

Palak Paneer in Tomato Curry with Spinach

Serves 4

Paneer, an Indian-style cottage cheese, is often used in the subcontinent to add substance to vegetarian dishes. Here, it partners spinach and a simple curry sauce in a dish that can accompany just about any other vegetarian or meat curry for a delightful weekday dinner.

1 tbsp	vegetable oil	15 mL
1 cup	diced tomatoes	250 mL
3/4 cup	very finely chopped spinach	175 mL
1/2 cup	Basic Gravy (see recipe, page 7)	125 mL
1/2 cup	milk	125 mL
1 1/2 cups	cubed paneer	375 mL
	Salt	

1. In a skillet, heat oil over medium heat. Add tomatoes and cook, stirring, until starting to soften, about 1 minute. Add spinach and gravy; cook, stirring, until saucy, 1 to 2 minutes. Stir in milk and heat just until bubbling.

2. Add paneer and gently fold into sauce. Reduce heat to medium-low and cook gently, stirring, until piping hot, 1 to 2 minutes. Season to taste with salt.

Matar Paneer Curry with Green Peas

Serves 4

The combination of plain-tasting cheese and peas sounds rather dull, until you begin adding the recommended spices, when it becomes a treat. Never underestimate the power of spice: empires have been based on it.

Variation

If paneer is not available, substitute an equal amount of firm tofu.

3 tbsp	vegetable oil	45 mL
1 tbsp	all-purpose flour	15 mL
7 oz	paneer, cut into $\frac{1}{2}$-inch (1 cm) cubes (about 1$\frac{1}{2}$ cups/375 mL)	210 g
$\frac{1}{2}$ tsp	cumin seeds	2 mL
1 cup	diced tomatoes	250 mL
2	hot green chile peppers, chopped	2
$\frac{1}{2}$ cup	Basic Gravy (see recipe, page 7)	125 mL
$\frac{1}{2}$ cup	water	125 mL
1 cup	frozen green peas, thawed	250 mL
	Salt	
	Chopped fresh cilantro	

1. In a large skillet, heat oil over medium-high heat. Spread flour in a shallow dish. Dip one side of each paneer cube in flour and place floured side in hot oil, in batches as necessary. Cook, without turning, until well browned. Using tongs, transfer paneer cubes to a plate, browned side up. Set aside.

2. Return the skillet to medium heat and heat for 15 seconds. Add cumin seeds and cook, stirring, until starting to pop, about 1 minute. Add tomatoes and cook, stirring, until starting to soften, about 2 minutes. Add chile peppers and gravy; cook, stirring, until saucy and bubbling, 2 to 3 minutes. Stir in water and bring to a boil.

3. Stir in peas and return paneer cubes to pan, browned side up. Reduce heat and simmer, without stirring, until piping hot, about 2 minutes. Season to taste with salt. Serve sprinkled with cilantro.

Pyaza Paneer and Navy Bean Curry

Serves 4

Beans, cheese and lots of onion combine for a hearty and versatile dish. Served with rice, it provides a satisfying lunch or light supper.

Variation

If paneer is not available, substitute an equal amount of firm tofu or pressed dry-curd cottage cheese. If using dry-curd cottage cheese, break into pieces and be very careful when stirring to prevent it from breaking up too much.

2 tbsp	vegetable oil	25 mL
1 cup	diced onion	250 mL
1 cup	diced tomatoes	250 mL
1 tbsp	minced garlic	15 mL
1 tbsp	minced gingerroot	15 mL
1 tsp	ground cumin	5 mL
1 tsp	ground coriander	5 mL
½ tsp	salt	2 mL
¼ tsp	ground turmeric	1 mL
1 cup	cooked or canned navy (cannellini) beans, drained and rinsed	250 mL
1 cup	boiled cubed peeled potato (½-inch/1 cm cubes)	250 mL
1 cup	water	250 mL
5 oz	paneer, cut into ½-inch (1 cm) cubes (about 1 cup/250 mL)	150 g
½ cup	chopped fresh cilantro	125 mL

1. In a skillet, heat oil over medium-high heat. Add onion and cook, stirring, until starting to soften, about 2 minutes. Add tomatoes and cook, stirring, until starting to soften, about 2 minutes.

2. Reduce heat to medium. Add garlic, ginger, cumin, coriander, salt and turmeric; cook, stirring, until softened and fragrant, 1 to 2 minutes. Stir in navy beans, potato and water; cook, stirring gently, until piping hot and bubbling, 2 to 3 minutes.

3. Gently fold in paneer and cilantro. Reduce heat to low and simmer, stirring gently, until paneer is heated through, about 3 minutes. Season to taste with salt.

Curried Paneer with Mixed Peppers and Zucchini

Serves 4

This composed dish, prepared in two easy steps, tops a curried cheese base with freshly fried peppers and zucchini that are lively with chiles. It can be served simply or as a worthy element of an articulated buffet of curries and special rices.

Tip

Cut paneer into sticks 1½ inches long by ½ inch square (4 by 1 by 1 cm) or into thinner sticks 1½ inches long by ¼ inch square (4 by 0.5 by 0.5 cm).

2 tbsp	vegetable oil, divided	25 mL
1	onion, finely chopped	1
3	cloves garlic, minced	3
1 tbsp	minced gingerroot	15 mL
1 tsp	ground cumin	5 mL
1 tsp	ground coriander	5 mL
½ tsp	salt	2 mL
¼ tsp	ground turmeric	1 mL
1½ cups	paneer sticks (about 8 oz/250 g) (see tip, at left)	375 mL
½ cup	water	125 mL
2 tbsp	freshly squeezed lemon juice	25 mL
2 to 3	hot green chile peppers, thinly sliced	2 to 3
1	zucchini, thinly sliced	1
1	red bell pepper, thinly sliced	1
1 tsp	garam masala	5 mL
	Chopped fresh cilantro	

1. In a large nonstick skillet, heat half the oil over medium heat. Add onion and cook, stirring, until starting to soften, about 2 minutes. Add garlic, ginger, cumin, coriander, salt and turmeric; cook, stirring, until onion is softened and spices are fragrant, about 2 minutes.

2. Add paneer and stir gently until coated with spices. Add water and lemon juice; bring to a boil, scraping up bits stuck to pan. Reduce heat and simmer, stirring gently occasionally, until liquid is almost evaporated, about 5 minutes. Transfer to a shallow serving dish.

3. Add remaining oil to skillet and heat over medium-high heat. Add chile peppers, zucchini and red pepper; cook, stirring, until just tender and slightly browned, about 10 minutes. Season to taste with salt. Spoon over paneer in dish. Serve sprinkled with garam masala and cilantro.

Paneer with Chickpeas in Creamy Tomato Curry

Serves 4

Cheese and chickpeas, a double dose of vegetarian proteins, are coddled in a rich tomato curry sauce and finished with cream. It's luxuriously suitable for a festive table.

Tip

Whipping cream adds a delightfully rich taste and texture; however, a lower-fat cream with a minimum of 10% milk fat can be used instead.

1 tbsp	vegetable oil	15 mL
3	green onions, sliced	3
½ tsp	ground cumin	2 mL
2 tbsp	Indian yellow curry paste or masala blend	25 mL
1 cup	canned crushed (ground) tomatoes	250 mL
½ cup	water	125 mL
5 oz	paneer, cut into ½-inch (1 cm) cubes (about 1 cup/250 mL)	150 g
1 cup	cooked or canned chickpeas, drained and rinsed	250 mL
⅓ cup	whipping (35%) cream	75 mL
	Chopped fresh cilantro	

1. In a skillet, heat oil over medium heat. Add green onions, cumin and curry paste; cook, stirring, until onions are softened and spices are fragrant, about 2 minutes. Stir in tomatoes and water; bring to a boil, scraping up bits stuck to pan.
2. Stir in paneer and chickpeas. Reduce heat and simmer, stirring often, until hot and flavorful, about 10 minutes. Stir in cream until heated through. Serve sprinkled with cilantro.

Vegetables

— ◆ —

continued on next page

Roasted Curried Asparagus with Warm Vinaigrette

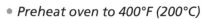

Serves 4 to 6

Here's a zesty new way to enjoy asparagus, the affordable luxury vegetable of all gourmets. It gets baked, instead of the more usual steaming, but turns out memorably tender-crisp and ever so flavorful.

Tip

If you prefer to use a coarse sea salt, such as fleur de sel, don't add the remaining salt to the dressing; instead, sprinkle a small amount over the finished dish to get the maximum effect.

- Preheat oven to 400°F (200°C)
- Large shallow baking dish

1 tsp	curry powder	5 mL
½ tsp	salt, divided	2 mL
Pinch	cayenne pepper	Pinch
¼ cup	olive oil, divided	50 mL
1 lb	asparagus, trimmed	500 g
1	small clove garlic, minced	1
3 tbsp	white wine vinegar	45 mL
½ tsp	Dijon or dry mustard	2 mL
Pinch	granulated sugar	Pinch
	Freshly ground black pepper	
	Chopped fresh cilantro	

1. In a small bowl, combine curry powder, half the salt, the cayenne and 1 tbsp (15 mL) of the oil. Drizzle over asparagus in baking dish and toss gently to coat.

2. Roast in preheated oven, stirring once, until asparagus is tender-crisp, about 15 minutes.

3. Meanwhile, in a small skillet, heat remaining oil over medium-low heat. Add garlic and cook, stirring, until softened and fragrant, about 2 minutes. Remove from heat. Whisk in vinegar and mustard. Season with remaining salt, sugar and pepper to taste. Keep warm.

4. Transfer asparagus to a serving platter and drizzle with warm dressing. Serve sprinkled with cilantro.

Malaysian Banana Curry

Serves 4 to 6

Delightfully fruity and fresh, this sweet-spicy banana side dish will enhance any menu, both as a side dish and as a condiment. It's best served with savory main courses for meaningful contrast.

Tips

Traditionally, this type of curry is made with unripe bananas. This version, using ripe but firm bananas, adds a level of sweetness that we North Americans expect in our bananas.

This is lovely served hot, but leftovers are surprisingly delicious cold and even served as a chutney.

1 tbsp	vegetable oil	15 mL
1	stick cinnamon, about 2 inches (5 cm) long	1
1 tsp	fennel seeds	5 mL
½ tsp	fenugreek seeds	2 mL
1	onion, finely chopped	1
1	Thai bird chile pepper, minced	1
1 tbsp	minced gingerroot	15 mL
5	curry leaves	5
½ tsp	salt	2 mL
⅛ tsp	ground turmeric	0.5 mL
1	can (14 oz/400 mL) coconut milk	1
4	firm ripe bananas	4
3 tbsp	freshly squeezed lime juice	45 mL
	Chopped fresh mint and/or cilantro	

1. In a large skillet, heat oil over medium heat until hot but not smoking. Add cinnamon, fennel seeds and fenugreek seeds; cook, stirring, until seeds are toasted and fragrant but not yet popping, about 30 seconds. Add onion and cook, stirring, until starting to soften, about 2 minutes. Add chile pepper, ginger, curry leaves, salt and turmeric; cook, stirring, until onion is soft and spices are fragrant, about 1 minute.

2. Add coconut milk and bring to a boil, scraping up bits stuck to pan. Reduce heat and simmer, stirring occasionally, until reduced by about half, about 10 minutes.

3. Meanwhile, cut bananas into thick slices and sprinkle with lime juice. Add to pan and fold gently until coated in sauce. Simmer, stirring very gently once or twice, just until bananas are heated through but still hold their shape, about 3 minutes. Discard cinnamon stick, if desired. Season to taste with salt. Serve sprinkled with mint and/or cilantro.

Curried Plantain with Raisins and Pecans

Serves 4

Banana's sturdier, less sweet cousin, the plantain, is widely available, and ever so pleasing when properly cooked. Give it its due and enjoy this offbeat delight, made festive with the added appeal of raisins and pecans.

1 lb	plantain (about 2)	500 g
2 tbsp	vegetable oil	25 mL
1 tsp	mustard seeds	5 mL
1	onion, sliced lengthwise	1
3	cloves garlic, minced	3
1 tbsp	minced gingerroot	15 mL
½ tsp	salt	2 mL
½ tsp	ground turmeric	2 mL
½ tsp	hot pepper flakes	2 mL
½ tsp	cracked black peppercorns	2 mL
¼ cup	chopped pecans	50 mL
2 tbsp	raisins	25 mL
½ cup	boiling water	125 mL

1. Peel plantain and cut into ¼-inch (0.5 cm) thick rounds. Immerse in a bowl of cold water to prevent discoloration. Let soak for 2 minutes. Drain and refresh water two more times, letting soak for 2 minutes each time. Drain and set aside.

2. In a large skillet, heat oil over medium-high heat until hot but not smoking. Add mustard seeds and cook, stirring, until starting to pop, about 1 minute. Add onion and cook, stirring, until starting to soften, about 2 minutes. Add garlic, ginger, salt, turmeric, hot pepper flakes and peppercorns; cook, stirring, until softened and fragrant, about 1 minute.

3. Stir in reserved plantain and cook, stirring gently often, until tender and browned, about 5 minutes. Add pecans, raisins and boiling water; cook, stirring, for 1 minute. Season to taste with salt.

Curried Green Beans Masala

Serves 4 to 6

Cooked through but still textured green beans in a fragrant sauce make for an easy side course to more substantial curries. The beans will get softer the longer they wait in their sauce, so they should be served as soon as they are ready.

Tips

Blanching the beans before adding them to the sauce ensures that they will have a nice, tender-crisp texture. Acid in the tomatoes can prevent them from softening.

If you want to blanch the beans ahead of time, rinse immediately in cold water until chilled after step 1. Drain, cover and refrigerate for up to 1 day.

8 oz	green beans, trimmed	250 g
1 tbsp	vegetable oil	15 mL
1 tsp	mustard seeds	5 mL
½ tsp	cumin seeds	2 mL
1	large tomato, diced	1
10	fresh curry leaves	10
½ cup	Basic Gravy (see recipe, page 7)	125 mL
¼ cup	water	50 mL
	Salt	

1. In a saucepan of boiling salted water, cook green beans just until bright green and slightly tender, about 3 minutes. Drain and set aside.

2. In a large skillet, heat oil over medium heat until hot but not smoking. Add mustard seeds and cumin seeds; cook, stirring, until toasted and fragrant but not yet popping, about 30 seconds. Add tomato and curry leaves; cook, stirring, until tomato is softened, about 2 minutes.

3. Add gravy and cook, stirring, for 1 minute. Add water and bring to a boil, stirring. Reduce heat and boil gently for 3 minutes. Add green beans and cook, stirring often, just until tender-crisp, about 3 minutes. Season to taste with salt.

Serving Suggestion

Serve with Filipino Chicken Adobo (page 59), Meatballs in Zesty Coconut Curry (page 105) or Spicy Kovalam Fish Curry (page 154). For a vegetarian option, serve with Yellow Lentil Curry with Vegetables (page 188) or Tofu with Lime, Lemongrass and Coconut Curry (page 198).

Green Curry and Basil Green Beans

Serves 4 to 6

Thai-style green beans means fiery green curry, coconut milk and all the other usual suspects of Thai curries. It ends up as a delicious vegetable side course that will eclipse the main course. Beans have never had it so good.

Tip

This version definitely has some kick. For a milder taste, reduce the curry paste to 1 tsp (5 mL).

1 tbsp	vegetable oil	15 mL
1	small onion, sliced lengthwise	1
2 tsp	Thai green curry paste	10 mL
1/2 cup	coconut milk	125 mL
1/2 cup	water	125 mL
2 tsp	fish sauce (nam pla) or 1/4 tsp (1 mL) salt	10 mL
8 oz	green beans, trimmed and halved	250 g
2 tbsp	chopped fresh Thai or sweet basil	25 mL

1. In a saucepan, heat oil over medium heat. Add onion and curry paste; cook, stirring, until onion is softened, about 5 minutes. Add coconut milk, water and fish sauce; bring to a boil.

2. Add green beans, cover, reduce heat and simmer until green beans are tender-crisp, about 5 minutes. Stir in basil.

Serving Suggestion

Create a Thai feast with Thai Sweet-and-Sour Curried Pork (page 124), Green Mango Fish Curry (page 157), Marinated Cucumber Carrot Salad (page 22) and jasmine rice.

Cashew Green Beans with Mustard Seeds

Serves 8

Green beans and cashews are such a good match that they taste wonderful all on their own. Served with these perky spices, they are unbeatable.

1 lb	green beans, cut into 1-inch (2.5 cm) pieces	500 g
2 tbsp	vegetable oil	25 mL
1 tsp	mustard seeds	5 mL
1	onion, thinly sliced	1
6	cloves garlic, minced	6
½ tsp	ground turmeric	2 mL
½ tsp	hot pepper flakes	2 mL
½ tsp	cracked black peppercorns	2 mL
½ tsp	salt	2 mL
½ cup	boiling water	125 mL
¼ cup	chopped unsalted roasted cashews	50 mL

1. In a saucepan of boiling water, cook green beans just until bright green, about 2 minutes. Drain and set aside.

2. In a large skillet, heat oil over medium-high heat until hot but not smoking. Add mustard seeds and cook, stirring, until starting to pop, about 1 minute. Add onion and cook, stirring, until starting to soften, about 2 minutes. Add garlic, turmeric, hot pepper flakes, peppercorns and salt; cook, stirring, until softened and fragrant, about 1 minute.

3. Stir in reserved green beans and boiling water. Reduce heat to medium and cook, stirring often, until beans are tender-crisp and most of the liquid is evaporated, about 5 minutes. Stir in cashews. Season to taste with salt.

> ### Serving Suggestion
>
> Serve with Chicken Vindaloo Curry (page 70), Beef Curry with Many Onions (page 92) or Spicy Pork Curry with Ginger (page 122).

Broccoli in Creamy Tomato Curry

Serves 4 to 6

We believe that anything we can do to turn ordinary broccoli into something special is worth the effort. This recipe accomplishes the mission and does so quickly and easily.

Tip

A lower-fat yogurt will work, but avoid fat-free yogurt and any with added gelatin. When cooked, gelatin in yogurt can cause the yogurt to split and create a curdled texture.

1 tsp	cornstarch	5 mL
½ cup	plain yogurt (not fat-free) (see tip, at left)	125 mL
1 tbsp	vegetable oil	15 mL
1 tsp	minced hot green chile pepper	5 mL
8	curry leaves	8
1 tsp	cumin seeds	5 mL
½ tsp	fenugreek seeds	2 mL
1	bunch broccoli, cut into small florets and stems sliced (about 5 cups/1.25 L)	1
¼ cup	water	50 mL
½ cup	Basic Gravy (see recipe, page 7)	125 mL
1 cup	milk	250 mL
½ tsp	salt, or to taste	2 mL

1. In a bowl, stir cornstarch and yogurt until blended and smooth. Set aside at room temperature.

2. In a saucepan, heat oil over medium heat until hot but not smoking. Add chile pepper, curry leaves, cumin seeds and fenugreek seeds; cook, stirring, until seeds start to pop, about 1 minute. Add broccoli and water; cover quickly. Cook, covered, until broccoli is starting to soften, about 5 minutes.

3. Add gravy and cook, stirring, for 30 seconds. Gradually stir in milk and bring to a simmer. Reduce heat and simmer gently, stirring occasionally, until broccoli is tender-crisp and sauce is slightly thickened, about 3 minutes.

4. Reduce heat to low and stir in yogurt mixture. Cook, stirring, until slightly thickened, about 2 minutes. Season to taste with salt.

Dry Curry of Shredded Cabbage

Serves 4 to 6

Here's an Asian version of sauerkraut, that European standby cabbage side course. Like its European cousin, this cabbage works best with pork or fowl dishes, especially duck.

Tip

Leftovers can be tossed with a white wine vinaigrette or lemon juice salad dressing for an interesting twist on coleslaw.

2 tbsp	vegetable oil	25 mL
1 tbsp	mustard seeds	15 mL
1 tsp	cumin seeds	5 mL
1 tsp	fenugreek seeds	5 mL
½ tsp	fennel seeds	2 mL
1	onion, sliced lengthwise	1
3	cloves garlic, minced	3
1	hot green chile pepper, minced	1
½ tsp	salt	2 mL
½ tsp	ground turmeric	2 mL
4 cups	shredded green cabbage (about ½ small head)	1 L
2 tbsp	water	25 mL
2 tbsp	freshly squeezed lime or lemon juice	25 mL

1. In a large skillet, heat oil over medium heat until hot but not smoking. Add mustard seeds, cumin seeds, fenugreek seeds and fennel seeds; cook, stirring, until slightly darker but not yet popping, about 30 seconds. Add onion and cook, stirring, until softened, about 3 minutes. Add garlic, chile pepper, salt and turmeric; cook, stirring, until onion is soft and starting to brown, about 5 minutes.

2. Add cabbage and water; cook, stirring often, until evenly coated in spices and wilted to desired consistency, about 3 minutes for tender-crisp. Add lime juice and toss to coat evenly. Season to taste with salt.

Cauliflower in Tomato Curry

Serves 4 to 6

Al dente cauliflower in a fragrant tomato sauce will tastefully accompany any meat or fish curry in your repertoire. A must-try recipe when the floral vegetable is in season.

Tip

If very ripe fresh tomatoes aren't available, substitute 1½ cups (375 mL) drained canned diced tomatoes. Underripe tomatoes won't add enough flavor or moisture.

1 tbsp	vegetable oil	15 mL
2 tsp	mustard seeds	10 mL
1 tsp	cumin seeds	5 mL
4 cups	small cauliflower florets (about 1 small head)	1 L
½ cup	water	125 mL
1½ cups	chopped tomatoes	375 mL
1 tsp	minced hot green chile pepper	5 mL
8	curry leaves	8
½ cup	Basic Gravy (see recipe, page 7)	125 mL
½ tsp	salt, or to taste	2 mL

1. In a saucepan, heat oil over medium heat until hot but not smoking. Add mustard seeds and cumin seeds; cook, stirring, until seeds start to pop, about 1 minute.
2. Add cauliflower and water; cover quickly. Cook, covered, until cauliflower is starting to soften, about 5 minutes.
3. Uncover and add tomatoes, chile pepper and curry leaves. Cook, stirring, until tomatoes are softened, about 2 minutes. Stir in gravy and cook, stirring once, until cauliflower is tender, about 5 minutes. Season to taste with salt.

Serving Suggestion

Serve with Chicken Korma Curry (page 60), Curried Lamb with Sweet Corn and Spinach (page 135), Grilled Fish Tikka (page 152) or Dal Curry with Chiles and Coconut (page 187).

Golden Curried Cauliflower with Green Peas

Serves 4 to 6

Cauliflower is a big favorite in India, and they have invented many recipes to honor it. This one is brightly colorful and textured, especially if not overcooked.

Tip

When buying whole and ground spices, purchase from a source that has a high turnover to make sure you are getting fresh spices with maximum flavor. Purchase small amounts at a time and store in an airtight jar or container in a cool, dark place for up to 1 year.

2 tbsp	vegetable oil	25 mL
1 tsp	cumin seeds	5 mL
1 tsp	mustard seeds	5 mL
1 tsp	fenugreek seeds	5 mL
1/2 tsp	fennel seeds	2 mL
3	cloves garlic, minced	3
1	hot green chile pepper, minced	1
1/2 tsp	ground turmeric	2 mL
1/2 tsp	salt	2 mL
1/2 tsp	cracked black peppercorns	2 mL
4 cups	cauliflower florets (about 1 small head)	1 L
1/2 cup	water	125 mL
1 cup	frozen green peas	250 mL

1. In a large skillet, heat oil over medium heat until hot but not smoking. Add cumin seeds, mustard seeds, fenugreek seeds and fennel seeds; cook, stirring, until starting to pop, about 1 minute. Add garlic, chile pepper, turmeric, salt and pepper; cook, stirring, until softened and fragrant, about 1 minute.

2. Stir in cauliflower until coated in spices. Add water and cover quickly. Reduce heat to medium-low and simmer until cauliflower is almost tender, about 8 minutes. Stir in peas, cover and cook until peas are hot and cauliflower is tender, about 3 minutes. Uncover and simmer, stirring gently, just until liquid evaporates, 2 to 3 minutes. Season to taste with salt.

Curried Cauliflower and Sweet Corn with Yogurt

Serves 4 to 6

Full of sunshine and happiness from golden corn and zestfully spiced, crisply textured cauliflower, this vegetable side course has a light sauce and will therefore work best alongside saucier curries.

Tips

A lower-fat yogurt will work, but avoid fat-free yogurt and any with added gelatin. When cooked, gelatin in yogurt can cause the yogurt to split and create a curdled texture.

Use frozen thawed, canned drained or cooked fresh corn kernels.

1 tbsp	cornstarch	15 mL
¾ cup	plain yogurt (not fat-free) (see tip, at left)	175 mL
1 tbsp	vegetable oil	15 mL
1 tsp	cumin seeds	5 mL
1	hot green chile pepper, minced	1
1 tsp	Indian yellow curry paste or masala blend	5 mL
4 cups	small cauliflower florets	1 L
½ cup	water	125 mL
½ tsp	salt	2 mL
1 cup	corn kernels	250 mL
1 tbsp	chopped fresh cilantro	15 mL

1. In a bowl, stir cornstarch and yogurt until blended and smooth. Set aside at room temperature.

2. In a saucepan, heat oil over medium heat until hot but not smoking. Add cumin seeds and cook, stirring, until toasted and fragrant but not yet popping, about 30 seconds. Add chile pepper and curry paste; cook, stirring, until blended and fragrant, about 30 seconds.

3. Add cauliflower, water and salt; cover quickly. Cook, covered, until cauliflower is almost tender, about 5 minutes. Stir in corn and cook, uncovered, until cauliflower is tender and liquid is almost all absorbed, about 2 minutes.

4. Reduce heat to low and stir in yogurt mixture. Cook, stirring, until sauce is thickened and vegetables are coated, about 2 minutes. Season to taste with salt. Serve sprinkled with cilantro.

Eggplant (Brinjal) Curry

Serves 4

Eggplant is so luxurious when lightly fried that it sparkles brightly even in this simple recipe.

Tips

Any Asian- or Italian-style eggplant will work well in this recipe. When purchasing an eggplant, choose one that is shiny and firm without any blemishes and with a fresh-looking green stem.

If the skin seems thick, you may want to peel the eggplant; if the skin is tender, leave it on.

3 tbsp	vegetable oil	45 mL
2 cups	cubed eggplant (1/2-inch/1 cm cubes)	500 mL
1 cup	sliced tomato	250 mL
8	curry leaves	8
1/2 cup	Basic Gravy (see recipe, page 7)	125 mL
1/4 cup	water	50 mL
	Salt	

1. In a large skillet, heat oil over high heat. Add eggplant and cook, stirring, until browned on all sides, about 3 minutes. Transfer to a bowl. Set aside.

2. Return pan to medium heat. Add tomato and curry leaves; cook, stirring, until tomato starts to soften, about 2 minutes. Stir in gravy and water; bring to a boil.

3. Return eggplant to pan and fold gently until coated in sauce. Cook, stirring very gently, until eggplant is tender and sauce is slightly thickened, 3 to 4 minutes. Season to taste with salt.

Serving Suggestion

For a satisfying and colorful vegetarian meal, serve with Red Lentil Curry with Coconut and Cilantro (page 190) and Spinach Rice Pilau (page 255).

Thai Green Curry Shrimp and Vegetables (page 174)

Caribbean Red Bean, Spinach and Potato Curry (page 185)

Red Lentil Curry with Coconut and Cilantro (page 190)

Curried Plantain with Raisins and Pecans (page 215)

Eggplant (Brinjal) with Green Chiles

Serves 4

Coddled in a fiery sauce, this eggplant turns out tender and flavorful, tasty enough to be lunch alongside plain rice or the most popular part of a multi-course dinner.

Tip

The long, tender Asian-style eggplant works best for this recipe. Cut crosswise into thin slices of even thickness for even cooking.

3 tbsp	vegetable oil	45 mL
1	onion, diced	1
½ tsp	salt	2 mL
½ tsp	hot pepper flakes	2 mL
½ tsp	freshly ground black pepper	2 mL
½ tsp	ground cumin	2 mL
2	hot green chile peppers, thickly sliced	2
1 tsp	ground turmeric	5 mL
½ cup	water	125 mL
2 cups	thinly sliced eggplant	500 mL
8	curry leaves	8
	Chopped fresh cilantro	

1. In a large skillet, heat oil over medium heat. Add onion, salt, hot pepper flakes, black pepper and cumin; cook, stirring, until onion starts to soften, about 2 minutes. Add chile peppers and turmeric; cook, stirring, for 30 seconds.

2. Stir in water and bring to a simmer. Gently fold in eggplant and curry leaves until coated in sauce. Cover, reduce heat to medium-low and simmer, without stirring, until eggplant is tender, about 6 minutes. Season to taste with salt. Serve sprinkled with cilantro.

Eggplant (Brinjal) Coconut Curry

Serves 4

A multidimensional sauce and creamy coconut are an appropriate backdrop for the smooth luxury of sautéed eggplant. This dish will impress even your most difficult dinner guest.

Tip

This version is definitely on the fiery side. For a milder curry, decrease the cayenne to ½ tsp (2 mL) and/or omit the chile peppers.

1½ tsp	ground turmeric	7 mL
1 tsp	cayenne pepper	5 mL
1 tsp	salt	5 mL
2 cups	cubed eggplant (1-inch/2.5 cm cubes)	500 mL
¼ cup	vegetable oil, divided	50 mL
½ tsp	mustard seeds	2 mL
¼ tsp	cumin seeds	1 mL
¼ tsp	aniseeds	1 mL
½ cup	thinly sliced onion	125 mL
4	cloves garlic, thinly sliced	4
1 tbsp	julienned gingerroot	15 mL
½ tsp	ground cinnamon	2 mL
2	hot green chile peppers, slit in half lengthwise	2
8	curry leaves	8
1	can (14 oz/400 mL) coconut milk	1
1 tbsp	white wine vinegar	15 mL

1. In a bowl, combine turmeric, cayenne and salt. Add eggplant and toss to coat evenly. Let stand at room temperature for 15 minutes.

2. In a large skillet, heat 3 tbsp (45 mL) of the oil over high heat. Add eggplant mixture and cook, stirring, until eggplant is browned on all sides, about 3 minutes. Transfer to a bowl. Set aside.

3. Return pan to medium heat. Add the remaining oil and heat until hot but not smoking. Add mustard seeds, cumin seeds and aniseeds; cook, stirring, until seeds start to pop, about 15 seconds. Add onion and cook, stirring, until starting to soften, about 1 minute. Add garlic, ginger and cinnamon; cook, stirring, until softened and fragrant, about 1 minute. Add chile peppers and curry leaves; cook, stirring, for 1 minute.

4. Stir in coconut milk and vinegar; bring to a boil. Boil, stirring often, until sauce is slightly thickened, about 3 minutes.

5. Return eggplant to pan and fold gently until coated in sauce. Reduce heat and simmer, stirring gently, until eggplant is tender, 5 to 8 minutes.

Roasted Curried Eggplant

Serves 4

Silky and smoky roasted eggplant is the prime element of Lebanese baba ghanoush and Greek melitzanosalata. This dish is based on the grandparent of those recipes, from the heart of courtly Indian cuisine.

Tip

This is fairly spicy when made with 1 tsp (5 mL) hot pepper flakes. To tone it down, decrease the amount to ½ tsp (2 mL) or even ¼ tsp (1 mL) for just a hint of heat.

• Preheat oven to 350°F (180°C)
• Rimmed baking sheet

1	large eggplant (about 1½ lbs/750 g)	1
2 tbsp	vegetable oil	25 mL
1 tsp	mustard seeds	5 mL
1 cup	diced onion	250 mL
½ cup	diced red bell pepper	125 mL
1 tsp	hot pepper flakes	5 mL
½ cup	Basic Gravy (see recipe, page 7)	125 mL
¼ cup	water	50 mL
2 tbsp	ghee or melted butter, optional	25 mL
	Salt, optional	
	Chopped fresh cilantro	

1. Place whole eggplant on baking sheet and bake in preheated oven until skin is charred and a knife pierces the flesh easily, about 45 minutes. Let cool. Peel off the skin (it comes off in easy strips), and cut the flesh in half. Discard any excess liquid. Using a spoon, scrape out the seed pods in the center and discard. Cut flesh crosswise into 1-inch (2.5 cm) thick slices (handle delicately; the flesh is very soft). Set aside.

2. In a large skillet, heat oil over medium heat until hot but not smoking. Add mustard seeds and cook, stirring, until starting to pop, about 30 seconds. Add onion, red pepper and hot pepper flakes; cook, stirring, until starting to soften.

3. Add gravy and cook, stirring, for 1 minute. Stir in water and bring to simmer. Simmer, stirring often, until slightly thickened, about 3 minutes.

4. Carefully add roasted eggplant and ghee, if using. Spoon sauce over eggplant. Reduce heat and simmer gently until eggplant is hot and flavorful, about 5 minutes. Season to taste with salt, if using. Serve sprinkled with cilantro.

Okra (Bindi) with Tamarind

Serves 4

The most sunbelt of all vegetables, okra occupies an honored position in the cuisines of tropical and subtropical locations. It is widely used in curries, such as this one, that use ingredients that grow in the same climates.

Tip

To make tamarind water, break 3 oz (90 g) of block tamarind into pieces and place in a heatproof bowl. Pour in 1½ cups (375 mL) boiling water. Let stand until very soft, at least 30 minutes or up to 8 hours. Press through a fine-mesh sieve, discarding seeds and skins.

2 tbsp	vegetable oil	25 mL
8 oz	okra, stems removed and pods thinly sliced on the diagonal	250 g
¼ tsp	mustard seeds	1 mL
2	hot green chile peppers, slit in half lengthwise	2
1 cup	diced onion	250 mL
6	cloves garlic, chopped	6
8	curry leaves	8
½ tsp	ground turmeric	2 mL
1 tsp	packed brown or palm sugar	5 mL
1½ cups	tamarind water (see tip, at left)	375 mL
	Salt, optional	

1. In a large skillet, heat oil over high heat. Add okra and cook, stirring occasionally, until browned on both sides, 2 to 3 minutes. Using a slotted spoon, transfer to a bowl, leaving as much oil in the pan as possible. Set okra aside.

2. Return pan to medium heat. Add mustard seeds and cook, stirring, until starting to pop, about 30 seconds. Add chile peppers and onion; cook, stirring, until onion is softened, about 2 minutes. Add garlic, curry leaves and turmeric; cook, stirring, until softened and fragrant, about 30 seconds. Stir in sugar and tamarind water; bring to a simmer, scraping up bits stuck to pan.

3. Return okra to pan and fold until coated in sauce. Reduce heat and simmer, stirring gently occasionally, until okra is tender and sauce is slightly thickened, about 15 minutes. Season to taste with salt, if using.

Curried Okra (Bindi) Masala

¼ cup	vegetable oil	50 mL
8 oz	okra, stems removed and pods sliced lengthwise	250 g
1	onion, finely chopped	1
1	small onion, cut into rings	1
6	cloves garlic, minced	6
2	hot green chile peppers, minced	2
2 tbsp	minced gingerroot	25 mL
½ tsp	salt	2 mL
1 cup	chopped tomato	250 mL
½ cup	water	125 mL
	Chopped fresh cilantro	

1. In a large skillet, heat oil over high heat. Add okra, in batches as necessary, and cook, stirring, until browned on both sides, 2 to 3 minutes. Using a slotted spoon, transfer to a bowl, leaving as much oil in the pan as possible. Set okra aside.

2. Return pan to medium heat. Add chopped onion and onion rings; cook, stirring, until starting to soften, about 2 minutes. Add garlic, chile peppers, ginger and salt; cook, stirring, until softened and fragrant, about 1 minute. Add tomato and water; cook, stirring, until saucy, 2 to 3 minutes.

3. Return okra to pan and fold until coated in sauce. Reduce heat and simmer, stirring gently occasionally, until okra is tender and sauce is slightly thickened, 20 to 25 minutes. Season to taste with salt. Serve sprinkled with cilantro.

Northern India

I revel in the views of Mussoorie, 6,000 feet (1,800 m) above the Doon Valley in northern India, which stretches before me in an endless twinkle. Behind me are the Himalayas, majestic and forbidding, and behind them are Nepal, Tibet and China. Mussoorie, an improbably beautiful town built vertically into the floral, woodsy face of the mountain, is an ancient hill station of the Raj. This is where heat-weary colonizers retired for the cooler summer of the Himalayan foothills. It is now equally in demand as a yuppie retreat from Delhi's inhuman heat.

It is best to give Mussoorie a miss "in season" (May to July), when it is swamped by Delhi holidaymakers and prices rise as steeply as the temperatures down in the valley. I have chosen February for my visit. It's spring-like in the daytime, with wafts of clouds that sweep the town, only to be dispersed by sunlight. At night it might snow a little, but nothing like the storms in Montreal at this time of year. Best of all, I have the place to myself. It is fully open and functional — on hold, so to speak — reaping what little tourism trickles its way from the famous northern-Indian playgrounds of Agra's Taj Mahal and Rajasthan's theme-park desert towns (Jaipur, Jodhpur, Udaipur), with their carnival atmospheres and Technicolor clothes.

My vantage point is room 10 of Hotel Padmini Nivas, built in 1860 as a British summer estate, converted in 1930 into a vacation palace for Maharani Padmini of Rajpipla, and since 1964 the most congenial of Mussoorie's countless hotels, all with spectacular views, but none to equal mine. The room is a pentagonal alcove of large picture windows, giving out to valley and mountains as if its walls had evaporated. If you were to sit in front of this view to write postcards, you would mail home nothing but descriptions of it.

Within easy walking distance of the hotel there are many mosques, temples and churches, two lively markets, a municipal garden and the rambling, old-world-style Savoy Hotel with its beer garden, tennis courts and grand ballroom, worth a peek at for its historical, now faded, glitz.

The most immediately accessible and most leisurely attraction of the town is the five-minute ride on the cable car (called the "ropeway") to Gun Hill, a steep outcrop behind The Mall, the town's main street. The ride over roofs and treetops is inside a perfectly secure gondola and could only scare those with incurable vertigo. The view from the peak outdoes even room 10. In one direction lies the valley; in the other, a never-ending mountainous vista regenerates into higher and higher peaks that blend in blue-grays into the distant horizon.

A slightly more adventurous excursion waits at the other end of The Mall, near the library: Camel's Back Road, a sculpted 2-mile (3.5 km) walk that skirts the town, showering the eyes with a revolving view of chasm and mountain. If you're not up for a walk, the trip can be accomplished on horseback, albeit led by a groom and allowed to gallop only if you ask nicely.

For the more athletic, there are countless treks and climbs — not exactly Mount Everest (which is far away in northern Nepal), but plenty challenging. At Kempty Falls, 9 miles (15 km) away, you'll find waterworks, including an emerald pond at the bottom for natural whirlpool bathing. Another 12 miles (20 km) from there lie the rhododendron and oak forests at Dhanolti, from which one can see the taller, snow-capped Himalayas.

Mussoorie offers a few days of spectacular exploration, but what makes traveling here truly worthwhile is its proximity to two of the most famous Hindu holy towns on the spiritual map, right where the Ganges River gushes out of the mountains and enters the plain, bringing water and life to many millions of people. They are easily accessible by a two-hour, $30 taxi ride.

The closer of the two is Rishikesh, the heart of the global yoga and meditation business. The head offices of every famous international ashram are here, either on the left or the right bank of the Ganges. This is where the Beatles made a pilgrimage in the 1960s to seek divine guidance, and where they found artistic inspiration for their *White Album*. Rishikesh has many hotels from which to watch the penitent wander in saffron robes, especially around the playful Lakshman Jhula complex, where one also finds the German Bakery with its yak cheese sandwiches on whole wheat, a great relief from the Indian standard of white bread and processed cheese. The delicious local cuisine is, by law, vegetarian to conform with Hindu religious rites.

A mere 40 minutes from Rishikesh is the even holier town of Haridwar, where not even eggs are allowed. Haridwar is located at the most sacred point of the revered Ganges, and it is here that Kumb Mela, a giant convention of millions of sadhus (religious people), occurs every 12 years. In other years, Haridwar is a more easygoing but still bustling pilgrimage town, with multitudes of sadhus streaming up for a cleansing dunk in the Ganges and a Ganga Aarti pooja (river-worship service) in Har Ki Pairi, the epicenter of the sacred part of town.

The more modern India gets, the more determinedly it tries to preserve what it values most: its natural wonders and its soul. One day it might succumb to the West and turn itself into a mere parody of its 5,000-year-old culture and its timeless topography. Until that happens, it behooves every traveler to visit as often as possible. — B.A.

Red Curry of Bell Peppers with Cashews

Serves 4 to 6

Here's a lively dish for summer, when bell peppers are inexpensive (or even for other seasons, when they are not so cheap). It adds color and sweetness to dinner and gladdens the heart.

Tips

If lime leaves aren't available, substitute ½ tsp (2 mL) finely grated lime zest and stir in with lime juice in step 3.

The cashews give the best texture to the sauce if pulsed in a food processor to a coarse meal (without processing too much into butter). You may need to do more than ⅓ cup (75 mL), depending on the size of your food processor. Extra ground nuts can be frozen for future use.

1 tbsp	vegetable oil	15 mL
3	bell peppers (mixed colors), thinly sliced	3
2	wild lime leaves (see tip, at left)	2
⅓ cup	salted roasted cashews, ground or finely chopped (see tip, at left)	75 mL
2 tsp	packed brown or palm sugar	10 mL
½ tsp	salt	2 mL
1	can (14 oz/400 mL) coconut milk	1
2 tsp	Thai red curry paste	10 mL
1 tbsp	freshly squeezed lime juice	15 mL
	Chopped fresh cilantro	
	Salted roasted cashews	

1. In a skillet, heat oil over medium heat. Add bell peppers and lime leaves; cook, stirring, until starting to soften, about 2 minutes. Transfer peppers to a bowl, leaving lime leaves in pan.

2. Add ground cashews, brown sugar, salt, coconut milk and curry paste to pan and bring to a boil, stirring until blended. Reduce heat and boil gently, stirring often, until slightly thickened, about 5 minutes.

3. Return peppers to pan and cook, stirring, until tender, 3 to 4 minutes. Stir in lime juice and season to taste with salt. Serve sprinkled with cilantro and cashews.

Serving Suggestion

Serve with Curry Lime Roasted Chicken (page 52), Cilantro Mint Curry–Crusted Pork Loin Roast (page 114) or Green Mango Fish Curry (page 157), and with Thai Basil Sticky Rice (page 261) or jasmine rice.

Botswana Pumpkin Curry

Serves 4

Any curry lover who has read Alexander McCall Smith's No. 1 Ladies' Detective Agency novels has likely craved a steaming bowl of Mma Ramotswe's pumpkin curry. Now you can make it at home and follow it up with a refreshing cup of red bush tea.

• ◆ •

Tip
The peanuts give the best texture to the sauce if pulsed in a food processor to a coarse meal (without processing too much into butter). You may need to do more than ½ cup (125 mL), depending on the size of your food processor. Extra ground nuts can be frozen for future use.

• ◆ •

Variation
Substitute 1 small butternut squash or 6 cups (1.5 L) squash chunks for the pumpkin.

1	small pie pumpkin (about 3 lbs/1.5 g)	1
1 tbsp	vegetable oil	15 mL
2	carrots, chopped	2
1	large onion, chopped	1
1 tbsp	minced gingerroot	15 mL
1 tbsp	curry powder	15 mL
1 tsp	salt	5 mL
1 tsp	ground cumin	5 mL
1 tsp	dried thyme	5 mL
¼ tsp	ground cloves	1 mL
1 cup	drained canned diced tomatoes	250 mL
2 cups	vegetable stock	500 mL
½ cup	ground or finely chopped peanuts (see tip, at left)	125 mL
2 tbsp	freshly squeezed lime juice	25 mL

1. Cut pumpkin in half. Trim off stem and scoop out seeds. Cut flesh into 1½-inch (4 cm) thick wedges. Using a sharp vegetable peeler or paring knife, peel off rind. Cut wedges into 1½-inch (4 cm) chunks. Set aside.

2. In a large saucepan, heat oil over medium heat. Add carrots and onion; cook, stirring, until softened, about 5 minutes. Add ginger, curry powder, salt, cumin, thyme and cloves; cook, stirring, until softened and fragrant, about 1 minute.

3. Stir in tomatoes and stock; bring to a boil, scraping up bits stuck to pan. Stir in pumpkin and peanuts. Cover, reduce heat to medium-low and simmer, stirring occasionally, until pumpkin is tender but still holds its shape, 15 to 25 minutes. Stir in lime juice and season to taste with salt.

Serving Suggestion

This hearty vegetarian dish is perfect served with steamed brown rice and a crispy salad dressed with a light vinaigrette.

Coconut Cashew Pumpkin Curry

Serves 4 to 6

This royal treatment will satisfy the yearning for pumpkin, one of the brightest culinary stars of the fall season. It's great with other curries, but will also serve as an exotic way to punch up Thanksgiving or Christmas.

Variation
If pumpkin is not available, butternut squash is a good substitute.

1 tbsp	vegetable oil	15 mL
1 tbsp	mustard seeds	15 mL
1 tsp	cumin seeds	5 mL
½ cup	chopped red onion	125 mL
10	curry leaves	10
2	dried red chile peppers, crumbled	2
4 cups	cubed peeled pie pumpkin (1-inch/2.5 cm cubes)	1 L
1 tbsp	packed brown or palm sugar	15 mL
½ tsp	salt	2 mL
¼ tsp	ground turmeric	1 mL
1 cup	coconut milk	250 mL
1 cup	water	250 mL
¼ cup	cashew butter	50 mL
2 tbsp	freshly squeezed lemon juice	25 mL

1. In a large skillet, heat oil over medium heat until hot but not smoking. Add mustard seeds and cumin seeds; cook, stirring, until toasted and fragrant but not yet popping, about 30 seconds. Add onion, curry leaves and chile peppers; cook, stirring, until onion is softened and starting to brown, about 3 minutes.

2. Add pumpkin, brown sugar, salt and turmeric; stir until pumpkin is coated with spices. Add coconut milk, water and cashew butter; bring to a simmer, stirring. Cover, reduce heat to medium-low and boil gently, stirring occasionally, until pumpkin is tender but still holds its shape and sauce is thickened, about 15 to 25 minutes. Stir in lemon juice and season to taste with salt.

Curried Tomato with Chiles

Serves 4

This lively sweet-and-sour curry is possible only in tomato season and will please best with plain rice or noodles.

Tips

Tomatoes should be perfectly ripe but not overly soft. They should yield to gentle pressure when squeezed and should be fragrant.

Never refrigerate tomatoes, as the cold temperature destroys their flavor.

2 tbsp	vegetable oil	25 mL
3	cloves garlic, minced	3
1 tsp	mustard seeds	5 mL
½ tsp	ground turmeric	2 mL
4	hot green chile peppers, sliced lengthwise	4
2 lbs	ripe tomatoes (about 6), cut into ½-inch (1 cm) thick slices	1 kg
1 tsp	granulated sugar	5 mL
½ tsp	salt	2 mL
½ cup	chopped unsalted roasted cashews	125 mL

1. In a skillet, heat oil over medium-high heat until hot but not smoking. Add garlic, mustard seeds and turmeric; cook, stirring, until seeds start to pop, about 1 minute. Add chile peppers and cook, stirring, until softened, about 1 minute.

2. Stir in tomatoes, sugar and salt. Cover, reduce heat to medium and cook until tomatoes are starting to soften and a sauce forms, 2 to 3 minutes. Stir in cashews and cook, stirring gently, for 30 seconds. Season to taste with salt.

Serving Suggestion

Serve with Tandoori Chicken (page 66) or Tandoori Grilled Calamari (page 162) and Lemon Coriander Rice (page 257).

Curried Vegetables Masala

Serves 4

Earthy and colorful, this mixed vegetable curry is as fast to make as it is a perfect companion dish for complex meat or fish curries.

1 tbsp	vegetable oil	15 mL
1 cup	diced tomato	250 mL
8	curry leaves	8
½ cup	Basic Gravy (see recipe, page 7)	125 mL
¼ cup	water	50 mL
4 cups	cooked cubed vegetables (potato, peas, cauliflower florets or a combination)	1 L
	Salt	
Pinch	garam masala	Pinch

1. In a large skillet, heat oil over medium heat. Add tomato and curry leaves; cook, stirring until tomato starts to soften, about 2 minutes. Add gravy and cook, stirring, for 1 minute. Add water and bring to a boil, stirring.
2. Add vegetables and cook, stirring gently, until vegetables are heated through and sauce is flavorful, about 5 minutes. Season to taste with salt. Serve sprinkled with garam masala.

Mixed Vegetable Coconut Curry

Serves 4

Vegetables and a flavorful sauce softened by silken coconut milk become a great asset to any curry meal. A standard in Indian cuisine, Vegetable Khurma is a snap to make, allowing more time for you to concoct additional dishes.

1 tbsp	vegetable oil	15 mL
1	large tomato, chopped	1
8	curry leaves	8
½ cup	Basic Gravy (see recipe, page 7)	125 mL
¼ cup	water	50 mL
4 cups	cooked chopped vegetables (potatoes, peas, cauliflower florets, green beans, carrots, in any combination)	1 L
1 cup	coconut milk	250 mL
½ tsp	salt	2 mL

1. In a large skillet, heat oil over medium heat. Add tomato and curry leaves; cook, stirring, until tomato starts to soften, about 2 minutes. Add gravy and cook, stirring for 1 minute. Add water and bring to a boil, stirring.
2. Stir in vegetables and return to a boil. Stir in coconut milk and salt; simmer, stirring gently, until vegetables are heated through and sauce is flavorful, about 5 minutes. Season to taste with salt.

Vegetable Curry with Poppy Seeds

Serves 4

A festive vegetable course, deeply scented with spices and nicely textured from poppy and mustard seeds, this one is for when you're in the mood to create something special.

• ◆ •

Tips

If using a mixture of vegetables, chop tender vegetables slightly larger and harder vegetables a little smaller to ensure even cooking.

Use a high-quality coconut milk for the best flavor and texture.

6	cloves garlic, minced	6
1 tbsp	minced gingerroot	15 mL
1 tbsp	poppy seeds	15 mL
1 tsp	coriander seeds	5 mL
1½ cups	water	375 mL
1 cup	coconut milk	250 mL
2	hot green chile peppers, sliced lengthwise	2
4 cups	chopped vegetables (potatoes, peas, cauliflower florets, squash, carrots, in any combination)	1 L
1 cup	diced tomato	250 mL
½ cup	chopped onion	125 mL
½ tsp	salt	2 mL
2 tbsp	vegetable oil	25 mL
8	curry leaves	8
1 tsp	mustard seeds	5 mL

1. In a mortar or a bowl, combine garlic, ginger, poppy seeds and coriander seeds. Using a pestle or the back of a wooden spoon, grind into a paste. Set aside.

2. In a large, deep skillet or saucepan, heat water and coconut milk over medium-high heat until bubbling. Stir in paste until blended. Stir in chile peppers, vegetables, tomato, onion and salt; reduce heat and simmer, stirring occasionally, until vegetables are tender and sauce is thickened, 15 to 20 minutes. Remove from heat, cover and let stand for 5 minutes.

3. Meanwhile, in a small skillet, heat oil over medium-high heat until hot but not smoking. Add curry leaves and mustard seeds; cook, stirring, until seeds start to pop, about 30 seconds. Drizzle oil and spices over the vegetable curry and stir until blended. Season to taste with salt.

Vegetable Curry with Fruit

Serves 4

This celebratory vegetable curry with fruit and cashew enhancements might adorn a buffet or become the centerpiece of a curry dinner for the family.

Tip

Leftover cooked vegetables are perfect for this dish. Mixed frozen vegetables will also work, and there are many interesting blends available now. Be sure to let them thaw, and drain well before using.

1 tbsp	vegetable oil	15 mL
8	curry leaves	8
2 tbsp	raisins	25 mL
2 tbsp	raw cashews	25 mL
½ cup	Basic Gravy (see recipe, page 7)	125 mL
¼ cup	water	50 mL
4 cups	cooked chopped vegetables (potatoes, peas, cauliflower florets, green beans, carrots, in any combination)	1 L
1 cup	coconut milk	250 mL
1	banana, cut into ½-inch (1 cm) thick slices	1
1	apple, peeled and cut into ½-inch (1 cm) cubes	1
½ tsp	salt, or to taste	2 mL
¼ cup	grapes	50 mL

1. In a large skillet, heat oil over medium heat. Add curry leaves and cook, stirring, for 15 seconds. Add raisins and cashews; cook, stirring, until raisins start to puff and cashews start to brown, about 30 seconds. Add gravy and cook, stirring, for 1 minute. Add water and bring to a boil, stirring.

2. Stir in vegetables and return to a boil. Stir in coconut milk and simmer, stirring gently, until vegetables are heated through and sauce is flavorful, about 5 minutes. Stir in banana and apple; cook, stirring very gently, just until fruit is hot, about 2 minutes. Season to taste with salt. Serve garnished with grapes.

Vegetable Croquette Kofta in Malai Curry

Serves 4

This vegetarian main course item features lightly fried vegetable patties in a mild sauce. It is fail-safe for all palates, including those of children, who will enjoy the crisp texture so much they won't even realize they are eating their vegetables.

Tip

Do not be tempted to use a food processor or another appliance to mash the bread and vegetables — the mixture will get mushy and watery. Your hands are the best tool for the job.

4	slices whole wheat bread	4
2 cups	cooked chopped vegetables (potatoes, peas, cauliflower florets, green beans, carrots, in any combination)	500 mL
1/4 cup	vegetable oil	50 mL
1	large tomato, thinly sliced	1
1/2 cup	Basic Gravy (see recipe, page 7)	125 mL
1/2 cup	milk	125 mL
	Salt	
	Chopped fresh cilantro	

1. Tear bread into small pieces. In a bowl, using your hands, mash bread with vegetables until well blended. Form into 4 patties about 3½ inches (8.5 cm) in diameter and ¾ inch (2 cm) thick.

2. In a large skillet, heat oil over high heat until hot but not smoking. Add patties, in batches as necessary, and cook, turning once, until well browned, 2 to 3 minutes per side. Transfer to a warmed dish in a single layer and keep warm. Repeat with remaining patties, adjusting heat as necessary between batches to prevent burning.

3. Return pan to medium-high heat. Add tomato and cook, stirring, until softened, about 2 minutes. Add gravy and cook, stirring, for 1 minute. Gradually stir in milk. Simmer, stirring, until sauce is slightly thickened and flavorful, about 2 minutes. Season to taste with salt. Spoon sauce over koftas and serve sprinkled with cilantro.

Jal-Frezi-Style Vegetable Curry with Cilantro

Serves 4

Quick and easy, this articulated vegetable curry will round out a meal with just one other dish, such as a vegetarian lentil or bean or any meat curry.

•◆•

Variation

Substitute 1½ cups (375 mL) thawed and drained frozen vegetables for the cooked carrot, green beans and cauliflower. Use your favorite vegetable blend or just one vegetable.

1 tbsp	vegetable oil	125 mL
½	green bell pepper, cut into ½-inch (1 cm) pieces	½
½ cup	diced onion	125 mL
¼ tsp	cayenne pepper	1 mL
½ cup	Basic Gravy (see recipe, page 7)	125 mL
1 tsp	granulated sugar	5 mL
¼ cup	water	50 mL
1 tsp	soy sauce	5 mL
½ cup	cooked diced carrot	125 mL
½ cup	cooked chopped green beans	125 mL
½ cup	cooked cauliflower florets	125 mL
	Chopped fresh cilantro	

1. In a large skillet, heat oil over medium-high heat. Add green pepper and onion; cook, stirring, until starting to brown, about 2 minutes. Add cayenne and gravy; cook, stirring, for 1 minute. Stir in sugar, water and soy sauce; bring to a boil.

2. Stir in carrot, green beans and cauliflower. Reduce heat and simmer, stirring gently, until vegetables are heated through and sauce is flavorful, about 5 minutes. Serve sprinkled with cilantro.

Jaipur-Style Curried Vegetables with Cheese

Serves 4

Jaipur is the extravagantly royal city of Rajasthan, as famous for its sites as for its vegetarian cooking. This simple vegetable dish is enriched with cheese, which in its homeland would be paneer, but mozzarella melts so much better.

Tip

Cooking the cauliflower, carrot and green beans in advance ensures that they stay tender-crisp and retain the most flavor. You can use 2 cups (500 mL) leftover cooked vegetables of any variety or thawed and drained frozen mixed vegetables instead.

1 tbsp	vegetable oil	15 mL
½ cup	diced onion	125 mL
½ cup	chopped green bell pepper	125 mL
½ cup	Basic Gravy (see recipe, page 7)	125 mL
1 cup	milk	250 mL
1 cup	cooked small cauliflower florets	250 mL
½ cup	cooked diced carrot	125 mL
½ cup	cooked chopped green beans	125 mL
½ cup	shredded mozzarella cheese	125 mL

1. In a large skillet, heat oil over medium-high heat. Add onion and green pepper; cook, stirring, until slightly browned, about 3 minutes. Add gravy and cook, stirring, for 1 minute. Gradually stir in milk and bring to a simmer.

2. Reduce heat to medium and add cauliflower, carrot and green beans. Cook, stirring gently, until vegetables are heated through and sauce is flavorful, about 5 minutes. Remove from heat. Sprinkle with cheese and let stand until cheese is melted, about 1 minute.

Serving Suggestion

For a vegetarian meal, serve with Tomato Onion Curry of Brown Lentils (page 189), Okra (Bindi) with Tamarind (page 228) and basmati rice.

Dry Curry of Potatoes and Onions

Serves 4

This easy curry is designed to contain its sauce inside the potato, allowing it to stand out in a meal that has a saucy main course. It also works as the potato of a Western-style meal, alongside roasted or grilled meat.

Tip

Do not use the oblong, baking type of potato for this recipe. They tend to break up and get mushy. Round, waxy boiling or all-purpose potatoes are the key to a nice texture. Choose red-skinned or yellow-fleshed potatoes to add a splash of color.

2 tbsp	sesame seeds	25 mL
2 tbsp	vegetable oil	25 mL
1 tbsp	coriander seeds, crushed	15 mL
1½ tsp	cumin seeds	7 mL
½ tsp	fenugreek seeds	2 mL
2	dried red chile peppers, crumbled	2
1	large onion, chopped	1
1 tsp	salt	5 mL
4	boiling or all-purpose potatoes, cut into ½-inch (1 cm) cubes	4
¾ cup	water	175 mL
	Chopped fresh cilantro	

1. Heat a dry large skillet over medium heat until hot but not smoking. Toast sesame seeds, stirring constantly, until fragrant and light brown, about 2 minutes. Transfer to a bowl and set aside.

2. Add oil to pan and swirl to coat. Add coriander seeds, cumin seeds and fenugreek seeds; cook, stirring, until toasted and fragrant but not yet popping, about 30 seconds. Add chile peppers, onion and salt; cook, stirring, until onion is starting to soften, about 2 minutes.

3. Stir in potatoes until coated with spices. Pour in water and cover pan quickly. Reduce heat to medium-low and simmer, stirring occasionally, until potatoes are tender and liquid is almost absorbed, about 20 minutes.

4. Uncover and cook, stirring often, until liquid is absorbed and potatoes start to brown, 5 to 10 minutes. Season to taste with salt. Serve sprinkled with reserved sesame seeds and cilantro.

Cauliflower and Potato Curry

Serves 4

This simple curry, traditionally known as Aloo Gobi, is arguably the most popular vegetarian recipe in India. Potato and cauliflower were made for each other, and cook up in a jiffy if preboiled, as in this recipe.

1 tbsp	vegetable oil	15 mL
½ tsp	cumin seeds	2 mL
1 cup	diced tomato	250 mL
½ cup	Basic Gravy (see recipe, page 7)	125 mL
½ cup	water	125 mL
1 cup	cooked or frozen cauliflower florets (thawed and drained if frozen)	250 mL
1 cup	cooked cubed potato (½-inch/1 cm cubes)	250 mL
	Salt	
	Chopped fresh cilantro	

1. In a skillet, heat oil over medium heat until hot but not smoking. Add cumin seeds and cook, stirring, until seeds start to pop, about 1 minute. Add tomato and cook, stirring, until starting to soften, about 2 minutes. Add gravy and cook, stirring, for 1 minute. Add water and bring to a boil, stirring.
2. Add cauliflower and potato; simmer, stirring occasionally, until heated through and flavorful, about 5 minutes. Season to taste with salt. Serve sprinkled with cilantro.

Potato and Spinach Curry

Serves 4

This curry, traditionally known as Aloo Palak, is a tasty way to fill up on spinach, especially as it is bolstered by the comforts of softly cooked potato and a tasty sauce.

1 tbsp	vegetable oil	15 mL
1 cup	sliced tomato	250 mL
½ cup	Basic Gravy (see recipe, page 7)	125 mL
1 cup	cooked cubed potato (½-inch/1 cm cubes)	250 mL
1 cup	lightly packed finely chopped fresh spinach	250 mL
¼ cup	milk	50 mL
	Salt	

1. In a skillet, heat oil over medium heat. Add tomato and cook, stirring, until starting to soften, about 2 minutes. Add gravy and cook, stirring, for 1 minute.
2. Stir in potato and spinach; bring to a simmer, stirring gently. Add milk and cook, stirring, until potatoes are heated through and sauce is flavorful, about 3 minutes. Season to taste with salt.

Curried Spinach and Potatoes with Yogurt

Serves 4 to 6

A balanced meal all on its own, this articulated recipe of spuds and healthful spinach in a creamy, lusty sauce becomes a good lunch simply accompanied by plain rice, but also serves well alongside other curries for dinner.

Tip

Full-fat yogurt provides the best texture in this recipe. A lower-fat yogurt will work, but avoid fat-free yogurt and any with added gelatin. When cooked, gelatin in yogurt can cause the yogurt to split and create a curdled texture.

1 tbsp	cornstarch	15 mL
1 cup	plain yogurt, preferably full-fat (see tip, at left)	250 mL
2 tbsp	vegetable oil	25 mL
1 tbsp	mustard seeds	15 mL
1 tsp	cumin seeds	5 mL
½ cup	chopped red onion	125 mL
2	cloves garlic, minced	2
½ tsp	salt	2 mL
1 tbsp	Indian yellow curry paste or masala blend	15 mL
2	boiling or all-purpose potatoes, cut into ½-inch (1 cm) cubes	2
½ cup	water	125 mL
6 cups	fresh spinach, trimmed (about 6 oz/175 g)	1.5 L

1. In a bowl, stir cornstarch and yogurt until blended and smooth. Set aside at room temperature.

2. In a large skillet, heat oil over medium heat until hot but not smoking. Add mustard seeds and cumin seeds; cook, stirring, until toasted and fragrant but not yet popping, about 30 seconds. Add red onion and cook, stirring, until softened and starting to brown, about 5 minutes. Add garlic, salt and curry paste; cook, stirring, until blended and fragrant, about 1 minute.

3. Stir in potatoes until coated with spices. Pour in water and cover pan quickly. Reduce heat to medium-low and boil gently, stirring occasionally, until potatoes are tender and most of the liquid is absorbed, about 20 minutes.

4. Stir in yogurt mixture. Gradually add spinach to skillet, one handful at a time, stirring just until wilted. Season to taste with salt.

Spinach Potato Fry with Curried Yellow Lentils

2	boiling or all-purpose potatoes, peeled and cut into ½-inch (1 cm) cubes	2
2 tbsp	vegetable oil	25 mL
1 tsp	mustard seeds	5 mL
2 tbsp	small yellow lentils (toor dal)	25 mL
1	onion, sliced lengthwise	1
2	hot green chile peppers, sliced lengthwise	2
2 tbsp	minced gingerroot	25 mL
8	curry leaves	8
2 cups	lightly packed chopped fresh spinach	500 mL
¼ cup	fresh or frozen unsweetened shredded coconut	50 mL
	Salt	

Serves 4

Spinach, potato, lentils and coconut combine in a zesty recipe that will delight vegetarians and meat eaters alike. Serve with other curries or on its own, alongside plain rice.

Tips

To shred fresh coconut, peel off brown outer layer and use the coarse side of a box cheese grater or pulse in a food processor until finely chopped but not smooth. Frozen coconut is available at Asian specialty stores; thaw and drain well before using.

In a pinch, packaged dried shredded unsweetened coconut can be used. Soak about 3 tbsp (45 mL) in boiling water for 1 hour, drain well and measure ¼ cup (50 mL).

1. In a saucepan of boiling salted water, boil potatoes until slightly tender, about 10 minutes. Drain and set aside.

2. In a large skillet, heat oil over medium-high heat until hot but not smoking. Add mustard seeds and cook, stirring, until slightly darker but not yet popping, about 15 seconds. Add lentils and cook, stirring, until golden brown, 1 to 2 minutes.

3. Add onion and cook, stirring, until softened, about 3 minutes. Add chile peppers, ginger and curry leaves; cook, stirring, until softened and fragrant, about 1 minute. Add spinach and cook, stirring, just until wilted, about 2 minutes.

4. Stir in reserved potatoes. Reduce heat to medium and cook, stirring often, until potatoes are tender, about 5 minutes. Add coconut and cook, stirring, for 2 minutes. Season to taste with salt.

Cilantro Lime Sweet Potatoes

Here's a colorful, fresh take on mashed potatoes to accompany curry-flavored roasts and meaty curries. It combines white and sweet potatoes for a taste that is familiar and exotic all at once.

Tip

Oblong baking potatoes or all-purpose potatoes give the best fluffy texture for mashing. Round, waxy boiling potatoes will have a gluey texture.

2	sweet potatoes (about 2 lbs/1 kg), peeled and cut into chunks	2
1	large oblong baking potato or all-purpose potato, peeled and cut into small chunks	1
1 tsp	salt	5 mL
1/2 tsp	ground coriander	2 mL
1/4 tsp	ground cumin	1 mL
	Cold water	
1/4 cup	butter, cut into cubes	50 mL
1 tsp	grated lime zest	5 mL
1 tbsp	freshly squeezed lime juice	15 mL
	Freshly ground black pepper	
2 tbsp	chopped fresh cilantro	25 mL

1. In a pot, combine sweet potatoes, baking potato, salt, coriander and cumin. Add enough cold water to cover and bring to a boil over high heat. Reduce heat and boil gently until potatoes are fork-tender, about 20 minutes. Drain and return to pot.

2. Return pot to low heat. Mash potatoes, adding butter, lime zest and lime juice, until blended and smooth. Remove from heat. Season to taste with salt and pepper. Stir in cilantro.

> ### Serving Suggestion
>
> Serve with Filipino Pork Adobo (page 121), Thai Tamarind Curry–Braised Lamb Shanks (page 136) or Curry Lime Roasted Chicken (page 52).

Dry Curry of Roasted Root Vegetables

Serves 6 to 8

A snap to assemble and let bake on its own, this collection of spicily roasted root vegetables accompanies just about any main course on your menu, and does so with gusto.

Tip

The vegetables are cut into different sizes depending on their density so they'll all cook in the same amount of time.

- *Preheat oven to 400°F (200°C)*
- *Rimmed baking sheet, ungreased*

3	cloves garlic, minced	3
1½ tsp	salt	7 mL
1½ tsp	ground coriander	7 mL
1 tsp	ground cumin	5 mL
½ tsp	ground turmeric	2 mL
¼ tsp	ground cinnamon	1 mL
¼ tsp	cayenne pepper	1 mL
¼ cup	vegetable oil	50 mL
2 tbsp	cider or white wine vinegar	25 mL
4	beets, peeled and cut into ½-inch (1 cm) chunks	4
2	all-purpose potatoes, cut into ¾-inch (2 cm) chunks	2
2	carrots, cut into ¾-inch (2 cm) chunks	2
1	small sweet potato, cut into 1-inch (2.5 cm) chunks	1
1	large onion, chopped	1
2 tbsp	chopped fresh cilantro	25 mL
½ tsp	garam masala	2 mL

1. In a small bowl, combine garlic, salt, coriander, cumin, turmeric, cinnamon, cayenne, oil and vinegar.

2. On baking sheet, combine beets, potatoes, carrots, sweet potato and onion. Drizzle with spice mixture and toss to coat evenly. Roast in preheated oven, stirring twice, until tender and golden brown, 45 to 60 minutes. Let stand for 5 minutes.

3. Using a spatula, transfer vegetables to a warmed serving dish, scraping any oil and spices from baking sheet and drizzling over top. Serve sprinkled with cilantro and garam masala.

Curried Root Vegetables Masala

Serves 4

Earthy and substantial, this curry is based on long-life root vegetables for those late-autumn and winter days when more fragile vegetables are at a premium.

Tip

Traditionally, whole spices are left in curries when serving, but they aren't meant to be eaten. Be sure to let your guests know not to eat the whole cloves in this dish.

¼ cup	vegetable oil, divided	50 mL
1	small sweet potato, cut into ½-inch (1 cm) cubes	1
1	boiling or all-purpose potato, cut into ½-inch (1 cm) cubes	1
1	large carrot, cut into ½-inch (1 cm) thick slices	1
1	beet, cut into ½-inch (1 cm) cubes	1
1	small onion, thinly sliced	1
¼ cup	minced garlic (about 8 cloves)	50 mL
1 tsp	ground cumin	5 mL
1 tsp	hot pepper flakes	5 mL
½ tsp	whole cloves	2 mL
2 tbsp	raisins	25 mL
2 cups	canned or fresh diced tomatoes with juice	500 mL
½ cup	water	125 mL
2 tbsp	freshly squeezed lemon juice	25 mL
	Salt	

1. In a large skillet, heat half the oil over high heat. Add sweet potato, potato, carrot and beet, in batches as necessary; cook, stirring, until vegetables start to brown and soften, about 5 minutes. Using a slotted spoon, transfer to a bowl, leaving as much oil in the pan as possible and adding more oil between batches as necessary. Set vegetables aside.

2. Return pan to medium-high heat. Add onion and cook, stirring, until starting to brown, about 2 minutes. Add garlic, cumin, hot pepper flakes and cloves; cook, stirring, for 1 minute.

3. Stir in raisins, tomatoes with juice, water and lemon juice; bring to a simmer. Simmer, stirring often, until tomatoes are softened, about 2 minutes.

4. Stir in reserved vegetables and cook, stirring occasionally, until vegetables are tender and sauce is slightly thickened, about 20 minutes. Season to taste with salt.

Rice & Noodles

◆

Vegetable Rice Biryani

Serves 8

Biryani is the ultimate expression of the Indian culinary imagination. A majestic dish that offers its rice and curry all in one, it was invented for maharajas but is now accessible to all. It's a bit of a production to create, but it goes fairly fast once you start, and it will certainly impress family and friends.

Tips

Steps 1 and 2 can be done 1 day ahead. Cover cooled rice and refrigerate. Steps 4 and 5 can be done 1 day ahead. Cool onion mixture, cover and refrigerate. Bring both rice and onion mixture to room temperature before assembling in step 7.

Traditionally, the pot lid is sealed to the pot with a flour-and-water dough-like paste. That does create a tight seal, but is a little messy. If you'd like to try it, add just enough water to whole wheat flour to make a smooth but moldable paste and squeeze around pot rim of casserole to seal lid on top.

- • *Baking sheet*
- • *12- to 16-cup (3 to 4 L) casserole dish or large ovenproof pot, preferably with a lid, greased*
- • *Parchment paper*
- • *Foil and kitchen string, if necessary*

2 cups	basmati rice	500 mL
	Cold water	
1½ tsp	salt, divided	7 mL
1¼ cups	vegetable stock	300 mL
½ tsp	saffron threads	2 mL
3 tbsp	vegetable oil, divided	45 mL
6	whole cloves	6
2	sticks cinnamon, broken in half	2
1 tsp	aniseed	5 mL
4	large onions, sliced lengthwise	4
6	cloves garlic, thinly sliced	6
2 tbsp	minced gingerroot	25 mL
2 tsp	garam masala, divided	10 mL
½ tsp	ground turmeric	2 mL
½ tsp	freshly ground black pepper	2 mL
¼ tsp	ground cardamom	1 mL
2	red bell peppers, chopped	2
2	carrots, diced	2
4 cups	small cauliflower florets	1 L
2 cups	chopped green beans	500 mL
½ cup	lightly packed cilantro leaves	125 mL
¼ cup	raw cashews or chopped almonds	50 mL
¼ cup	raisins	50 mL

1. In a sieve, rinse rice under cool running water until water runs fairly clear. Transfer rice to a bowl and cover with cold water. Let soak for 20 minutes. Drain well.

2. In a large pot of boiling water, boil drained rice and 1 tsp (5 mL) of the salt until rice is slightly softened on the outside but firm inside, about 3 minutes. Drain and spread out on baking sheet to cool.

3. In a glass measuring cup or a small saucepan, heat stock until almost boiling. Remove from microwave or stovetop and stir in saffron. Let stand until softened, about 15 minutes, or for up to 1 hour.

4. In a large skillet, heat 2 tbsp (25 mL) of the oil over medium heat until hot but not smoking. Add cloves, cinnamon sticks and aniseed; cook, stirring, until cloves are puffed, about 30 seconds.

5. Add onions and cook, stirring, until starting to soften, about 5 minutes. Reduce heat to medium-low and cook, stirring often, until onions are very soft and deep golden brown, 45 to 60 minutes. Add garlic, ginger, remaining salt, 1½ tsp (7 mL) of the garam masala, the turmeric, pepper and cardamom; cook, stirring, until softened and fragrant, about 3 minutes. Set aside.

6. Preheat oven to 375°F (190°C).

7. *To assemble:* Spread half the onion mixture in bottom of prepared casserole. Sprinkle with half each of the red peppers, carrots, cauliflower and green beans. Spread half the rice lightly over top (do not pack down). Pour half the stock mixture over top, drizzling slowly to coat rice as evenly as possible. Sprinkle with half the cilantro leaves. Repeat with remaining onion mixture, vegetables, rice and stock mixture. Sprinkle with remaining cilantro and ½ tsp (2 mL) garam masala.

8. Place a large piece of parchment over top of dish, leaving an overhang of 1 to 2 inches (2.5 to 5 cm). Fit lid on as tightly as possible over parchment. If there is no lid, fit a large piece of foil over parchment, pinching at edges to seal as tightly as possible. Tie kitchen string around sides of dish to secure foil.

9. Bake for 75 minutes. Remove from oven and let stand, without lifting lid, for 10 minutes.

10. Meanwhile, in a small skillet, heat remaining oil over medium heat until hot but not smoking. Add cashews and raisins; cook, stirring, until cashews are toasted and raisins are puffed. Transfer to a bowl.

11. Using two large bamboo or rubber spatulas, carefully transfer biryani to a warmed serving platter, trying not to disrupt layers. Serve sprinkled with cashews and raisins.

Tips

It is very difficult to remove the whole cloves and cinnamon sticks before serving without disturbing the presentation of this dish. Be sure to alert your guests to watch for the whole spices and avoid eating them.

When buying saffron, look for long threads that are mostly red in color, with just a few yellow ones. This high-quality saffron is more expensive, but it is worth the price for the excellent, true flavor.

Potato and Green Peas Rice Biryani

Serves 4

A combination of rice, peas and potatoes might not sound all that exciting, but when you factor in the spices and onions, as well as the slow bake in the oven, you achieve a deeply satisfying dish that will please alongside a simple salad, or even more as part of a festive meal with one or two curries and a dal.

Tips

Steps 1 and 2 can be done 1 day ahead. Cover cooled rice and refrigerate. Bring rice to room temperature before assembling in step 6.

To make this for a larger crowd, double the ingredients and follow the baking instructions for Vegetable Rice Biryani (page 250).

- *Baking sheet*
- *8-cup (2 L) casserole dish, preferably with a lid, greased*
- *Parchment paper*
- *Foil and kitchen string, if necessary*

1 cup	basmati rice	250 mL
	Cold water	
1 tsp	salt, divided	5 mL
2 tbsp	vegetable oil	25 mL
1	stick cinnamon, broken in half	1
2 tsp	mustard seeds	10 mL
1 tsp	cumin seeds	5 mL
2	boiling or all-purpose potatoes, cut into ½-inch (1 cm) cubes	2
2	large onions, sliced lengthwise	2
4	cloves garlic, minced	4
2 tsp	Indian yellow curry paste	10 mL
2 cups	frozen green peas	500 mL
¾ cup	vegetable stock	175 mL
2 tbsp	chopped fresh mint or cilantro	25 mL
½ tsp	garam masala	2 mL
	Lemon wedges	

1. In a sieve, rinse rice under cool running water until water runs fairly clear. Transfer rice to a bowl and cover with cold water. Let soak for 20 minutes. Drain well.

2. In a large pot of boiling water, boil drained rice and ½ tsp (2 mL) of the salt until rice is slightly softened on the outside but firm inside, about 3 minutes. Drain and spread out on baking sheet to cool.

3. In a large skillet, heat oil over medium-high heat until hot but not smoking. Add cinnamon, mustard seeds and cumin seeds; cook, stirring, until seeds start to pop, about 1 minute. Add potatoes and remaining salt; cook, stirring, until starting to soften and brown, about 3 minutes. Using a slotted spoon, transfer potatoes to a bowl, leaving as much oil and spice in the pan as possible. Set potatoes aside.

4. Reduce heat to medium and add onions to pan. Cook, stirring, until starting to soften, about 2 minutes. Reduce heat to medium-low and cook, stirring, until very soft and golden brown, 15 to 20 minutes. Add garlic and curry paste; cook, stirring, until softened and fragrant, about 2 minutes. Set aside.

5. Preheat oven to 375°F (190°C).

6. *To assemble:* Spread half the onion mixture in bottom of prepared casserole. Sprinkle with half each of the reserved potatoes and the peas. Spread half the rice lightly over top (do not pack down). Pour half the stock over top, drizzling slowly to coat rice as evenly as possible. Sprinkle with half the mint. Repeat with remaining onion mixture, potatoes, peas, rice and stock. Sprinkle with remaining mint and the garam masala.

7. Place a large piece of parchment over top of dish, leaving an overhang of 1 to 2 inches (2.5 to 5 cm). Fit lid on as tightly as possible over parchment. If there is no lid, fit a large piece of foil over parchment, pinching at edges to seal as tightly as possible. Tie kitchen string around sides of dish to secure foil.

8. Bake for 45 minutes. Remove from oven and let stand, without lifting lid, for 10 minutes.

9. Using two large bamboo or rubber spatulas, carefully transfer biryani to a warmed serving platter, trying not to disrupt layers. Serve with lemon wedges to squeeze over top.

Serving Suggestion

Serve topped with Pickled Peach Chutney (page 38), Fresh Cilantro Mint Chutney (page 39) or Tomato Chutney (page 42).

Tip

Different brands of prepared vegetable stocks have vastly different flavors. Choose one with a subtle vegetable flavor and color for this recipe.

Variation

Chicken, Potato and Green Peas Rice Biryani: Add 8 oz (250 g) boneless skinless chicken thighs or breasts, cut into ½-inch (1 cm) pieces, in step 4 with the garlic and cook just until chicken starts to turn white. Assemble and bake dish immediately (do not make ahead, as in tip, opposite).

Roasted Bell Pepper Rice Pilau

Serves 4

Festive with the color and smoky taste of roasted red peppers, this rice will enliven a monochrome curry or a grilled meat, and will also add visual punch to a buffet.

Tip
You can use jarred or freshly roasted red bell peppers. If using fresh, 2 peppers will give you about ½ cup (125 mL) chopped. If using the jarred variety, which are usually smaller, you'll need about 4. Drain well and pat dry before measuring.

Variation
If curry leaves are not available, substitute 2 bay leaves and discard before serving.

1 cup	basmati rice	250 mL
	Cold water	
2 tbsp	vegetable oil	25 mL
10	curry leaves	10
1 tsp	coriander seeds, crushed	5 mL
½ tsp	cumin seeds	2 mL
1	onion, finely chopped	1
3	cloves garlic, minced	3
1	hot red or green chile pepper, minced	1
½ cup	drained chopped roasted red bell peppers	125 mL
1 tsp	salt	5 mL
1¾ cups	water	425 mL
½ tsp	garam masala	2 mL

1. In a sieve, rinse rice under cool running water until water runs fairly clear. Transfer rice to a bowl and cover with cold water. Let soak for 20 minutes. Drain well.

2. In a saucepan, heat oil over medium heat until hot but not smoking. Add curry leaves, coriander seeds and cumin seeds; cook, stirring, until seeds start to pop, about 1 minute. Add onion and cook, stirring, until very soft and starting to brown, about 5 minutes. Add garlic, chile pepper, roasted peppers and salt; cook, stirring, for 1 minute.

3. Stir in rice until well coated with spices. Stir in water and bring to a boil. Reduce heat to low, cover and simmer until rice is tender and liquid is absorbed, about 15 minutes. Remove from heat and let stand, covered, for 5 minutes. Fluff with a fork. Serve sprinkled with garam masala.

Spinach Rice Pilau

Serves 4

Spinach and rice have a well-exploited affinity for each other and are partnered in a number of cuisines to create rice dishes that nourish and satisfy. In this Indian version, their combined taste is enhanced with onion and spices.

Tip

The spinach adds about 2 tbsp (25 mL) moisture to the rice, so the total amount of liquid being added is 1¾ cups (425 mL). If your package of basmati rice specifies a different amount of liquid for 1 cup (250 mL) of rice, adjust the amount of water accordingly.

1 cup	basmati rice	250 mL
	Cold water	
2 tbsp	vegetable oil	25 mL
2 tsp	mustard seeds	10 mL
1 tsp	cumin seeds	5 mL
1 tsp	fennel seeds	5 mL
1	onion, finely chopped	1
1	hot green chile pepper, minced, optional	1
1 tsp	salt	5 mL
1⅔ cups	water	400 mL
2 cups	packed finely chopped fresh spinach (about 4 oz/125 g)	500 mL
2 tbsp	freshly squeezed lemon juice	25 mL

1. In a sieve, rinse rice under cool running water until water runs fairly clear. Transfer rice to a bowl and cover with cold water. Let soak for 20 minutes. Drain well.

2. In a saucepan, heat oil over medium heat until hot but not smoking. Add mustard seeds, cumin seeds and fennel seeds; cook, stirring, until seeds are toasted but not yet popping, about 30 seconds. Add onion and cook, stirring, until very soft and starting to brown, about 5 minutes. Add chile pepper, if using, and salt; cook, stirring, for 1 minute.

3. Stir in rice until well coated with spices. Stir in water, then spinach, and bring to a boil. Reduce heat to low, cover and simmer until rice is tender and liquid is absorbed, about 15 minutes. Remove from heat and let stand, covered, for 5 minutes. Sprinkle with lemon juice and fluff with a fork.

Tomato and Onion Rice Pilau

Serves 4

Rice is a chameleon, taking on the hues and taste nuances of whatever it is cooked in. In this recipe, it is tomato-tart and onion-sweet and spice-rich, and altogether a welcome addition to any curry meal.

Tip

Soaking the rice helps prevent it from breaking up and becoming mushy when you're making a pilau. It is an extra step, but well worth it.

1 cup	basmati rice	250 mL
	Cold water	
2 tbsp	vegetable oil	25 mL
2	bay leaves	2
½ tsp	cumin seeds	2 mL
1	small red onion, finely chopped	1
2	cloves garlic, minced	2
¾ tsp	salt	3 mL
1¼ cups	water	300 mL
1 cup	canned diced tomatoes with juice	250 mL

1. In a sieve, rinse rice under cool running water until water runs fairly clear. Transfer rice to a bowl and cover with cold water. Let soak for 20 minutes. Drain well.

2. In a saucepan, heat oil over medium heat until hot but not smoking. Add bay leaves and cumin seeds; cook, stirring, until seeds start to pop, about 1 minute. Add onion and cook, stirring, until very soft and starting to brown, about 5 minutes. Add garlic and salt; cook, stirring, for 1 minute.

3. Stir in rice until well coated with spices. Stir in water and tomatoes with juice; bring to a boil. Reduce heat to low, cover and simmer until rice is tender and liquid is absorbed, about 15 minutes. Remove from heat and let stand, covered, for 5 minutes. Fluff with a fork. Discard bay leaves.

Lemon Coriander Rice

Serves 4

It doesn't take much to transform rice into a delight without depriving it of its essential wholesome nature. Here, it's a double dose of the coriander plant, in both seed form and leaf form. Add a little bit of lemon, and it sings.

Tip

Use the fine side of a box cheese grater or a fine, sharp grater designed for zest to get a nicely textured zest that will blend in with the rice.

1 cup	basmati rice	250 mL
	Cold water	
1 tsp	coriander seeds, crushed	5 mL
½ tsp	salt	2 mL
1¾ cups	water	425 mL
1 tsp	finely grated lemon zest	5 mL
2 tbsp	freshly squeezed lemon juice	25 mL
	Chopped fresh cilantro	

1. In a sieve, rinse rice under cool running water until water runs fairly clear. Transfer rice to a bowl and cover with cold water. Let soak for 20 minutes. Drain well.

2. In a saucepan, combine rice, coriander seeds, salt and water; bring to a boil over high heat. Cover, reduce heat to low and simmer until rice is tender and liquid is absorbed, about 15 minutes. Remove from heat and sprinkle with lemon zest and juice. Let stand, covered, for 5 minutes. Fluff with a fork. Serve sprinkled with cilantro.

Serving Suggestion

This is the perfect rice to serve with fish and seafood curries or any tomato-based curry.

Saffron Curried Pear and Raisin Basmati Rice

Serves 4

This royal rice dish is highlighted by the elegant color and smoky taste of saffron and embellished with fruit and almonds. It is a fitting centerpiece for a holiday buffet, and an absolute treat for the family dinner.

Tips

If your package of basmati rice specifies a different amount of water for 1 cup (250 mL) of rice, adjust the amount accordingly.

Choose a pear variety that keeps its flavor when cooked, such as Bartlett, Bosc or Packham.

1 cup	basmati rice	250 mL
	Cold water	
1/8 tsp	saffron threads	0.5 mL
1 3/4 cups	hot water	425 mL
1 tbsp	butter or vegetable oil	15 mL
1/2	small onion, finely chopped	1/2
1 tbsp	minced gingerroot	15 mL
1 tsp	ground coriander	5 mL
1/2 tsp	salt	2 mL
1/4 tsp	ground cumin	1 mL
1	firm ripe pear, chopped	1
1/4 cup	raisins	50 mL
1 tsp	grated lemon zest	5 mL
2 tbsp	freshly squeezed lemon juice	25 mL
	Toasted sliced almonds	

1. In a sieve, rinse rice under cool running water until water runs fairly clear. Transfer rice to a bowl and cover with cold water. Let soak for 20 minutes. Drain well.

2. Meanwhile, in a measuring cup or bowl, combine saffron and hot water. Let stand until saffron is softened, about 15 minutes, or for up to 1 hour.

3. In a saucepan, melt butter over medium heat. Add onion and cook, stirring, until softened, about 3 minutes. Add ginger, coriander, salt and cumin; cook, stirring, until onion is softened and spices are fragrant, about 1 minute. Add pear and raisins; cook, stirring, just until pear starts to release its juices, about 2 minutes.

4. Stir in rice until well coated with spices. Stir in saffron water and lemon zest; bring to a boil. Reduce heat to low, cover and simmer until rice is tender and liquid is absorbed, about 15 minutes. Remove from heat and let stand, covered, for 5 minutes. Sprinkle with lemon juice and fluff with a fork. Serve sprinkled with almonds.

Golden Curried Pineapple Rice

Serves 4

This rice works well with any hot and spicy curry, while bringing sweet pineapple's promise of sunshine to your table. It has pep, it has taste, and it has the tart fruitiness of its star ingredient.

• ◆ •

Tips

If your package of basmati rice specifies a different amount of water for 1 cup (250 mL) of rice, adjust the amount accordingly.

It is traditional to serve whole spices in the rice, but they are not meant to be eaten. You can discard them if you prefer.

1 cup	basmati rice	250 mL
	Cold water	
1 tbsp	vegetable oil	15 mL
8	curry leaves	8
1	stick cinnamon, about 2 inches (5 cm) long	1
1 tsp	cumin seeds	5 mL
1 tsp	mustard seeds	5 mL
3	cloves garlic, minced	3
1/2 tsp	salt	2 mL
1/2 tsp	ground turmeric	2 mL
1 cup	chopped fresh pineapple	250 mL
1 3/4 cups	water	425 mL
1/4 tsp	garam masala	1 mL

1. In a sieve, rinse rice under cool running water until water runs fairly clear. Transfer rice to a bowl and cover with cold water. Let soak for 20 minutes. Drain well.

2. In a saucepan, heat oil over medium heat until hot but not smoking. Add curry leaves, cinnamon, cumin seeds and mustard seeds; cook, stirring, until seeds start to pop, about 1 minute. Add garlic, salt and turmeric; cook, stirring, until blended and softened, about 1 minute. Add pineapple and cook, stirring, until pineapple starts to release its juices, about 2 minutes.

3. Stir in rice until well coated with spices. Stir in water and bring to a boil. Reduce heat to low, cover and simmer until rice is tender and liquid is absorbed, about 15 minutes. Remove from heat and let stand, covered, for 5 minutes. Fluff with a fork. Discard cinnamon stick, if desired. Serve sprinkled with garam masala.

Basil and Mint–Scented Coconut Jasmine Rice

Serves 4

This truly comforting rice is cooked in coconut milk and scented with fresh herbs. Serve it with any curry you like. With its rich texture and subtle flavors, it blends into curry sauces seamlessly.

Tip

For the best results when cooking rice, use a saucepan with a tight-fitting lid. If the lid on your saucepan doesn't fit tightly, place a piece of parchment or waxed paper between the lid and the pot, just hanging over the edge; this will create a tight seal.

1 cup	jasmine rice	250 mL
½ tsp	salt	2 mL
1 cup	water	250 mL
¾ cup	coconut milk	175 mL
2 tsp	chopped fresh Thai or sweet basil	10 mL
1 tsp	chopped fresh mint	5 mL

1. In a sieve, rinse rice under cool running water until water runs fairly clear. Drain well.

2. In a saucepan, combine rice, salt, water and coconut milk; bring to a boil over high heat. Cover, reduce heat to low and simmer until rice is tender and liquid is absorbed, about 15 minutes. Remove from heat and let stand, covered, for 5 minutes. Sprinkle with basil and mint. Fluff with a fork, gently combining herbs.

Serving Suggestion

This rice is a wonderful base for saucy Thai curries, such as Red Curry Beef with Thai Basil (page 88), Yellow Curry Pork with Pineapple (page 128) or Green Mango Fish Curry (page 157).

Thai Basil Sticky Rice

Serves 4

Thai rice is meant to be sticky because Thai curries work better on rice that is wet and bound together. Lime leaves and basil enhance it with their combined perfumes.

Tips

Sticky rice is usually cooked in a cone-shaped basket steamer or a rice cooker. This stovetop method is a good substitute that doesn't require any special equipment. If you have a steamer or rice cooker, just add the lime leaves with the water and follow your usual method.

It is traditional not to salt sticky rice, but feel free to add it if you prefer.

If lime leaves aren't available, substitute ½ tsp (2 mL) grated lime zest and sprinkle over rice just after cooking, then cover and let stand as directed.

1 cup	Thai sticky rice	250 mL
	Cold water	
2	wild lime leaves (see tip, at left)	2
½ tsp	salt, optional	2 mL
2 cups	water	500 mL
2 tbsp	shredded fresh Thai or sweet basil	25 mL

1. In a sieve, rinse rice under cool running water until water runs fairly clear. Transfer rice to a bowl and cover with cold water. Let soak for at least 4 hours or overnight. Drain well.

2. In a saucepan, combine rice, lime leaves, salt, if using, and water. Bring to a boil over high heat. Cover, reduce heat to low and simmer until rice is tender and liquid is absorbed, about 20 minutes. Remove from heat and let stand, covered, for 5 minutes.

3. Using a broad bamboo or rubber spatula, transfer to a warmed shallow serving dish, being careful not to mush the rice. Serve sprinkled with basil.

Serving Suggestion

Serve with Thai Green Curry Chicken (page 71), Pork Meatballs with Red Curry Peanut Sauce (page 132) or Tofu and Snow Peas in Tamarind Ginger Curry (page 194).

Caribbean Curry Rice and Peas

Serves 4 to 6

A good scoop of this rich and deliciously messy rice accompanies most meals of local food down in the islands. It is essential with Caribbean curries and adds substance to grills and roasts. Serve a crisp salad on the side for textural counterpoint.

• ◆ •

Tips

If you prefer to cook dried pigeon or black-eyed peas, soak and cook 1 cup (250 mL) dried peas.

The texture of parboiled (converted) rice stays nice and firm when used in this dish. Regular long-grain white rice will work, but may have a softer texture.

• ◆ •

Variation

Omit vegetable oil and cook 4 slices bacon, chopped, until almost crisp. Drain off all but 1 tbsp (15 mL) fat, then add onions and seasonings and proceed with step 1. Decrease salt to ¼ tsp (1 mL).

1 tbsp	vegetable oil	15 mL
4	green onions, sliced	4
3	cloves garlic, minced	3
1	whole Scotch bonnet pepper	1
1	bay leaf	1
2 tsp	chopped fresh thyme (or ½ tsp/2 mL dried)	10 mL
1 tsp	curry powder, preferably Caribbean-style	5 mL
½ tsp	salt	2 mL
1	can (14 to 19 oz/398 to 540 mL) pigeon peas or black-eyed peas, rinsed and drained	1
1 cup	long-grain white rice	250 mL
1 cup	coconut milk	250 mL
1 cup	chicken or vegetable stock or water	250 mL

1. In a large saucepan, heat oil over medium heat. Add green onions, garlic, Scotch bonnet pepper, bay leaf, thyme, curry powder and salt; cook, stirring, until onions are softened, about 3 minutes.

2. Stir in peas and rice until well coated with spices. Stir in coconut milk and stock; bring to a boil. Reduce heat to low, cover and simmer until rice is tender and liquid is absorbed, about 20 minutes. Remove from heat and let stand, covered, for 5 minutes. Fluff with a fork. Discard bay leaf and Scotch bonnet.

Serving Suggestion

Use as a filling wrapped in Chickpea Flatbreads (page 271) or store-bought roti skins, along with Fresh Cilantro Mint Chutney (page 39) or Fresh Mango Pineapple Relish (page 47).

Spicy Singapore Curried Noodles

Serves 4

The Cody Inn in Buckhorn, Ontario, inspired this version of these spicy rice noodles, a staple of Chinese noodle houses. They are showy to prepare, with various appetizing enhancements that get added in quick stages. It is a good party dish, and can be prepared in front of the guests, who will get hungrier for it the closer it comes to its appetizing completion.

Tip

Precooked barbecued pork is often available at Asian grocery stores. If it's not available, substitute leftover grilled pork tossed with 1 tsp (5 mL) soy sauce, or just omit.

4 oz	rice vermicelli	125 g
	Hot water	
2 tbsp	vegetable oil, divided	25 mL
2	eggs, beaten	2
2	carrots, thinly sliced on the diagonal	2
2	stalks celery, thinly sliced on the diagonal	2
1	onion, sliced lengthwise	1
4	cloves garlic, minced	4
2 tbsp	minced gingerroot	25 mL
2 tbsp	curry powder	25 mL
1/2 tsp	salt	2 mL
1	red bell pepper, thinly sliced	1
6 oz	skinless boneless chicken breast, cut into thin strips (about 1 breast)	175 g
1 tsp	Asian chili sauce (approx.)	5 mL
8 oz	medium or large shrimp, peeled and deveined	250 g
2 tbsp	water	25 mL
4 oz	Chinese-style barbecued pork, julienned, optional	125 g
2	green onions, thinly sliced	2

1. In a large bowl, cover noodles with hot water by at least 2 inches (5 cm). Let soak until softened, about 5 minutes, or according to package directions. Drain and set aside.

2. In a large wok, heat half the oil over medium-high heat. Add eggs and cook, stirring, just until set. Transfer to a bowl.

3. Increase heat to high. Add remaining oil to wok and swirl to coat. Add carrots, celery and onion; cook, stirring, just until starting to soften, about 1 minute. Add garlic, ginger, curry powder and salt; cook, stirring, until softened and fragrant, about 1 minute.

4. Add red pepper, chicken and chili sauce; cook, stirring often, for 2 minutes. Add shrimp and cook, stirring, just until starting to curl and turn pink, about 1 minute. Pour in water.

5. Add noodles and pork, if using, and cook, folding gently but thoroughly with two large spatulas, until noodles are well coated in spices and steaming hot, 2 to 3 minutes. Return eggs to wok and toss to combine. Season to taste with chili sauce and salt. Serve sprinkled with green onions.

Malaysian Curry Noodles and Seafood

Serves 4 to 6

Some winter evening, when memories of a holiday in Penang or Kuala Lumpur get you in the mood, call up some friends and make a large batch of these party noodles, which are seafood-laced and doubly enriched by coconut and cashew. A salad and a chilled Chardonnay are all you'll need on the side.

Tip

Bags of mixed seafood are available in the frozen section of supermarkets and specialty fish shops. These are handy if you want a variety of seafood. You can substitute one type of your favorite seafood if you prefer.

Variation

Substitute 1 lb (500 g) boneless skinless chicken breast, thinly sliced, for the seafood and add in step 3 before the noodles. Simmer for 1 minute, then add noodles, cooking until chicken is no longer pink inside.

1 lb	mixed seafood, thawed, drained and patted dry	500 g
½ tsp	ground turmeric	2 mL
1 tbsp	vegetable oil	15 mL
3	cloves garlic, minced	3
2 or 3	hot red or green chile peppers, minced	2 or 3
1 tbsp	minced gingerroot	15 mL
2 tsp	ground coriander	10 mL
1 tsp	salt	5 mL
⅓ cup	cashew butter or natural peanut butter	75 mL
1	can (14 oz/400 mL) coconut milk	1
1 cup	water	250 mL
4 oz	rice vermicelli	125 g
3 tbsp	freshly squeezed lemon juice	45 mL
1 cup	bean sprouts	250 mL
	Chopped fresh mint	
	Thinly sliced cucumber	
	Chopped roasted salted cashews, optional	

1. In a bowl, combine seafood and turmeric; toss to coat evenly. Set aside at room temperature.

2. In a wok or large, deep skillet, heat oil over medium heat. Add garlic, chile peppers, ginger, coriander and salt; cook, stirring, until softened and fragrant, about 2 minutes. Stir in cashew butter until blended. Add coconut milk and water; bring to a simmer, scraping up bits stuck to pan and stirring until cashew butter is blended.

3. Stir in noodles and return to a boil, stirring gently just until noodles are immersed. Stir in seafood mixture and lemon juice; reduce heat and simmer, stirring gently often, just until seafood starts to firm up and noodles are softened, about 5 minutes. Gently stir in bean sprouts just until wilted. Divide among warmed serving bowls and serve sprinkled with mint and garnished with cucumber slices and cashews, if using.

Noodles in Mango Curry Cream

Serves 4 to 6

These creamy noodles, lively and sweet-sour with their chutney and spices, will turn a weekday meal into a special occasion.

Tips

This version has just a bit of heat; if you want a hot and spicy noodle dish, use a hot curry paste or add 1 or 2 hot green chile peppers, sliced, with the garlic.

A Major Grey–style chutney can be used but will give a different flavor because of its bitterness and tanginess. If you prefer that style of chutney over a sweeter, fruitier chutney, you may want to add a little sugar or honey to the sauce.

Variation

Add 8 oz (250 g) boneless skinless chicken or pork tenderloin, thinly sliced, just before adding the cream in step 3 and cook, stirring, for 1 minute. Cook sauce until chicken is no longer pink inside or just a hint of pink remains in pork.

8 oz	wide rice stick noodles	250 g
	Hot water	
1 tbsp	butter or vegetable oil	15 mL
1	onion, finely chopped	1
3	cloves garlic, minced	3
1 tbsp	minced gingerroot	15 mL
½ tsp	salt	2 mL
2 tbsp	mild Indian yellow curry paste	25 mL
1	red bell pepper, thinly sliced	1
1½ cups	whipping (35%) or table (18%) cream	375 mL
½ cup	mango chutney (Fruity Mango Papaya Chutney, page 37, or store-bought)	125 mL
	Chopped fresh cilantro	

1. In a large bowl, soak noodles in hot water until softened but not soft, about 20 minutes, or according to package directions.

2. Meanwhile, in a wok or large, deep skillet, melt butter over medium heat. Add onion and cook, stirring, until softened and starting to brown, about 5 minutes. Add garlic, ginger, salt and curry paste; cook, stirring, until softened and fragrant, about 1 minute. Add red pepper and cook, stirring, for 1 minute.

3. Add cream and chutney; bring to a boil, scraping up bits stuck to pan. Boil gently, stirring often, until slightly thickened and reduced, about 2 minutes.

4. Drain noodles well and add to sauce. Using two spatulas, toss gently just until coated in sauce. Reduce heat and simmer, stirring gently, until noodles are tender, about 3 minutes. Season to taste with salt and serve sprinkled with cilantro.

Serving Suggestion

These noodles are rich and should be served with a simple grill and a salad.

Coconut Curry Noodles with Crispy Vegetables

Serves 4

Soothing in their coconut mantle and crisply garnished by thinly sliced fresh vegetables, these noodles make for a quick lunch. If you prefer them for supper, top with cooked chicken, shrimp or fish.

Tips

If lime leaf is not available, substitute ½ tsp (2 mL) grated lime zest and add with the noodles in step 2.

To shred fresh coconut, peel off brown outer layer and use the coarse side of a box cheese grater or pulse in a food processor until finely chopped but not smooth. Frozen coconut is available at Asian specialty stores; thaw and drain well before using.

In a pinch, packaged dried shredded unsweetened coconut can be used. Soak about ⅓ cup (75 mL) in boiling water for 1 hour, drain well and measure ½ cup (125 mL).

1	can (14 oz/400 mL) coconut milk, divided	1
3	cloves garlic, minced	3
2 tbsp	minced gingerroot	25 mL
1	wild lime leaf (see tip, at left)	1
1 tbsp	Thai yellow curry paste	15 mL
1	onion, sliced lengthwise	1
½ cup	fresh or frozen unsweetened shredded coconut, divided (see tips, at left)	125 mL
½ cup	water	125 mL
1 tbsp	fish sauce (nam pla), or ½ tsp (2 mL) salt	15 mL
12 oz	thick precooked Asian noodles (such as udon or other stir-fry noodles)	375 g
	Salt, optional	
2	green onions, thinly sliced	2
1	carrot, julienned	1
½	yellow bell pepper, very thinly sliced	½
1 cup	julienned English cucumber	250 mL
2 tbsp	shredded Thai or sweet basil	25 mL
	Lime wedges	

1. In a wok or large saucepan, heat ¼ cup (50 mL) of the coconut milk over medium heat until bubbling. Add garlic, ginger, lime leaf and curry paste; cook, stirring, until softened and fragrant, about 2 minutes. Add onion and all but 1 tbsp (15 mL) of the coconut; cook, stirring, until onion starts to soften, about 2 minutes.

2. Stir in remaining coconut milk, water and fish sauce; bring to a boil, scraping up bits stuck to pan. Boil for 2 minutes. Add noodles and toss gently, using two spatulas, just until coated in sauce. Reduce heat and simmer, stirring gently, until noodles are hot, 2 to 3 minutes. Discard lime leaf. Season to taste with salt, if using.

3. Divide noodles and sauce among warmed serving bowls and sprinkle evenly with green onions, carrot, yellow pepper, cucumber, basil and remaining coconut. Serve garnished with lime wedges to squeeze over top.

Breads, Pancakes & Samosas

◆

Naan

Makes 8

The tandoori oven is used in India for grill-roasting meats and seafood and for baking naan, which sticks to the hot clay walls and bakes fluffy inside and charred outside. This recipe will yield naan that comes as close to the original as is possible using a barbecue or normal oven.

Tips

Full-fat yogurt works best to give a soft texture to the dough. Avoid yogurt that contains gelatin, as it does not react well in baked goods.

If the yeast mixture doesn't foam in step 2, it means the yeast is inactive (dead) and should be discarded. Dough made with dead yeast will not rise.

The dough will be quite elastic as you roll it. Let it rest often, and it will roll out nicely. If you try to roll too quickly, it will spring back and frustrate you!

- Pizza stone, optional
- Baking sheets, ungreased

3 cups	all-purpose flour (approx.), divided	750 mL
1¼ tsp	salt	6 mL
1 tsp	baking powder	5 mL
2 tsp	granulated sugar	10 mL
¾ cup	warm water (100°F/38°C)	175 mL
1½ tsp	active dry yeast	7 mL
¼ cup	plain yogurt, preferably full-fat, at room temperature (see tip, at left)	50 mL
¼ cup	butter, melted, divided	50 mL

1. In a bowl, combine 2¾ cups (675 mL) of the flour, the salt and baking powder.

2. In a large bowl, dissolve sugar in warm water. Sprinkle yeast over top and let stand until foamy, about 10 minutes. Whisk in yogurt and 2 tbsp (25 mL) of the butter. Using a wooden spoon, stir in flour mixture until a soft dough forms.

3. Turn dough out onto a floured surface and knead, adding just enough of the remaining flour to prevent dough from sticking (it should still be softer than traditional bread dough). Continue to knead until smooth and elastic, 10 to 15 minutes total. Place in an oiled bowl, turning to coat. Cover with plastic wrap and let rise in a warm, draft-free place until doubled in bulk, about 1 hour.

4. *To grill:* Preheat barbecue to medium-high and grease grill rack.

5. *To bake:* Preheat oven to 400°F (200°C) and position rack in the lower third of oven. If using pizza stone, preheat according to manufacturer's directions. Otherwise, place a large, heavy baking sheet in oven for 10 minutes.

6. Punch dough down and divide into 8 equal pieces. Roll each into a ball and let rest for 5 minutes. On a clean work surface, working with 1 or 2 balls at a time, roll out to a 5-inch (12.5 cm) circle, lifting dough and letting it rest often while rolling. Let circles rest for 1 minute. Hold on to one side of each circle and use your other hand to gently pull opposite side to make a teardrop shape about 8 inches (20 cm) long. Place on baking sheets, covered with a dry towel, while rolling remaining pieces.

7. *To grill:* Cooking a few pieces at a time as necessary, place breads directly on greased grill, at least 2 inches (5 cm) apart, and close lid. Grill until brown spots form on the bottoms and tops start to puff, 1 to 2 minutes. Turn, cover and grill until brown spots form on the other side and tops spring back when touched, about 1 minute. Transfer to a large piece of foil and lightly brush both sides with some of the remaining melted butter. Wrap loosely with the foil. Repeat with remaining breads. Serve warm.

8. *To bake:* Cooking a few pieces at a time as necessary, place breads on preheated stone or baking sheet, leaving at least 2 inches (5 cm) between each piece. Bake until brown spots form on the bottoms and tops start to look dry, about 3 minutes. Turn and bake until brown spots form on the other side and tops spring back when touched, about 2 minutes. Transfer to a large piece of foil and lightly brush both sides with some of the remaining melted butter. Wrap loosely with the foil. Repeat with remaining breads. Serve warm.

Tips

Shaping the naan on a clean (unfloured) surface prevents it from getting dry and tough. The dough shouldn't be sticky, but variations in weather might cause it to be moist on particularly humid days. If the dough does stick, roll it out on a silicone rolling mat or a piece of parchment paper anchored to the counter with tape.

Naan are best served immediately after cooking, but can be cooled completely, wrapped in plastic wrap and stored at room temperature for up to 1 day. To reheat, remove plastic and wrap in foil. Reheat in a 350°F (180°C) oven for 5 to 10 minutes.

Chapati

Chapati is the primordial bread of curry cuisine and is served in India with every meal, much like the tortilla in Mexico or the baguette in France.

• ◆ •

Tips

Traditionally, a finely ground whole wheat chapati flour called atta is used for chapati. It can be difficult to find, but the combination of regular whole wheat and all-purpose is a good substitute. If you have atta, use 1½ cups (375 mL).

You may want to start rolling 2 or 3 balls and alternate rolling and letting them rest, as the dough tends to spring back quite a bit and benefits from the rest.

Chapati are best served immediately after cooking, but can be wrapped in foil and stored at room temperature for up to 1 day. Reheat in foil in a 350°F (180°C) oven for 5 to 10 minutes.

1 cup	whole wheat flour	250 mL
½ cup	all-purpose flour (approx.)	125 mL
¼ tsp	salt	1 mL
1 tbsp	melted butter or vegetable oil	15 mL
⅓ cup	lukewarm water (approx.)	75 mL
	Vegetable oil	
	Melted butter, optional	

1. In a bowl, combine whole wheat flour, all-purpose flour and salt. Drizzle in butter and stir until blended. Drizzle in water, stirring, adding just enough water to make a ragged, but not dry, dough.

2. Turn dough out onto a surface dusted lightly with all-purpose flour and knead until dough is smooth and no longer sticky, about 5 minutes. Return dough to bowl and cover dough with a damp towel. Let rest at room temperature for 1 hour.

3. Divide dough into 8 equal pieces. Roll each piece into a ball and cover with a damp towel. On a clean, dry surface, roll out each ball to a very thin 6-inch (15 cm) circle, lifting dough often to prevent sticking. Let dough rest periodically while rolling if it is too elastic. Cover rolled chapati with a damp towel. Do not stack.

4. Heat a large nonstick skillet over medium heat until small drops of water splashed on the surface evaporate almost immediately. Brush lightly with oil. Working with one chapati at a time, cook until brown spots appear on the bottom, about 1 minute. Turn and cook the other side until lightly browned, about 30 seconds. Transfer to a plate and lightly brush both sides with melted butter, if using, or more oil. Cover with a clean dry towel or foil. Repeat with remaining chapati, oiling pan and adjusting heat as necessary to prevent browning too quickly. Serve warm.

Chickpea Flatbread (Roti)

Makes 8

Crispy and nutty-tasting, these flatbreads are a delight alongside any curry. They are delicate, yet sturdy, and will add a gourmet dimension to dinner.

Tips

To keep the bowl from spinning around when you're adding the water and stirring, nestle it in a scrunched-up damp tea towel.

The dough can be rolled and cooked after resting for 1 hour, but it improves in texture if made a day ahead.

Roti are best served immediately after cooking, but can be wrapped in foil and stored at room temperature for up to 1 day. Reheat in foil in a 350°F (180°C) oven for 5 to 10 minutes.

1 cup	chickpea flour (besan)	250 mL
2/3 cup	all-purpose flour (approx.)	150 mL
1/2 cup	whole wheat flour	125 mL
1/2 tsp	salt	2 mL
2 tbsp	vegetable oil (approx.), divided	25 mL
1/2 cup	water (approx.)	125 mL

1. In a large bowl, combine chickpea flour, all-purpose flour, whole wheat flour and salt. Drizzle in 1 tbsp (15 mL) of the oil and stir until blended. Drizzle in water, stirring, adding just enough water to make a ragged, but not dry, dough.

2. Turn dough out onto a surface dusted lightly with all-purpose flour and knead until dough is smooth and no longer sticky and springs back slowly when squeezed, about 5 minutes. Wrap dough in plastic wrap. Let rest at room temperature for 1 hour, or refrigerate for up to 1 day. Bring to room temperature before rolling.

3. Divide dough into 8 equal pieces. Roll each piece into a ball and cover with a damp towel. On a surface dusted lightly with all-purpose flour, roll out each ball to a very thin 8-inch (20 cm) circle, lifting dough often and keeping surface and rolling pin floured. Let dough rest periodically while rolling if it is too elastic. Do not stack rolled roti.

4. Heat a large nonstick skillet over medium heat until small drops of water splashed on the surface evaporate almost immediately. Working with one roti at a time, cook, pressing down edges with a spatula, until brown spots appear on the bottom and bubbles appear in dough, 45 to 60 seconds. Turn and cook the other side, pressing edges, until brown spots appear, about 30 seconds. Transfer to a large piece of foil and brush both sides lightly with oil. Wrap loosely with the foil. Repeat with remaining roti, adjusting heat as necessary to prevent browning too quickly. Serve warm.

Chile Pepper Cornbread

Serves 6 to 8

This easy-to-make, spicy cornbread is common in African and Caribbean cuisines. Serve thick slices with saucy curries to mop up every last drop of flavor.

Tips

A whole Scotch bonnet pepper gives this bread a definite kick. For a milder flavor, use half a Scotch bonnet or a milder jalapeño or other type of chile pepper. If you don't want any heat at all, leave out the chile pepper and enjoy the pure corn flavor.

To make ahead, let bread cool completely. Wrap in plastic wrap and store at room temperature for up to 1 day. To reheat, remove plastic and wrap in foil. Reheat in a 350°F (180°C) oven for about 15 minutes (if whole) or less for smaller pieces.

- Preheat oven to 400°F (200°C)
- 9-inch (23 cm) round metal cake pan, buttered

1 cup	cornmeal	250 mL
1 cup	all-purpose flour	250 mL
1 tbsp	granulated sugar	15 mL
2 tsp	baking powder	10 mL
½ tsp	baking soda	2 mL
½ tsp	salt	2 mL
¼ tsp	dried thyme	1 mL
2	eggs	2
1	Scotch bonnet or other hot chile pepper, minced	1
1 cup	buttermilk	250 mL
½ cup	butter, melted	125 mL
1 cup	corn kernels	250 mL

1. In bowl, combine cornmeal, flour, sugar, baking powder, baking soda, salt and thyme.

2. In a separate bowl, whisk together eggs, Scotch bonnet pepper, buttermilk and butter. Pour over dry ingredients, sprinkle with corn and stir just until moistened. Spread batter in prepared pan, smoothing top.

3. Bake in preheated oven until a tester inserted in the center comes out clean and edges are crispy and golden, about 30 minutes. Let cool in pan on rack for 10 minutes. Run a knife around edge of pan and turn bread out onto rack. Serve warm.

Curried Okra (Bindi) Masala (page 229)

Vegetable Curry with Fruit (page 238)

Vegetable Rice Biryani (page 250)

Baked Samosas (page 280)

Zucchini Pancakes

Makes about 12

These refreshingly light and fluffy pancakes feature the juicy texture of shredded zucchini, but are sturdy enough to be used as scoops for saucy curries.

Tip

Use the coarse side of a box cheese grater to shred zucchini. You'll need about 1 medium zucchini to get 1 cup (250 mL) lightly packed.

Variation

Make about 36 silver-dollar-sized pancakes using 1 tbsp (15 mL) batter each and cooking for 1 to 2 minutes per side. Use as a base for appetizers, topped with Marinated Cucumber Carrot Salad (page 22), Curry Chicken, Apple and Raisin Salad (page 28), Curry Shrimp and Papaya Salad (page 30) or Sweet Onion and Date Chutney (page 43).

1¼ cups	all-purpose flour	300 mL
½ tsp	salt	2 mL
½ tsp	baking soda	2 mL
1	green onion, finely chopped	1
1 cup	lightly packed shredded zucchini	250 mL
1 tbsp	chopped fresh cilantro	15 mL
1 cup	water or milk	250 mL
1 tbsp	freshly squeezed lemon juice	15 mL
	Vegetable oil	

1. In a bowl, combine flour, salt and baking soda.

2. In a separate bowl, combine green onion, zucchini, cilantro, water and lemon juice. Pour over dry ingredients and stir until well blended. Let stand at room temperature for 15 minutes.

3. Preheat oven to 300°F (150°C).

4. Heat a large nonstick skillet over medium heat until small drops of water splashed on the surface evaporate almost immediately. Brush lightly with oil. Add a scant ¼ cup (50 mL) of batter per pancake and, using the bottom of a metal ladle or flat-bottomed metal measuring cup, gently spread to about 3½ inches (8.5 cm) in diameter.

5. Cook until bubbles just start to break in batter and bottom is golden brown, 2 to 3 minutes. Flip and cook the other side until golden brown, about 1 minute. Keep warm on rack in oven. Repeat with remaining batter, oiling pan and adjusting heat as necessary between batches. Serve hot.

Sweet Potato Pancakes

Makes 8

These pancakes are an adaptation of a favorite Kerala yam dish, erissery. Serve as an accompaniment to tangy curries or topped with chutney as a snack.

Tips

To shred fresh coconut, peel off brown outer layer and use the coarse side of a box cheese grater or pulse in a food processor until finely chopped but not smooth. Frozen coconut is available at Asian specialty stores; thaw and drain well before using.

In a pinch, packaged dried shredded unsweetened coconut can be used. Soak about ¼ cup (50 mL) in boiling water for 1 hour, drain well and measure ⅓ cup (75 mL).

Variation

Substitute 1½ cups (375 mL) leftover mashed cooked sweet potato for the fresh and add ¼ tsp (1 mL) turmeric with the curry leaves in step 2.

1	large sweet potato, peeled and cut into chunks	1
1 tsp	salt, divided	5 mL
½ tsp	ground turmeric	2 mL
	Cold water	
2 tbsp	vegetable oil (approx.), divided	25 mL
1	dried red chile pepper, crumbled	1
½ cup	minced shallots or red onion	125 mL
5	curry leaves, finely chopped	5
1 tbsp	mustard seeds	15 mL
⅓ cup	fresh or thawed frozen unsweetened shredded coconut (see tips, at left)	75 mL
¾ cup	all-purpose flour	175 mL

1. In a saucepan, combine sweet potato, half the salt and the turmeric. Add enough cold water to cover and bring to a boil over high heat. Reduce heat and boil gently until potatoes are soft, about 20 minutes. Drain well, return to pot and mash until smooth. Measure out 1½ cups (375 mL) and transfer to a bowl. Set aside and let cool. Reserve any remainder for another use.

2. In a small skillet, heat 1 tbsp (15 mL) of the oil over medium heat. Add chile pepper, shallots, curry leaves and mustard seeds; cook, stirring, until shallots are softened, about 3 minutes. Add to mashed potatoes. Stir in coconut and remaining salt. Sprinkle with flour and stir until blended.

3. Preheat oven to 300°F (150°C).

4. Heat a large nonstick skillet over medium heat until small drops of water splashed on the surface evaporate almost immediately. Brush lightly with some of the remaining oil. With moistened hands, shape one-eighth of the potato mixture into a ball. Place in pan and flatten with a moistened spatula to about ¼ inch (0.5 cm) thickness.

5. Cook 2 or 3 of these pancakes at a time until well browned on bottom, about 2 minutes. Flip and cook until the other side is browned, about 2 minutes. Keep warm on rack in oven. Repeat with remaining potato mixture, oiling pan and adjusting heat as necessary between batches. Serve hot.

Uthappam

Makes about 16

A dressy version of dosa, uthappam incorporates its "stuffing" onto the pancake itself, making it easier to assemble. Serve with Cold Coconut Chutney (page 34).

Tips

Be sure pancakes do not cook too quickly, or they won't get cooked through.

Each topping variation makes enough for one whole batch of batter. If you want a variety of flavors, reduce each topping by half and make half of the uthappam with onion and half with tomato.

These are best served freshly made, but leftovers can be cooled, wrapped in plastic wrap and refrigerated for up to 1 day. To reheat, remove plastic and wrap in foil. Reheat in a 350°F (180°C) oven for 5 to 10 minutes.

Variation

For plain uthappam, omit toppings and serve topped with your favorite chutney.

• *Preheat oven to 300°F (150°C)*

2 cups	white rice flour	500 mL
¾ cup	white lentil flour (urid dal)	175 mL
1 tsp	salt	5 mL
1 tsp	fenugreek seeds, ground or finely crushed	5 mL
2½ cups	water (approx.)	625 mL
	Vegetable oil	

Onion Topping (for 1 batch)

¾ cup	finely chopped sweet or red onion	175 mL
1 tsp	minced hot green chile pepper	5 mL
⅛ tsp	salt	0.5 mL

Tomato Topping (for 1 batch)

¾ cup	diced seeded tomatoes, well drained	175 mL
1 tbsp	chopped fresh cilantro	15 mL
⅛ tsp	salt	0.5 mL

1. In a large bowl, whisk together rice flour, lentil flour, salt and fenugreek. Whisk in water, adding more if necessary to make a smooth, thick batter. Set aside at room temperature.

2. *Prepare the topping:* Onion: In a small bowl, combine onion, chile pepper and salt. Tomato: In a small bowl, combine tomatoes, cilantro and salt.

3. Heat a large nonstick skillet over medium heat until small drops of water splashed on the surface evaporate almost immediately. Brush lightly with oil. Reduce heat to medium-low. Pour ¼ cup (50 mL) of the batter into pan for each pancake and, using the bottom of a metal ladle or flat-bottomed metal measuring cup, gently spread to about 3½ inches (8.5 cm) in diameter. Sprinkle with a scant tablespoon (15 mL) of the topping mixture, pressing lightly.

4. Cook until batter on top is no longer shiny, bubbles just start to break in batter and bottom is golden brown, 2 to 3 minutes. Flip carefully and cook the other side until golden brown, about 1 minute. Flip onto a plate, topping side up, and slide from the plate to rack in oven; keep warm. Repeat with remaining batter, oiling pan and adjusting heat as necessary between batches. Serve hot.

Easy Masala Dosa

Makes about 12

As an Indian guru once said, "Masala dosa: good for breakfast, good anytime." A pancake made of rice and lentil flours that is browned in a little oil and stuffed with a zesty filling, masala dosa is the tiffin of choice even when one is not all that hungry. This is a simplified version of the classic, but just as tasty.

• ◆ •

Tips

Grind the fenugreek seeds in a spice grinder or using a mortar and pestle. Or place the seeds on a cutting board and crush with the bottom of a heavy saucepan.

It may take a little practice to spread the batter in the pan. The dosa should be very thin and lacy; don't worry if you have a couple of small holes.

While cooking dosas, the batter may thicken as it sits. Gradually add a little more water to the remaining batter as necessary to keep the consistency thin.

2 cups	white rice flour	500 mL
3/4 cup	white lentil flour (urid dal)	175 mL
1 tsp	salt	5 mL
1 tsp	fenugreek seeds, ground or finely crushed	5 mL
3 cups	water (approx.), divided	750 mL
	Vegetable oil	

Chutney Options

Fresh Cilantro Mint Chutney (page 39)

Cold Coconut Chutney (page 34)

Any other chutney of choice

Filling Options

Golden Curried Cauliflower with Green Peas (page 222)

Dry Curry of Potatoes and Onions (page 242)

Nepalese Potato, Cauliflower and Egg Curry (page 204)

Curried Tofu and Green Onion Samosa Filling (page 289)

1. In a large bowl, whisk together rice flour, lentil flour, salt and fenugreek. Whisk in $2\frac{1}{2}$ cups (625 mL) of the water. Gradually whisk in just enough water to make a smooth, thin batter similar to a crêpe or thin pancake batter. Cover and let stand in a warm, draft-free place for at least 1 hour or for up to 24 hours. (It may start to ferment and bubble; this is normal. If it doesn't ferment, it will still work.)

2. Stir batter and add just enough water to make a very thin, pourable batter, about the consistency of thin cream.

3. Heat a large nonstick skillet over medium heat until small drops of water splashed on the surface evaporate almost immediately. Brush lightly with oil. Pour about $\frac{1}{3}$ cup (75 mL) of the batter into pan and, working quickly, spread batter as thin as possible by swirling pan as when making crêpes, or using the bottom of a metal ladle or flat-bottomed metal measuring cup.

4. Cook until top is no longer shiny, about 30 seconds. Drizzle 1 tsp (5 mL) oil around edge of dosa and cook until edges are golden brown, about 30 seconds. Carefully flip and cook the other side for 15 seconds. Flip onto a plate and lightly brush lighter side with oil. Cover with a dry towel to keep warm. Repeat with remaining batter, oiling pan and adjusting heat as necessary between each dosa, stacking on the same plate. Be sure the dosas do not cook too quickly and get crispy; they should remain pliable.

5. With lighter side of a dosa facing up, spread half with a thin layer of chutney. Spoon desired amount of filling on top of chutney. Fold over other side to make a half-moon shape. Repeat with remaining dosas, chutney and filling. Serve hot.

Serving Suggestion

For an elaborate Indian-style feast, serve with Indian-Style Butter Chicken (page 65), Red Curry Lamb Rogan Josh (page 137), Matar Paneer Curry with Green Peas (page 207), Mixed Vegetable Coconut Curry (page 236), Saffron Curried Pear and Raisin Basmati Rice (page 258) and a simple dessert of fresh fruit, dates and raw almonds.

Tip

These are best served freshly made, but leftovers can be cooled, wrapped in plastic wrap and refrigerated for up to 1 day. To reheat, remove plastic and wrap in foil. Reheat in a 350°F (180°C) oven for 5 to 10 minutes.

Vegetable Pakora

Makes about 24

A sinfully delicious deep-fried snack, this perky fritter is practically addictive: it's impossible to have just one. The addition of beer is a little unconventional, but it makes for a tender-crisp texture. Serve with cold beer.

Tips

Chickpea flour should have a fresh, nutty aroma. To preserve its freshness, store it in an airtight container in the freezer and bring to room temperature before using.

The texture of a waxy boiling potato or all-purpose potato is essential to the batter. A drier oblong baking potato won't provide enough "glue."

When frying pakoras, be sure the oil stays as close to the correct temperature as possible to make sure the inside gets cooked but the outside doesn't burn. Frying at the correct temperature also prevents soggy, greasy fried foods.

- Large wok or deep fryer
- Candy/deep-fry thermometer

	Vegetable oil for frying	
2½ cups	chickpea flour (besan)	625 mL
1 tsp	salt	5 mL
1 tsp	ground cumin	5 mL
½ tsp	baking powder	2 mL
½ tsp	granulated sugar	2 mL
½ tsp	ground coriander	2 mL
¼ tsp	baking soda	1 mL
1	boiling or all-purpose potato	1
1 or 2	hot green chile peppers, minced	1 or 2
1	onion, finely chopped	1
1 cup	finely chopped cauliflower and/or broccoli	250 mL
¼ cup	chopped fresh cilantro	50 mL
½ cup	beer	125 mL
½ cup	water (approx.)	125 mL
	Chutney for dipping (see Serving Suggestion, opposite)	

1. In wok or deep fryer, heat at least 2 inches (5 cm) of vegetable oil to 350°F (180°C) or until a small amount of batter dropped in turns light golden in about 15 seconds.

2. Meanwhile, in a large bowl, whisk together chickpea flour, salt, cumin, baking powder, sugar, coriander and baking soda. Set aside.

3. Line a bowl with a triple layer of paper towels. Peel potato and shred on the coarse side of a box cheese grater into the bowl. Roll paper towel up jellyroll-style and gently squeeze out excess moisture from potato. Discard liquid.

4. Sprinkle shredded potato over flour mixture. Add chile peppers, onion, cauliflower and/or broccoli and cilantro. Stir in beer and water, adding just enough water to make a thick, spoonable batter, similar to cookie dough.

5. Using two spoons, one to hold batter and one to slide it into oil, carefully drop about 2 tbsp (25 mL) of the batter into hot oil for each pakora. Add 4 or 5 at a time (without crowding pan) and fry, turning once, until deep golden brown, about 3 minutes. Using a slotted spoon, transfer to a paper towel–lined tray. Repeat with remaining batter, adjusting heat as necessary between batches. Serve hot with chutney.

> *Serving Suggestion*
>
> Serve with Tomato Chutney (page 42), Banana Tamarind Chutney (page 40), Fresh Banana Mint Chutney (page 39), Sweet Onion and Date Chutney (page 43) or Fresh Cilantro Mint Chutney (page 39) or your favorite store-bought chutney.

Tip

If you have a side burner on your outdoor gas barbecue, this is a good time to use it, so you won't fill your house with the somewhat overpowering aroma of frying oil.

● ◆ ●

Variation

Replace beer with soda water or ginger ale. If using ginger ale, omit the sugar.

Baked Samosas

Makes 28

Ever so easy to make at home with this snappy recipe, the subcontinent's favorite snack satisfies with crispy crust and flavorful filling. The use of untraditional phyllo pastry for the crust makes the procedure even faster, and baking rather than frying limits the calories. Ideas for stuffings are on pages 284–290.

Tips

If the samosa filling has been made ahead and refrigerated, let stand at room temperature for 15 to 30 minutes before assembling samosas to ensure even baking.

Samosas can be prepared up to the end of step 2 and frozen on baking sheets until solid. Transfer frozen samosas to a rigid airtight container and freeze for up to 2 months. Let stand on baking sheets at room temperature for 15 minutes. Decrease baking temperature to 400°F (200°C) and increase baking time to about 20 minutes.

- Preheat oven to 425°F (220°C)
- Baking sheets, ungreased

7	sheets phyllo pastry, thawed	7
¼ cup	butter, melted, or olive oil	50 mL
1	recipe samosa filling (see recipes, pages 284–290)	1
	Chutney (store-bought or see recipes, pages 34–43)	

1. Place one sheet of phyllo on work surface, with long side facing you, keeping remaining sheets covered with plastic wrap and a damp cloth. Brush sheet lightly with butter. Cut vertically into four strips. Place a heaping tablespoon (15 mL) of filling about 1 inch (2.5 cm) from bottom of each strip.

2. Starting at the bottom right corner of strip, fold pastry over filling to the left side, making a triangle. Continue folding from left to right and back all the way along the strip to enclose filling and make a neat triangular bundle (like folding a flag). Tuck end underneath and brush top lightly with butter. Place on baking sheet. Repeat with remaining pastry and filling, placing samosas at least 1 inch (2.5 cm) apart on baking sheets.

3. Bake one baking sheet at a time in preheated oven until samosas are golden brown and crispy, 12 to 15 minutes. Serve warm with chutney for dipping.

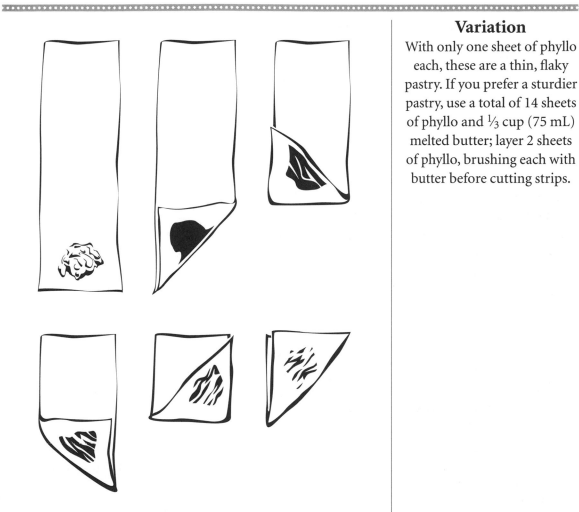

Variation

With only one sheet of phyllo each, these are a thin, flaky pastry. If you prefer a sturdier pastry, use a total of 14 sheets of phyllo and ⅓ cup (75 mL) melted butter; layer 2 sheets of phyllo, brushing each with butter before cutting strips.

Fried Samosas

Makes 28

These snack pockets are deep-fried as per the originals. The use of Asian spring roll wrappers is unconventional, but results in a very crispy crust and makes the samosas less fatty, as these wrappers absorb less oil than ordinary crusts. Any kind of curried filling works; we've offered seven examples to get you started (see pages 284–290).

Tips

If the samosa filling has been made ahead and refrigerated, let stand at room temperature for 15 to 30 minutes before assembling samosas to ensure even cooking.

Keep spring roll wrappers covered with a slightly damp cloth while assembling the samosas. They dry out quickly and can become to brittle to fill and fold.

Press out the air from around the filling when folding the samosas. Trapped air can cause the wrappers to open when they are being fried.

• *Baking sheet, lined with a slightly damp, lint-free towel*

28	spring roll wrappers (about 6 inches/ 15 cm square), thawed if frozen	28
1	egg, beaten	1
1	recipe samosa filling (see recipes, pages 284–290)	1
	Chutney (store-bought or see recipes, pages 34–43)	
	Vegetable oil	

1. Place one wrapper on work surface with one corner pointed toward you. Brush all around edges with egg. Place a heaping tablespoon (15 mL) of filling in the center of the square. Fold the corner closest to you over the filling to meet the opposite corner, making a triangle. Brush the left and right angled edges with egg.

2. Bring the left-hand point across the triangle toward the center, creating a straight edge at the top of the new folded layer. Repeat with the right-hand point. You will now have an envelope with slightly slanted sides. Fold the top point down to meet the center of the bottom edge, pressing to seal. Place on prepared baking sheet and cover with another slightly damp towel. Repeat with remaining wrappers and filling.

3. In a large, deep skillet or wok, heat about 1½ inches (4 cm) of oil over medium heat until a small piece of spring roll wrapper or bread turns golden in about 15 seconds. Fry samosas, in batches of 3 or 4 (without crowding pan), turning once, until golden brown, about 4 minutes per batch. Using a slotted spoon, transfer to a paper towel–lined plate. Repeat with remaining samosas, adjusting heat and adding oil between batches as necessary. (Make sure the oil does not get too hot; otherwise, the wrappers may burn before the filling is heated through.)

4. Serve hot with chutney for dipping.

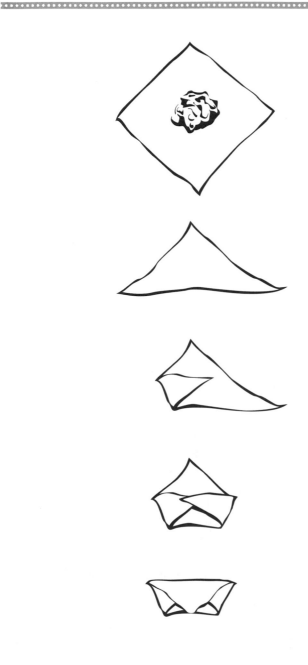

Tips

Keeping the oil hot enough when frying prevents soggy, greasy samosas, but make sure it's not so hot that the wrappers burn quickly. For perfectly fried samosas, you may need to adjust the burner frequently to let the oil heat up or cool down.

Samosas are best served immediately after frying, but can be wrapped in foil and refrigerated for up to 1 day. Reheat in foil in a 350°F (180°C) oven for 10 to 15 minutes.

Curried Potato and Green Pea Samosa Filling

**Makes enough
filling for
28 samosas**

❦

This is the classic vegetarian samosa filling that is available all over India, one of the very few recurring themes in that infinitely varied, continent-size country. Use to fill Baked Samosas (page 280) or Fried Samosas (page 282).

● ◆ ●

Tips

A lower-fat yogurt will work, but avoid fat-free yogurt and any yogurt that contains gelatin, as it does not react well in baked goods.

Filling can be made ahead, covered and refrigerated for up to 1 day.

1 tsp	cornstarch	5 mL
½ cup	plain yogurt, preferably full-fat (see tip, at left)	125 mL
2 tbsp	vegetable oil	25 mL
1 tsp	cumin seeds	5 mL
1	small onion, finely chopped	1
2	cloves garlic, minced	2
¾ tsp	salt	3 mL
1 tbsp	Indian yellow curry paste or masala blend	15 mL
2 cups	diced peeled boiling or all-purpose potatoes (about 2)	500 mL
¾ cup	water	175 mL
½ cup	frozen green peas, thawed and drained	125 mL

1. In a bowl, stir cornstarch and yogurt until blended and smooth. Set aside at room temperature.

2. In a large skillet, heat oil over medium heat until hot but not smoking. Add cumin seeds and cook, stirring, until toasted and fragrant but not yet popping, about 30 seconds. Add onion and cook, stirring, until softened and starting to brown, about 3 minutes. Add garlic, salt and curry paste; cook, stirring, until fragrant, about 1 minute.

3. Stir in potatoes until coated with spices. Pour in water and cover pan quickly. Reduce heat to medium-low and boil gently, stirring occasionally, until potatoes are tender, 15 to 20 minutes. Uncover and simmer, if necessary, until liquid is absorbed. Season to taste with salt. Let cool completely. Stir in peas and yogurt mixture.

Curried Chicken Samosa Filling

Makes enough filling for 28 samosas

For more satisfying samosas, try this tasty chicken stuffing. All you need for a complete lunch is 3 or 4 chicken samosas, plus a salad. Use to fill Baked Samosas (page 280) or Fried Samosas (page 282).

◦ ◄► ◦

Tips
Grilled or roasted chicken adds a nice flavor to this filling, but any cooked chicken will work. You'll need about 1 lb (500 g) raw chicken to get the right amount.

Chicken minced in the food processor keeps a better texture if it is cold. Chill chopped chicken for about 30 minutes before using.

Filling can be made ahead, covered and refrigerated for up to 1 day.

1 tsp	cornstarch	5 mL
½ cup	plain yogurt, preferably full-fat (see tip, page 284)	125 mL
2 tbsp	vegetable oil	25 mL
1 tsp	cumin seeds	5 mL
1 tsp	mustard seeds	5 mL
1	small onion, finely chopped	1
2	cloves garlic, minced	2
1 tbsp	minced gingerroot	15 mL
1 tsp	salt	5 mL
1 tbsp	Indian yellow curry paste or masala blend	15 mL
¼ cup	water	50 mL
2½ cups	coarsely chopped cooked chicken (about 12 oz/375 g), chilled	375 mL
¾ cup	diced red bell pepper	175 mL
2 tbsp	chopped fresh cilantro	25 mL

1. In a bowl, stir cornstarch and yogurt until blended and smooth. Set aside at room temperature.

2. In a small skillet, heat oil over medium heat until hot but not smoking. Add cumin seeds and mustard seeds; cook, stirring, until toasted and fragrant but not yet popping, about 30 seconds. Add onion and cook, stirring, until softened and starting to brown, about 3 minutes. Add garlic, ginger, salt and curry paste; cook, stirring, until fragrant, about 1 minute. Add water and bring to a boil, scraping up bits stuck to pan. Boil for 1 minute. Remove from heat and let cool.

3. In a food processor, pulse chicken until coarsely chopped (to keep the texture, avoid processing too fine). Add onion mixture and pulse just until combined. Transfer to a bowl and stir in yogurt mixture, red pepper and cilantro. Season to taste with salt.

Curried Beef and Peas Samosa Filling

1 tbsp	vegetable oil	15 mL
1 tsp	cumin seeds	5 mL
1	onion, finely chopped	1
1 lb	lean ground beef	500 g
4	cloves garlic, minced	4
1	hot green chile pepper, minced	1
2 tbsp	minced gingerroot	25 mL
2 tsp	garam masala	10 mL
½ tsp	salt	2 mL
¼ tsp	ground turmeric	1 mL
½ cup	water	125 mL
½ cup	frozen green peas, thawed	125 mL
2 tbsp	chopped fresh cilantro	25 mL
1 tbsp	freshly squeezed lemon juice	15 mL

1. In a large skillet, heat oil over medium-high heat until hot but not smoking. Add cumin seeds and cook, stirring, until toasted and fragrant but not yet popping, about 30 seconds. Add onion and cook, stirring, until softened and starting to brown, about 3 minutes.

2. Add ground beef, garlic, chile pepper, ginger, garam masala, salt and turmeric; cook, breaking up beef with a spoon, until beef is no longer pink, about 7 minutes. Stir in water, reduce heat and simmer, stirring often, until mixture is fairly dry and starting to brown and flavors are blended, about 10 minutes.

3. Remove from heat and stir in peas, cilantro and lemon juice. Season to taste with salt. Let cool completely.

Coconut Green Curry Pork Samosa Filling

Makes enough filling for 28 samosas

This Thai-influenced filling was inspired by the scrumptious curry-filled buns available at Minh's Chinese grocery store in Peterborough, Ontario. It's a delicious departure from the usual samosa fillings. Use to fill Baked Samosas (page 280) or Fried Samosas (page 282).

Tip

Filling can be made ahead, covered and refrigerated for up to 1 day.

Variation

To serve as a saucy curry, increase the coconut milk to 1 can (14 oz/400 mL) and simmer just until slightly thickened and serve over rice. Serves 4 to 5.

1 lb	lean ground pork	500 g
2	cloves garlic, minced	2
1 tbsp	minced gingerroot	15 mL
1/4 cup	sliced green onions	50 mL
4 tsp	Thai green curry paste	20 mL
1/2 cup	coconut milk	125 mL
1/2 cup	water	125 mL
1 tbsp	fish sauce (nam pla)	15 mL
1/2 cup	diced red bell pepper	125 mL
2 tbsp	chopped fresh Thai basil	25 mL
1 tbsp	freshly squeezed lime juice	15 mL
	Salt, optional	

1. In a large skillet over medium-high heat, cook ground pork, garlic and ginger, breaking up pork with a spoon, until pork is no longer pink, about 8 minutes. Add green onions and curry paste; cook, stirring, until onions are softened, about 2 minutes. Drain off any fat.

2. Stir in coconut milk, water and fish sauce; bring to a boil, scraping up bits stuck to pan. Reduce heat and simmer, stirring often, until most of the liquid is absorbed and flavors are blended, about 10 minutes.

3. Remove from heat and stir in red pepper, basil and lime juice. Season to taste with salt, if using. Let cool completely.

Curried Lamb and Eggplant Samosa Filling

Makes enough filling for 28 samosas

This filling transforms the modest samosa into a gourmet item. It's perfect for parties, especially if there are samosas with other fillings to provide variety. Use to fill Baked Samosas (page 280) or Fried Samosas (page 282).

Tips

This is a flavorful filling, but it's not particularly hot; if you like more heat, use a medium or hot curry paste or masala blend.

Filling can be made ahead, covered and refrigerated for up to 1 day.

1 tbsp	vegetable oil	15 mL
1½ tsp	cumin seeds	7 mL
1	onion, finely chopped	1
1 cup	diced peeled eggplant	250 mL
1 lb	lean ground lamb	500 g
4	cloves garlic, minced	4
1	hot green chile pepper, minced	1
1 tbsp	minced gingerroot	15 mL
1 tbsp	curry powder, Indian yellow curry paste or masala blend	15 mL
½ tsp	salt	2 mL
½ cup	water	125 mL
2 tbsp	chopped fresh mint or cilantro	25 mL
1 tbsp	freshly squeezed lime or lemon juice	15 mL

1. In a large skillet, heat oil over medium-high heat until hot but not smoking. Add cumin seeds and cook, stirring, until toasted and fragrant but not yet popping, about 30 seconds. Add onion and eggplant; cook, stirring, until softened and starting to brown, about 3 minutes.

2. Add ground lamb, garlic, chile pepper, ginger, curry powder and salt; cook, breaking up lamb with a spoon, until lamb is no longer pink, about 7 minutes. Stir in water, reduce heat and simmer, stirring often, until mixture is fairly dry and starting to brown and flavors are blended, about 10 minutes.

3. Remove from heat and stir in mint and lime juice. Season to taste with salt. Let cool completely.

Curried Tofu and Green Onion Samosa Filling

2	packages (each 10 oz/300 g) soft tofu, drained	2
2 tbsp	vegetable oil	25 mL
1 tsp	mustard seeds	5 mL
1 tsp	cumin seeds	5 mL
½ tsp	fenugreek seeds	2 mL
4	green onions, chopped	4
3	cloves garlic, minced	3
1	hot green or red chile pepper, minced	1
1 tsp	salt	5 mL
4 tsp	Indian yellow curry paste or masala blend	20 mL
2 tbsp	freshly squeezed lime or lemon juice	25 mL
½ cup	dry bread crumbs	125 mL
2 tbsp	chopped fresh cilantro	25 mL

1. In a bowl, using a fork, mash tofu until broken up but not smooth. Set aside.

2. In a small skillet, heat oil over medium heat until hot but not smoking. Add mustard seeds, cumin seeds and fenugreek seeds; cook, stirring, until toasted and fragrant but not yet popping, about 30 seconds. Add green onions, garlic, chile pepper, salt and curry paste; cook, stirring, until onions are softened and spices are fragrant, about 2 minutes. Remove from heat and stir in lime juice, scraping up bits stuck to pan.

3. Add spice mixture, bread crumbs and cilantro to tofu and stir until evenly blended.

Curried Chickpea and Paneer Samosa Filling

Makes enough for 28 samosas

This filling is nutty with chickpeas and creamy with paneer, for a double dose of nutrition. The resulting samosas can be served hot or at room temperature, and will be as much of a hit on a party buffet as in a lunchbox. Use to fill Baked Samosas (page 280) or Fried Samosas (page 282).

Tips

If using dried chickpeas, soak and cook 1 cup (250 mL). One 19-oz (540 mL) can of chickpeas yields 2 cups (500 mL).

Filling can be made ahead, covered and refrigerated for up to 1 day.

½ tsp	cornstarch	2 mL
½ cup	plain yogurt, preferably full-fat (see tip, page 284)	125 mL
2 tbsp	vegetable oil	25 mL
1 tsp	cumin seeds	5 mL
1 tsp	coriander seeds, crushed	5 mL
¼ tsp	fenugreek seeds	1 mL
1	small onion, finely chopped	1
3	cloves garlic, minced	3
½ tsp	salt	2 mL
4 tsp	Indian yellow curry paste or masala blend	20 mL
¼ cup	water	50 mL
2 cups	cooked or canned chickpeas, drained and rinsed (see tip, at left)	500 mL
8 oz	paneer or dry-pressed cottage cheese, broken into chunks	250 g

1. In a bowl, stir cornstarch and yogurt until blended and smooth. Set aside at room temperature.

2. In a small skillet, heat oil over medium heat until hot but not smoking. Add cumin seeds, coriander seeds and fenugreek seeds; cook, stirring, until toasted and fragrant but not yet popping, about 30 seconds. Add onion and cook, stirring, until softened and golden brown, about 5 minutes. Add garlic, salt and curry paste; cook, stirring, until fragrant, about 1 minute. Add water and bring to a boil, scraping up bits stuck to pan. Remove from heat and let cool.

3. In a food processor, pulse chickpeas and paneer until coarsely chopped (to keep the texture, rather than make a paste, avoid processing too fine). Add onion mixture and pulse just until combined. Transfer to a bowl and stir in yogurt mixture. Season to taste with salt.

Ingredients Glossary

Cardamom: The seed pod of a tropical plant grown primarily in India and Sri Lanka. The whole pods are available in black, green and white, with green being the most common. The flavor of cardamom is warm, slightly hot and very aromatic. Whole pods are simmered in curries. Inside the pods are tiny, round black seeds. These seeds are ground and used in curries, curry powders, curry pastes and spice blends. "Ground cardamom" refers to just the ground black seeds, not the ground pod. It is a fairly expensive spice, but because of its bold flavor, a small amount goes a long way. It is worth the price for the depth of flavor it adds to curries.

Chickpeas: The seed of a plant native to the Mediterranean. The buff-colored seeds have a mild, nutty flavor and grow in many areas around the world. They are prized for their protein content and versatility and are used in curries in many cuisines. Sold dried or precooked in cans, they are an economical and convenient food. Also known as channa or garbanzo beans.

Chickpea flour: Dried chickpeas are ground into flour and used in Indian breads, to coat foods before frying and as a thickener for sauces. Chickpea flour is available in Indian and Asian grocery stores and some well-stocked supermarkets. Look for fine, straw yellow–colored flour with no visual impurities and a fresh, nutty aroma. Store in a tightly sealed container in the refrigerator or freezer for up to 1 year. Also called besan.

Chile peppers: There are a vast number of hot chile peppers available. Though they have varying heat levels, most can be used interchangeably as long as you adjust the number added based on the heat level. The recipes in this book were tested mainly with Indian-style long green chiles, unless otherwise specified. Even chile peppers of the same variety vary in heat level, so in recipes that call for a range, you may want to start with the lower number if you're not sure how hot the peppers you're using are. You can always add hot pepper sauce to taste at the end of a recipe if you want more heat, but it's difficult to calm a dish that is too hot.

Jalapeño peppers: Medium-hot, commonly available peppers used in Mexican and Southwestern dishes. If using jalapeños in place of long green chiles or other hot chiles, you may need to increase the amount to create a hot dish.

Long hot green or red chiles: The most commonly used chiles in Indian cuisines. They are 4 to 5 inches (10 to 12.5 cm) long and about $\frac{1}{2}$ inch (1 cm) thick at the stem.

Scotch bonnet peppers: Extremely hot peppers used in Caribbean cuisines. They come in red, yellow, orange and green and look like tiny, wrinkled bell peppers with a pointed bottom. They are closely related to, and sometimes interchangeably labeled as, habanero chile peppers.

Cilantro: The delicate, bright green leaves of a plant native to southern Europe and the Middle East. The leaves have a fresh, slightly citrusy, herbaceous flavor that some people find a little soapy. Cilantro is used abundantly as an herb in many curry cuisines. In Indian cooking, it is used in chutneys, cooked into curries and added as a fresh garnish. It is also used in many other Asian and Latin American cuisines. For people who truly dislike the taste, fresh mint or basil can be substituted; they will provide the necessary fresh green herb flavor, though a slightly different one. Cilantro leaves should be washed well, patted dry and chopped just before using. They are very soft and delicate and deteriorate quickly, turning black and mushy and losing flavor if prepared ahead. Also known as fresh coriander or Chinese parsley.

Cinnamon: Cinnamon sticks (or quills) are pieces of bark from two related evergreen trees that are members of the laurel family (as are bay leaves), native to Asia. There are two types: true, or Ceylon, and cassia. True cinnamon is a pale tan, higher-quality, mild bark; cassia is a darker, reddish brown, stronger bark. Most of the cinnamon sticks and ground cinnamon sold in North America are, in fact, cassia. Sticks are simmered in curries to lend a warm, spicy, sweet flavor. Ground cinnamon is used in curry pastes and powders, in spice blends such as garam masala and in quick-cooking curries that don't simmer long enough to extract the flavor from whole sticks.

Coconut milk: Coconut meat is grated and pressed to extract the thick, milky liquid. Use unsweetened, higher-quality coconut milk for the best flavor. Check the Nutrition Facts table on the label and make sure the fat content is at least 14 grams per ¼ cup (50 mL). Lower-fat products are usually of inferior quality, with more added water and much less flavor and body.

Coriander seeds: The seeds of the cilantro plant, native to southern Europe and the Middle East. The small, round, light tan–colored seeds are harvested and dried, and are sold whole and ground. Along with cumin, coriander seeds are one of the most common spices in curries. They have a mild, sweet, slightly citrusy flavor that is completely different from the flavor of cilantro leaves, though they're from the same plant. The seeds are often toasted, dry or in oil, before other ingredients are added.

Cumin: Small, grayish brown, oblong seeds of a flowering plant with ancient Egyptian origins. One of the most commonly used spices in Indian curries, cumin has an aromatic, slightly medicinal flavor. It is used both whole and ground. Ground cumin is a dark tan color with a slight greenish yellow tint. Whole seeds are often toasted, dry or in oil, to add depth to their flavor before they are used.

Curry leaves: Small, shiny green leaves sold fresh in large sprigs on woody branches. Available in Indian and Asian grocery stores, curry leaves add an herbaceous, slightly citrusy flavor to curries. Also called kari leaves.

To store fresh curry leaves: Wrap the branches in a paper towel or a lint-free tea towel and place in a plastic bag. Do not tie tight. Store in a crisper drawer in the refrigerator for 1 to 2 weeks, replacing the towel if it gets too wet. Curry leaves are best used fresh but can be frozen or dried. To dry, place branches in a single layer on a paper towel–lined baking sheet in a cool, dark, dry place for 3 to 6 days. Remove the dried leaves from the branches and store in an airtight container in a cool, dark place for up to 1 year. To use dried leaves, pour a small amount of boiling water over them and let soak for 15 to 30 minutes, until softened. Drain and squeeze out water; use as directed in the recipe.

Fennel seeds: The seeds of the fennel plant, prized for its mildly licorice-flavored bulbous stalk, used fresh as a vegetable. The seeds are harvested and dried and have a mild licorice flavor. The pale green and tan, oblong seeds are relatively soft and are commonly used whole.

Fenugreek seeds: Small, golden brown, irregular-shaped seeds of a plant native to southern Europe and western Asia. The seeds add a characteristic bitterness to Indian curries. Toasting the seeds in oil before adding the other ingredients softens the bitterness and adds a depth of flavor.

Garam masala: A blend of warmly flavored spices commonly used in northern Indian cuisine. It is often sprinkled as a garnish on cooked curries and rice dishes. The combination of spices in the blend varies; each Indian family has its own signature blend, often passed down from generation to generation. Typical spices include cardamom, cinnamon, coriander, cumin, cloves and black peppercorns. When buying a prepared garam masala blend, choose well-packaged spices and try different blends until you find one you prefer. Guyanese garam masala is a similar blend of spices that are roasted for a deeper flavor.

Gingerroot: A tropical rhizome originating in Southeast Asia. Sold in both fresh and dried, ground forms, ginger adds a unique flavor to many types of recipes. It contributes a sweet heat and is a base flavor in almost all curry cuisines. Fresh ginger is sold in knobs, or hands, and should have firm, shiny, light tan–colored skin and juicy, yellow flesh. Ground or powdered ginger should have a muted yellow hue and be very fragrant. Fresh ginger can be minced by hand with a knife or grated on a fine Microplane-style grater or the fine side of a box cheese grater. Jars of puréed ginger or cubes of frozen ginger are a convenient alternative, though the jarred variety does taste different from fresh. Store fresh gingerroot in a paper bag in the crisper section of the refrigerator for up to 2 weeks.

Jalapeño peppers: See Chile peppers.

Lentils: Dried lentils are legumes with the skins intact. Lentils with the skins removed and split are called dal and are a staple of Indian cuisine. All lentils (whole and split) should be rinsed in a sieve under running water and drained well. Check for and remove any stones or grit.

Toor dal: Small split yellow lentils with the skins removed. They can maintain their shape when cooked or can be cooked until very soft. Also called thoor, toover, tuvar, tur or arhar.

Brown lentils: Whole lentils with a thin, brownish green skin and a red interior. They maintain their shape when cooked and have a tender but firm texture. Also called green lentils or masoor lentils. When split, with the skins removed, they are red lentils (dal). They get very soft and turn a bright yellow when cooked. Also called masoor, masar, mussoor, masur or pink lentils.

Black lentils: Whole, small, oval lentils with a thin, shiny black skin and a white interior. They maintain their shape when cooked and have a tender but firm texture. Also called urad, urid, black gram or kali dal. When split, with the skins removed, they are white lentils, also called urad, urid and black gram dal.

Lemongrass: The stalks of a tall, tropical grass used widely in Thai and Vietnamese cuisines. Lemongrass is also ground to a paste and used in Thai and Indian curry pastes. Simmered into curries, it provides a delicate, sweet lemon flavor without acidity. Even cooked, the tough stalks are not intended to be eaten. Now grown in Florida and California, lemongrass is commonly available fresh in the herb section of well-stocked supermarkets and in Asian grocery stores. Fresh lemongrass stalks can be stored in a paper bag or wrapped in a paper towel in the refrigerator for up to 2 weeks. Also known as serah.

To prepare lemongrass: Trim off the tough outer layers and cut the remaining stalk into 2-inch (5 cm) sections. Smash each piece with the broad side of a knife to bruise; this will help release the flavor when the lemongrass is cooked.

Mustard seeds: The small, round seeds of the mustard plant, which are harvested and dried. They are available in yellow, brown and black varieties. The yellow variety, which is the most common, is used in these recipes.

Saffron: The stigma of a variety of crocus flower cultivated in Spain, Iran and India. The thin, red, thread-like stigmas are hand-picked and dried; thus, they are one of the most costly ingredients by weight. Saffron has a delicate floral flavor and aroma and adds a golden yellow color to foods. The best-quality saffron is made up of long red threads and is worth the price for its superior flavor. Be wary of too-good-to-be-true low-cost saffron; it likely isn't the real, high-quality product.

Scotch bonnet peppers: See Chile peppers.

Tamarind: The fruit of the tamarind tree, which grows in East Africa, Sri Lanka and India. After harvest, the ripe pods are peeled and the pulpy seeds are usually pressed into a block for packaging. The dark brown pulp is prized for the sour, fruity flavor it adds to curries. The seeds are inedible; tamarind is used in the form of tamarind water (see below) or as tamarind paste or concentrate, available in jars. It sometimes has salt added in processing, so check the label or taste a small amount before using it and adjust the salt in the recipe accordingly. It is commonly found in Asian grocery stores and well-stocked supermarkets. Also know as Indian date.

To make tamarind water: Break 2 oz (60 g) of block tamarind into pieces and place in a heatproof bowl. Pour in 1 cup (250 mL) boiling water. Let stand until very soft, at least 30 minutes or up to 8 hours. Press through a fine-mesh sieve, discarding seeds and skins. You may need to add a little more boiling water to the pulp and press well to get a full cup (250 mL) of tamarind water, depending on how much liquid is absorbed by the pulp.

Turmeric: A rhizome that is indigenous to India and related to ginger. It is generally sold dried and ground. The bright yellow powder gives curry powder its characteristic color.

Turmeric provides a desired bitterness and depth to curry recipes.

Thick yogurt: Full-fat, thick yogurt is available in some grocery stores, sometimes labeled Balkan-style or Greek. If thick yogurt is unavailable, drain regular 2% or 3% yogurt in a coffee filter– or cheesecloth-lined sieve set over a bowl. Cover and refrigerate for 4 to 12 hours to drain off excess liquid.

Tomatoes: Choose ripe but not soft tomatoes that yield slightly to gentle pressure. To peel tomatoes, drop into a pot of boiling water for 30 seconds. Using a slotted spoon, transfer tomatoes to a bowl or sink of ice-cold water and let cool. Using a sharp paring knife, remove cores and peel off skins.

Paneer: An Indian soft, unripened cheese made from cow's milk. It is lightly pressed into a block and generally sold in a vacuum package. It is available at Indian and Asian specialty stores and in some larger supermarkets. It resembles tofu in texture and has a mild taste with a pleasant tang. It softens slightly when cooked but holds its shape without melting. You can make paneer at home, but the result is usually a softer product than the commercially made one. We used store-bought paneer for these recipes.

Wild lime leaves: Fragrant, flavorful leaves of a lime tree species native to Southeast Asia and now grown in California. The tough leaf is simmered in curries to let the deep, floral lime flavor infuse into the sauce. The leaf is not meant to be eaten. In North America, lime leaves are generally available frozen at Asian grocery stores. Also known as Makrut, Kaffir or Kefir lime leaves.

Resources

Rolland, Jacques L., and Carol Sherman. *The Food Encyclopedia.* Toronto: Robert Rose, 2006.

Vaswani, Suneeta. *Complete Book of Indian Cooking.* Toronto: Robert Rose, 2007.

Acknowledgments

The production of this book truly was a collaborative effort. We would both like to thank our publisher, Bob Dees, and Marian Jarkovich of Robert Rose Inc. To our ever-efficient editor, Sue Sumeraj, your sharp eye and logical mind prove that a skilled editor is paramount to turning a good book into something fabulous. We thank you for doing just that! Thanks to the design team at PageWave Graphics, especially Kevin Cockburn, for creating a functional and beautiful book; photographer Colin Erricson, food stylist Kathryn Robertson and props stylist Charlene Erricson for creating such tantalizing photographs; and Kveta for saving us "a thousand words" with her illustrations. Proofreader Sheila Wawanash and indexer Gillian Watts also deserve thanks for their valuable contributions.

From Byron:
Great thanks to: Naushad Abubacker; Neesha Jhaveri; Algis Kemezys; Arjun Khubchandani; Lonely Planet Restaurant, Kovalam Beach; Chef Manju Nath; Chef T. Siva Prasannan; Rakesh Puri; Raheem's Shop, Lucknow; Lisa Spiro; Thampi of Karavayal Tours.

From Jennifer:
To Bob Dees, an extra thank you for recommending me for this project and for your continual support and trust in my work. To my co-author, Byron Ayanoglu, thank you for taking a chance on me and sharing your expertise.

To professional recipe testers and proofreaders extraordinaire, Kate Gammal and Teresa Makarewicz, thank you both. I'm fortunate to have you as colleagues and friends.

Thank you to my many friends and family members for tasting the curry creations, giving your extremely helpful critiques and suggestions and diligently returning your empty containers for refills.

To the staff at our shop, In a Nuttshell, and Nuttshell Next Door Café: Melanie, Barb, Eric, Laura, Miguel, Miranda, Rachel, Valerie, Victoria and Wendy. Thanks for keeping things running smoothly for Jay at work while our life at home was topsy-turvy (to say the least).

My family has always been there for me, no matter what, and I'm truly grateful. Mom, your passion and caring spirit inspire me daily. Dad, you are the biggest supporter a girl could ask for — it means the world to me. Brent, Alicia and John, I'm sure some of my early culinary creations were less than fantastic, but you ate them anyway. Thank you for that and so much more!

And to my husband, Jay Nutt, thank you for going above and beyond, not only with your emotional support, patience and love, but by doing daily grocery shopping for me, by lending your palate, expertise and objective opinion and by testing recipes on your precious few days off. To quote a famous (and admittedly a little cheesy) movie line, "You complete me." I truly believe that.

Library and Archives Canada Cataloguing in Publication

Ayanoglu, Byron
    Complete curry cookbook : 250 recipes from around the world / Byron Ayanoglu and Jennifer MacKenzie.

Includes index.
ISBN 978-0-7788-0184-9

1. Cookery (Curry). I. MacKenzie, Jennifer. II. Title.

TX819.C9A93 2008   641.3'384   C2007-907055-8

Index